FIRST LADIES AND THE PRESS

Medill School of Journalism
VISIONS *of the* AMERICAN PRESS

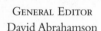

GENERAL EDITOR
David Abrahamson

Other titles in this series

HERBERT J. GANS
Deciding What's News: A Study of CBS Evening News,
NBC Nightly News, Newsweek, *and* Time

PATRICIA BRADLEY
Women and the Press: The Struggle for Equality

FIRST LADIES
AND THE PRESS
THE UNFINISHED
PARTNERSHIP OF
THE MEDIA AGE

Maurine H. Beasley

Foreword by Caryl Rivers

MEDILL SCHOOL OF JOURNALISM

Northwestern University Press

Evanston, Illinois

Northwestern University Press
www.nupress.northwestern.edu

Printed in the United States of America

10   9   8   7   6   5   4   3   2   1

ISBN 0-8101-2312-6

Library of Congress Cataloging-in-Publication Data

Beasley, Maurine Hoffman.
    First ladies and the press : the unfinished partnership of the media age / Maurine H. Beasley ; foreword by Caryl Rivers.
        p. cm. — (Visions of the American press)
    Includes bibliographical references and index.
    ISBN 0-8101-2312-6 (pbk. : alk. paper)
    1. Presidents' spouses—Press coverage—United States. 2. Mass media—Political aspects—United States. 3. Press and politics—United States. 4. Presidents' spouses—United States—Biography—Miscellanea. 5. United States—Politics and government—Miscellanea. I. Title. II. Series.
    E176.2.B43 2005
    973.91'092'2—dc22

                                                                        2005018040

To my husband, Henry R. Beasley,
with gratitude for his
never-failing encouragement

CONTENTS

FOREWORD

Caryl Rivers

Each election season, a Niagara of print is devoted to whether or not a prospective first lady is a replay of the original Eve, proffering poisoned fruit to an unsuspecting mate. Is she too mouthy and not attentive enough to her husband, as Teresa Heinz Kerry was said to be? (*New York Times* columnist Maureen Dowd wrote on July 8, 2004, that running mate John Edwards's adoring gaze at John Kerry was taking the place of the one Kerry *wasn't* getting from his wife. "Heaven knows Teresa was never going to do it," Dowd decreed. "Her attention rarely seems to light on her husband when she's at a microphone with him . . . she doesn't gaze like Nancy or glare like Lee Hart or look appraisingly at her husband like Elizabeth Edwards. She doesn't always seem to notice he's there. When Mr. Kerry moves in for a nuzzle or a kiss, she sometimes makes a little face. . . . She siphons attention from a husband who has a hard enough time getting it.")

Is a prospective first lady too powerful, as Hillary Clinton was proclaimed to be? Too intrusive, like Nancy Reagan, trying to get her astrologer's ideas into the Oval Office? The best sort of first lady, one would assume after reading the press, would be like Mr. Rochester's first wife in *Jane Eyre*—locked in the attic and neither seen nor heard, except for an occasional muffled shriek.

Why is there so much angst in the press over whether

a president will be influenced by his wife? Why is he in danger of being called a wimp if he barely nods in her direction? It seems odd that we don't worry half as much about the men to whom a president listens. Why don't we see cascades of print about a candidate's male political allies? Oh, there are the occasional "newsmaker" profiles now and then, but rarely do these view a male friend or ally with alarm.

In truth, it has been the President's Men, not his Lady, that have led him astray, from Teapot Dome to Watergate. Remember Ollie North slipping Iranian money to the contras? Remember the Happy Warriors—Haldeman, Ehrlichman, Hunt, Liddy, Mitchell, et al.—who almost managed to get Nixon impeached? LBJ had Bobby Baker, and Ike had Sherman Adams, both accused of having a blind spot where ethics were concerned. Harry Truman weathered the scandal of the "five-percenters."

By contrast, what influences have first ladies had on affairs of state? Eleanor Roosevelt made things better for blacks, coal miners, and poor people. Rosalynn Carter used her influence with her husband to help the mentally ill. Lady Bird Johnson pushed for environmental laws, Betty Ford tried to help alcoholics, and Hillary Clinton worked for universal health care. Perhaps it was only Edith Wilson whose actions could be called a potential threat. She concealed the grave illness of Woodrow Wilson for many months, becoming the de facto president while her husband was unable to perform his duties.

What is at play in the media's treatment of modern first ladies, I believe, is the Myth of Female Strength. In *Labeling Women Deviant,* Edwin Schur wrote that men have a tendency "to experience the very condition of femaleness as threatening . . . if femaleness itself possesses some kind of threat, then it becomes all the more important to keep it under control." In a report for Harvard's Shorenstein Center for Press, Politics, and Public Policy in May 1989, former *Newsweek* Boston bureau chief Bernice Buresh noted several themes that emerge in the press's attitudes toward women and political power:

> Women's demands are always excessive. No matter
>   what they are.
> Women's anger is terrifying.
> Once loosed, that power cannot be contained.

A woman close—as close as it is possible to get, in fact—to the holder of great power seems to start all sorts of media alarm bells to ring. Unless a first lady stays in the attic, she cannot win. Eleanor Roosevelt was cruelly mocked for her activities in behalf of minorities and women. Hillary Clinton was probably the most maligned female since Lady Macbeth. In fact, the *New York Times* reported on September 23, 1992, that "at least 20 articles in major publications this year involved some comparison between Mrs. Clinton and a grim role model for political wives: Lady Macbeth." That was just the beginning. Hillary was the "Yuppie wife from hell," said *US News & World Report* (April 27, 1992). *Spy* magazine put Hillary on its cover in a black-studs-and-leather domi-natrix outfit, holding a riding crop, with the headline: WHAT HILLARY PROBLEM? (February 1993). The Canadian news-magazine *MacLean's* declared flatly that "the First Lady has emasculated America" (April 1994). One syndicated cartoon showed Hillary, an evil grin on her face, sitting up in bed and thinking "Hillary Rodham . . . Bobbitt." (Lorena Bobbitt was the woman who made headlines around the world in the early 1990s by slicing off her husband's private parts.)

Castration, sadomasochism, witches, harridans, Lady Macbeth. It is the language of fear, dread, and loathing. Few males get this sort of terminology applied to them. How many male political candidates are called warlocks, devils, fiends, or sexual mutilators, no matter what their transgressions? "Three centuries after Salem, what's going on?" asked Patricia J. Williams in the *Village Voice*. "Why are we still burning witches, or even just simmering them to death? Why are these images so powerful?" (January 24, 1993).

While Hillary got the worst of it, Nancy Reagan, a traditional political wife who believed that her husband's career was her major career too, also came in for massive doses of critical coverage. Nancy, it seems, may have urged her husband to consider his place in history and take a step toward world peace. The vixen! And she was not kind to presidential aides whose egos and political ambitions were making her husband look bad. For this she should be stoned? Kitty Dukakis, wife of presidential candidate Michael Dukakis, was called a "Dragon Lady," while Rosalynn Carter was dubbed "The Steel Magnolia." Kitty's interests were in the welfare of refugees and in funding the arts. If Kitty got her hands on some dough, she would have given it to the National Symphony. Rosalynn Carter worked tirelessly for people who were mentally ill. Should the Republic have trembled?

The fear of an all-powerful female dominating a president seems unwarranted, given the sort of men who get to that office. They are almost always men with towering egos and rock-solid constitutions, with a strong belief in their own ideas. Few shrinking violets suddenly wake one morning and say, "By golly, I'd like to be president." So why, each political season, does the Dragon Lady specter arise? The very idea of a female with power has wellsprings deep in history and myth. Eve, after all, got blamed for losing Paradise. Even John Adams, who adored his Abigail, was not about to cede power to any other women when Abigail asked him to "remember the ladies" in his revolution (letter dated March 31, 1776). He replied, "We know better than to repeal our masculine systems. Although they are in full force, you know they are little more than theory. . . . In practice, you know we have only the name of master, and rather than give this up, which would completely subject us to the despotism of the petticoat, General Washington and all of our heroes would fight" (letter dated April 14, 1776). And this was when women could not vote or own property.

With such a long and venerable history, the press's fear of Dragon Ladies and Petticoat Despots will not fade overnight. The story that Maurine Beasley tells makes that clear. Perhaps, though, the media will call a moratorium on some clichés in the future: for example, iron fists in velvet gloves, flowers made of steel, and all manner of reptile life attached to a word indicating the female gender. Some traditions—even if they date back to Adam and Eve—are not worth keeping around.

Picture the scene. A drafty old house in a small town in central Missouri. A tired housewife is hunched over a hot-air register, trying to keep warm on a cold winter night while she reads her favorite columnist in the *Kansas City Star.* Suddenly, her face lights up, and she murmurs to her little daughter playing nearby, "I'm sure that SHE is better than HE is!"

That scene is etched indelibly on my memory. The woman was my mother, I was the child, the "SHE" was Eleanor Roosevelt, the "HE" Franklin D. Roosevelt, and the column "My Day." In "My Day," a simplistic, diary-like account of the people she met and the places she went, Eleanor Roosevelt offered women readers, such as my mother, a respite from their domestic drudgery and a glimpse of life in the far-off White House. My rock-ribbed Republican family hated the Roosevelts and everything they stood for in terms of social legislation (how they would have embraced George W. Bush!). Yet my mother, a former schoolteacher, admired Eleanor Roosevelt as a woman who wanted to educate other women so they could take charge of their own lives and not be totally dependent on fathers or husbands. My mother preached to me the importance of going to college and being able "to take care of yourself if you have to," and she hoped that I might someday go to Washington and see those important and interesting places that the first lady mentioned in her column. Eleanor Roosevelt held out the lure of a wider world for women.

Fast-forward a half century or so. I am teaching history of journalism and women's studies courses at the University of Maryland in College Park, just outside Washington, D.C. A friend invites me to visit the pressroom at the White House, where I see journalists vying for space and attention in very crowded quarters as they try to find out what is going on in the administration. Nobody talks about the first lady, and she isn't mentioned at the daily briefing. "Why not?" I ask. "Well, she has her own press staff, and we don't get much on her unless something special is going on," I'm told. I receive the distinct impression that the White House press corps doesn't think she is particularly newsworthy, which strikes me as somewhat odd.

When I go to the drugstore and look at a magazine rack, I frequently see pictures of first ladies on magazine covers, and I know they are there because they sell magazines. When I turn on morning network television shows while I'm getting dressed for work, I sometimes hear first ladies being interviewed. I assume they are sought-after guests whose presence boosts ratings. Of course, I see occasional front-page stories on them, particularly if there is some whiff of scandal or impropriety or news of an activity that seems to break through accustomed social roles. Mainly, though, these women seem a bit reclusive in terms of mainstream journalism—figures standing with sweet smiles beside their husbands.

Why is this? I wondered. The world and the media have changed since Eleanor Roosevelt's day, but first ladies still speak to women through the mass media. The first ladies who came after Roosevelt exhibited their own individualities, and not all chose to follow in her footsteps by any means. As a people, we Americans are far more sophisticated than we were in Roosevelt's era. Women have experienced the second wave of feminism, which has brought enormous opportunity for professional achievement.

Still, I began to suspect that the journalistic attention given to first ladies had not evolved much beyond my mother's observation that the SHE of a presidential couple was better than the HE. It seemed to me that first ladies were being given a somewhat dismissive deference that kept them from being looked at too carefully by the news media except when they appeared to be treading directly on their husbands' territories. By extension, I wondered if that was not the way the news media in general tended to treat women— as beings somewhat apart from the world of power and influence and as individuals centered on emotion, not reason, and more in tune with victimization than self-actualization. I also wondered if conventional news values of conflict and controversy almost by definition excluded the activities of many women—including first ladies, who seemed to be expected to adopt noncontroversial "good works" that did not meet the criteria for important news.

Therefore, I was delighted when Professor David Abrahamson of Northwestern University's Medill School of Journalism approached me about writing a book on first ladies and the press for the new Visions of the American Press series. I thank him and Northwestern very much for giving me the opportunity to explore my ideas by looking at the interaction between individual first ladies and mass media, from Martha Washington to Laura Bush. In this work,

I have attempted a thematic analysis concentrated on the press because it is the oldest form of the news media, but obviously, I have broadened the subject matter to include electronic media and new forms of media technology. In hopes of making the work accessible to the general reader, I have avoided using the academic vocabulary often associated with media studies. While I have used secondary sources, I have fleshed them out by examining hundreds of newspaper clippings and magazine articles (far, far more than I have cited here). I also have conducted personal interviews with journalists and representatives of the press staffs of various first ladies (as referred to in the text and bibliography). It was good of them to take time to talk to me, and I am in their debt.

In addition to Professor Abrahamson, I would like to thank my husband, Henry Beasley, who is the "better half" of our team, as well as our daughter, Susan Kim, and her family for their encouragement. I am grateful to Dean Thomas Kunkel and the Philip Merrill College of Journalism of the University of Maryland and the university's Graduate School for giving me research time apart from my teaching schedule. Also, it has been my pleasure to discuss the significance of first ladies with Professor Lisa M. Burns, who recently received her Ph.D. from the University of Maryland.

My basic premise is that coverage of first ladies reflects quandaries over news values related to women and incorporates societal strains over changing gender roles in American life. In the conclusion of the book, I argue that the news media need to take coverage of first ladies more seriously because the institutionalization of their role is having a greater effect on the country's political system than has been recognized. I have tried to depict individual first ladies in the context of shifting expectations for women during different periods of U.S. history, a fascinating story in itself.

Not surprisingly, the book starts with Eleanor Roosevelt and her women-only press conferences, which put the first lady into a symbiotic news-making relationship with the reporters who covered her. I point out how Roosevelt transformed the position of the first lady into a role measured mainly by the success or failure of the incumbent as a communicator in the venues open to women in her era. Roosevelt had the courage to put herself on a public stage, and that, in itself, was a marked departure from the practices of her predecessors. Through her interaction with reporters, she began a partnership between the press and the presidential wife that has influenced the development of the first lady as an institution.

Today, in the early years of the twenty-first century, I would ask if it is not time to update and rethink this partnership. Women constitute more than 50 percent of the U.S. population, and the first lady is the single most visible symbol of American womanhood. Those of us concerned about the future of journalism are well aware that there has been a decline in newspaper readership among women in recent decades and that women relate to mass media differently than men. By examining news values related to the first lady, I hope we can detect some of the outworn precepts of news conventions that keep women as a group from receiving equal treatment with men and that may influence women's attitudes toward the news product.

By no means am I trying to blame that amorphous force known as "the media" for mistreating women. Elements involved in producing media content converge from various philosophical and political points of view and encompass society's uncertainty about gender relationships. But I am suggesting that those of us involved with the mass media as journalists, teachers, and researchers should cast a more careful eye on our use of tired stereotypes in dealing with women.

The second chapter of this book moves backward in history to show how first ladies before Roosevelt, with some exceptions, did not enter the public sphere. This situation was in keeping with social conventions that restricted women to the private realm—restrictions that still operate to some degree to keep women as subordinate players in the fields of both news and politics. Subsequent chapters deal with twentieth-century first ladies as treated by the news media in several roles—as political wives and helpmates, advocates for causes, and personifications of politically palatable images. Hillary Rodham Clinton is pictured in the context of being a media polarizer. Laura Bush is presented as a media representation of caring for other Americans in the wake of the terrorist attacks of September 11, 2001.

The final chapter calls for a broader examination of the Office of the First Lady in the White House and for greater awareness of the first lady as a political force in raising funds and serving as a magnet for women voters. The chapter also touches on the symbolic importance of first ladies on the world stage, as well as the ways in which they and their professional staffs are making increased use of sophisticated public relations techniques and taking advantage of new media outlets and technology to bypass conventional media.

The book ends with a look at a future in which the first

lady may be replaced by a first gentleman, speculation that is particularly timely now that Rodham Clinton is expected to be a presidential contender in 2008. The final chapter also questions whether the gender-specific institution of the first lady is outmoded in terms of media coverage. Whether or not Rodham Clinton manages to become the first woman president, her emergence as a possible nominee shows that the first lady as an institution deserves more study. The first lady's position has become a quasi training ground for the presidency almost in spite of the news media, which have consigned it to a status less important than it deserves.

MAURINE BEASLEY

ONE

ELEANOR ROOSEVELT AND THE "NEWSPAPER GIRLS"

Eleanor Roosevelt said she never forgot her first press conference on March 6, 1933, only two days after the inauguration of her husband, Franklin D. Roosevelt, as president of the United States. Entering the Red Room on the first floor of the White House, "I could feel the disapproval of the ushers as I went in with fear and trembling," she wrote in her autobiography. Sensing that the staff considered it undignified for a first lady to speak directly to the press, she attempted to conceal her dismay by grabbing a box of candied grapefruit peel. She passed it to thirty-five women journalists, referred to as "newspaper girls" in the language of the day, who had been invited to attend the record-making event.

That gesture betrayed her ambivalence and conveyed a host of unspoken questions. Was she a hostess entertaining guests in the White House or a leader in her own right? Was it possible to script a role to fit both the needs of her husband's administration and her personal interests? What should she do in the White House? How should she try to portray herself? Should she put herself forward as an advocate or role model for other women? How much of a part should she play in setting the tone of the administration, if not its actual policies? What kind of a relationship should there be between her and the news media? Conversely, what did the news media want or expect of her?

Although three-quarters of a century have passed since Roosevelt's first halting effort to meet the press, these questions still confront presidents' wives today as they carve out roles in successive administrations. Each first lady who has followed Roosevelt has been forced by the exigencies of the political process to answer them for herself. The power and influence of the news media have increased over the decades, shining an ever more intense spotlight on the wives as well as on the actual occupants of the Oval Office. First ladies have become all too cognizant of the fact that the news media pass judgment on their success or failure in a demanding job lacking specific parameters. These presidential wives serve as case studies for understanding the evolution of both the presidency and the news media as each institution has attempted, with limited success, to relate to the changing roles of American women.

In facing reporters at her first press conference, Roosevelt realized she was treading on unplowed ground. Her immediate predecessors had minimized contact with the Washington women journalists Roosevelt now sought to make her allies in a mutually beneficial arrangement. Pressed to make remarks at a social event, Grace Coolidge, who had been ordered by her husband not to speak to reporters, communicated with them by sign language, drawing on her skills as a teacher of the deaf before her marriage. Lou Henry Hoover, a Stanford graduate, was active in the Girl Scout movement and involved in the cause of physical education for women, but she held reporters at bay. Determined to get a holiday feature story, the ingenious Bess Furman, the top woman reporter in the Associated Press's Washington bureau, slipped into the White House to sing Christmas carols in the disguise of a Girl Scout.

Aware of their potential to picture her unfavorably, Roosevelt greeted the reporters at her first press conference with trepidation. As she recalled in her autobiography, "Most of the women facing me were total strangers. . . . I only hope they did not know how terrified I was in entering this untried field." Although she had watched her husband hold press conferences and she herself had been interviewed frequently and published books and magazine articles, she still felt daunted by the prospect of dealing with a sizable group of journalists. She knew that "many people around my husband were doubtful whether I could handle press conferences without getting myself and him into trouble." Fortunately, she found a friendly audience, and the conferences continued. She held 348 in all, usually meeting the reporters weekly when she was at the White House during her twelve years as first lady from 1933 to 1945.

In her initial insecurity, Roosevelt ran head-on into a reality that has marked the lives of first ladies since Martha Washington: everything they do is scrutinized carefully and seen as a reflection on their husbands. As autonomous individuals, they face amorphous boundaries, defined partly by their own personalities and partly by shifts in public attitudes and perceptions of what women should be and should do. Roosevelt took a calculated risk that the press would endorse her effort to make her position more visible by holding face-to-face meetings with reporters. Many of the topics covered, such as social events and her own schedule, engendered little controversy; others promoted her husband's New Deal programs to alleviate suffering during the Great Depression. Nevertheless, the press conferences focused attention on the first lady in her own right—featuring "Mrs. Roosevelt" as a motherly figure who humanized bureaucratic policies, voiced her own opinions, and attempted to lead the nation's women in weathering first the Depression and then World War II.

Since Roosevelt's era, first ladies have functioned increasingly as an arm of the presidency. Today, the Office of the First Lady stands third in the White House hierarchy, just below the Office of the Vice President, which is outranked only by the Oval Office itself according to the White House organizational chart. Yet there are no guidelines for the uncompensated position of first lady, and the post itself is not mentioned in the Constitution. With their own paid staffs and hectic schedules, first ladies stand out as the nation's premier volunteers, surrendering much of their personal privacy to public scrutiny as they contribute to the success, or failure, of their husbands' administrations. Historically, they have faced all the drawbacks of political office with few of the benefits, although Hillary Rodham Clinton managed to use her tenure as the stepping-stone for election to the U.S. Senate from New York. As the institution of the first lady has gained prominence over the years, presidents' wives have drawn barrages of both criticism and praise and served as lightning rods for societal arguments over competing and confusing expectations for women in general.

Carrying out myriad ceremonies traditionally performed by monarchs, first ladies have become American-style royal consorts in an ill-defined position that seems out of tune with the twenty-first century. The glamour and applause surrounding them come with a high price. Presidents' wives today are forced to carefully weigh whatever they do against the possibility of adverse reaction from no-holds-barred media increasingly ready to ferret out gossip and scandalous tidbits.

Perhaps it is not surprising that Teresa Heinz expressed dismay about the possibility of becoming first lady when she married Senator John Kerry in 1995. She told a magazine writer that she preferred not to think about her new husband as a presidential prospect. "For anyone who loves life," she said, the idea of being first lady was "worse than going to a Carmelite convent." (The Carmelite order is marked by ascetic strictures.) By the time Kerry became the Democratic nominee for president in 2004, she apparently viewed the prospect differently and campaigned vigorously for his election, although he lost.

Following Roosevelt, first ladies have been expected to perform in the public arena, unlike many presidential wives in the nineteenth century who took refuge in illness. Roosevelt's successors have developed strategies to deal with journalists, including media-oriented projects such as the "Just Say No" antidrug campaign of Nancy Reagan. As a group, first ladies have proven to be committed helpmates, using their contacts with the press to support their husbands. With a few exceptions, most first ladies have displayed exemplary social skills, coming from upper-class or upper-middle-class backgrounds and accustomed to assisting their husbands in their drive for political power. Unlike some of the husbands, all of the wives apparently have been committed to their marriage vows as far as the public is aware. Some have remarried after their husbands' deaths, but as widows, all have exhibited loyalty to the memory of their presidential spouses.

In many ways, their unique sorority personifies mainstream values, which historically have included strong marital partnerships. Yet no first lady, not even Eleanor Roosevelt or Hillary Rodham Clinton, has been able to totally escape what historian Gil Troy called "the First Lady's gossamer shackles, the delicate, exquisitely feminine bind that thrust them close to power and into the maelstrom of American politics yet forbade them from flexing their muscles." Nevertheless, they have made an important impact on U.S. society as symbolic representations of American womanhood.

Consequently, their relationship with the news media assumes more importance than simply being part of White House political communication. What first ladies say and do, as interpreted by journalists, frames public perceptions of the part women should play in American life. Their position gives them special entrée into the news-making process in general, where women long have been subordinate elements. Even today, when women make up more than half the population and constitute 47 percent of the labor force, they are cited much less frequently than men in news stories, and they constitute a minority of news reporters in both print and broadcasting media. On the three main U.S. broadcast networks, for example, 87 percent of the sound bites from experts are provided by men, while women represent only 23 percent of the news directors at television stations and about 37 percent of newspaper staffs.

Against this backdrop of male domination of the news

media, first ladies arguably have stood out for decades as the single most visible group of American women, apart from actresses and other performers who also rise or fall by dint of publicity. Arguments over first ladies' performances exemplify the ongoing debate over women's options. As three authorities on women and politics put it, "The press coverage of women in politics is an artifact of this country's age-old but unresolved debate over women citizens' proper role versus 'proper women's' place." Because of their prestige, when first ladies appear in the news they provide an imprimatur for other women to bridge the gap that still exists between the public world of power and the private world of domesticity.

Certainly, a greater gap existed in Roosevelt's period than today. Yet her press conferences, peculiar products of their time, provide a good starting point for an examination of gender issues that are still pervasive in journalism. Traditionally, journalists have been conditioned to cover two kinds of news (described with terms that have obvious sexual connotations). "Hard" news, pegged to timeliness and actual events, emphasizes public conflict and controversy, long the staples of our political system. In contrast, "soft" news flatters, amuses, and entertains, masking the seriousness of the struggles for dominance played out in the hard news domain. More than hard news, soft news frequently involves cooperation between journalists and news sources, who work together to construct a particular news scenario. First ladies traditionally have belonged in the soft news category, unless they have been touched by rumors of scandal (as Hillary Rodham Clinton was when she was called to testify before a grand jury investigating the Whitewater affair). If that happens, they become hard news, subject to a more ad-

versarial type of journalistic treatment. In her news conferences, Roosevelt tried to straddle the line between the two
categories, assuming the male privilege of establishing herself
as a key figure in the White House but doing it in a feminine,
nonthreatening way.

The idea of holding the conferences came from
Eleanor Roosevelt's intimate friend Lorena Hickok, the top
woman reporter for the Associated Press before she was
forced to resign due to her closeness to Roosevelt. Hickok,
who subsequently worked directly for the Roosevelt administration as an investigator of welfare programs, told the first
lady that women reporters were losing their jobs in Depression cutbacks and that women-only press conferences might
allow them to hang on to their positions.

Uncertain of what would make news at the conferences, Roosevelt moved cautiously to establish her terrain.
She wrote in her autobiography, "I began to wonder if there
was anything besides the purely social doings that might be
of special interest and value to the women of the country
and that the women reporters might write up better than
the men." Apart from her husband's position, she had no
mandate to use the White House as the "bully pulpit" that
her uncle, President Theodore Roosevelt, had advocated, but
she contemplated making it a lectern from which to reach
the nation's women. By doing so, she set a standard for activism against which all successive first ladies have been
measured, foreshadowing her subsequent career as the U.S.
representative to the United Nations who was the guiding
force behind the UN Declaration of Human Rights.

As contemporary first ladies confront the same issue—
how to act in a pulpit not their own—they receive unrelent-

ing attention in a media-centered culture increasingly dependent on images in place of words. Print, television, cable, the Internet, and all other elements of the modern communications mix are brought to bear on their White House role today. They are prime subjects for soft news that may have hard news implications if they actually are perceived as presidential advisers.

In spite of intense media scrutiny, however, the extent of the first lady's counsel is difficult to assess because of the privacy of her marital relationship. As one writer, Kati Marton, put it, "The institution's outer face has never been the primary source of the first lady's power. The quality of her relationship with her husband has been the key factor in determining the extent of her influence." The picture is further clouded by the fact that the first lady's public activities may be integral to her relationship with her spouse. This appeared to be the case with Roosevelt, who served for years as her husband's political but not marital partner, following disclosure of his romantic attachment to her social secretary in the World War I era. According to their children, the Roosevelts decided to stay together for political and family reasons but never resumed a sexual relationship.

No hint of the unusual nature of the Roosevelt marriage emanated from the first lady's press conferences, even though there were rumors in the capital that the couple had once considered divorce. In an era of little investigation into the personal lives of public officials, the reporters probably would not have written the full story even if they had known it, as Mary Hornaday, who covered the first lady for the *Christian Science Monitor,* noted in 1979. The conferences succeeded in part because of a blandness geared to the sex-segregated sections of daily newspapers, which remained the dominant mode for disseminating news during the Roosevelt administration. These sections, called women's and society pages, were oriented toward middle- and upper-class women and were known for formulaic news of fashion, weddings, and club events. Scorned by male journalists, the sections had little prestige, and staffers who worked on them were paid far less than their male colleagues. Yet the sections were important because they drew both readers and advertising.

Although some who attended the press conferences, such as Bess Furman, wrote for general audiences, many of the regulars wrote for women's and society pages. Advised by Louis Howe, the president's chief political strategist, as well as by Hickok, Eleanor Roosevelt initially limited attendance to newspaper and press association women accredited by Stephen T. Early, Franklin Roosevelt's press secretary. Laying down guidelines similar to those used by her husband in his twice-weekly press conferences, which actually did not start until two days after her first halting effort, she did not allow reporters to use direct quotes without permission. In addition, she depended on the good faith of the group to spare her embarrassing publicity. A contemporary journalist noted, "The moment she grows spontaneous, a vigilant newspaper woman is sure to interrupt and say, 'This is off the record, isn't it?'" Roosevelt was said to quickly agree.

Before World War II broke out, more than one hundred women had received accreditation to attend the press conferences. A small number represented radio networks and government agencies. A more sizable group worked as part-time correspondents for their hometown newspapers. They wrote columns of Washington chitchat, giving readers across the United States a picture of Roosevelt graciously conversing with women reporters. No African American reporters, however, were allowed to attend. Early, who favored segregation, contended they were not eligible to participate in either the president's or the first lady's news conferences because they represented weekly, not daily, publications. During World War II, part-time writers were dropped and the number of accredited reporters fell to thirty-three. By that time, accreditation had been turned over to the women themselves, who organized as Mrs. Roosevelt's Press Conference Association and voted on new applicants.

Most topics brought up at the press conferences reflected news deemed suitable for women's and society pages—vignettes of White House life and events, the first lady's interest in various causes, her family, her schedule, her wardrobe, and her personal views on war and peace. Stories based on these themes, somewhat trivial and naive by today's standards, testified to the relatively narrow dimensions of women's sphere during the Depression and World War II. They conveyed a picture of Eleanor Roosevelt as a warm human being to large numbers of newspaper readers. In spite of growing competition from radio and the newsreels shown in movie theaters, newspapers still reached vast segments of the population, with aggregate circulation standing at 1.18 copies per day per household in 1940. They made up a far more pervasive medium in that era than they do today, when 42 percent of men and 47 percent of women do not read newspapers at all on a daily basis, according to the industry's own readership demographics. (In response to the gap in women readers, newspapers have been experimenting with the reintroduction of women's pages, most of which were transformed into lifestyle/leisure sections in the 1970s.)

Male reporters scoffed at the women-only press conferences. They dubbed the "newspaper girls" Roosevelt's "incense burners" when a picture taken at an early conference showed some of the women sitting on the floor clustered around the first lady's feet. Roosevelt, without commenting on the ridicule that ensued, soon moved the conferences to the Monroe Room on the second floor of the White House living quarters, where all attendees were furnished straight-backed chairs. At the appointed hour, the reporters dashed up the stairs from the Green Room, vying for front-row seats. After the group had assembled, Roosevelt entered, followed by her social secretary, Edith Helm, and her personal secretary, Malvina Thompson; she shook each woman's hand, announced her schedule, and entertained questions for an hour or more on assorted topics.

On occasion, Early would make sure that the first lady had some "real" news to present, illustrating how the press conferences fit into presidential political communication. When the White House decided to start serving beer to mark the end of Prohibition, President Roosevelt referred journalists to his wife, who brought up the topic on April 3, 1933. As a result, the newspaperwomen got a front-page news story, which helped elevate their professional standing. The approach also allowed the administration to handle a "hot potato" subject carefully. Eleanor Roosevelt, known to be against drinking, prepared a carefully worded statement indicating that she hoped the change would lead to temperance. With Eleanor rather than Franklin Roosevelt making the announcement, the administration hoped to appease those who still supported Prohibition. Another major story was the announcement on January 29, 1934, that wines (preferably American) but not distilled spirits would return to the White House.

Although Roosevelt formed close friendships with some of the journalists, her inner circle excluded women's page and society reporters, who viewed her as more interested in social causes than fashion and style. According to Hope Ridings Miller, society editor of the *Washington Post* during the Roosevelt administration, "Mrs. Roosevelt's closest friends were very homely girls and Lorena Hickok was one of them. Mrs. Roosevelt was homely herself and felt comfortable with them. She felt she could do something for them—build up their ego," although, Miller continued, "she gave us plenty to write about." Explaining that "the men were always prying around trying to get something nasty about her, and we did protect her," Miller said the women reporters believed Roosevelt "did the best she could for the country and herself with the gifts she had."

By deciding to meet reporters instead of relying on White House announcements describing social functions, Roosevelt repudiated the method of dealing with Washington women reporters set up by Edith Carow Roosevelt, the wife of Eleanor's uncle Theodore Roosevelt, who served as president from 1901 to 1909. Avoiding direct contact with reporters had been Edith Roosevelt's passion. She had hired a secretary to give the press handouts on formal entertaining, along with posed photographs of herself and her children.

Eleanor Roosevelt had no desire to follow her aunt's example. Just before Franklin's election as president in 1932, she had written a letter in which, according to two of her biographers, she confided "her fear that the White House would be a prison where she would serve a death sentence made up of endless receptions, formal dinners and teas." The press conferences evolved as one way she could mesh her own desire to play a meaningful role with the traditional expectations of a president's wife.

When Roosevelt moved far afield from the social, however, as she did when she served as a civil defense official at the start of World War II, she laid herself open to criticism. Questions were raised of the kind still asked today when a first lady is perceived as wielding political power. They boil down to speculation over how much influence she has by virtue of direct access to her husband, but they end with the succinct criticism: who elected her anyway?

In her opening statement at her first press conference, Roosevelt spelled out a practical reason for weekly press briefings—it would save time for her to see the journalists in one group. In her autobiography, she put it more bluntly. She decided that "everything that was legitimate news should be given out by me" to forestall reporters' efforts to gain information through bribery of White House staff and other "devious methods." At the same time, she believed that in the women reporters, she could have a channel through which she could reach the country on significant issues. She told them, "You are the interpreters to the women of the country as to what goes on politically in the legislative national life and also what the social and political life is at the White House." Still, she recognized that her press conferences should not, in her words, "trespass on my husband's prerogatives, that national and international news must be handled by him."

As a group, the women reporters were grateful to the first lady for holding the conferences and did not want to jeopardize their continuation by writing unfavorable stories. Hickok never covered them, but she did help Roosevelt gain rapport with the more influential women journalists such as Furman, whose position with the Associated Press meant that her stories appeared in hundreds of newspapers. Furman became one of Roosevelt's longtime allies, picturing her as an exemplary modern woman working tirelessly on behalf of her husband's administration. The press conferences sometimes were used to float trial balloons for New Deal programs, such as a proposal to set up training camps for unemployed women; the idea received such adverse reaction that the camps were limited to the unmarried.

Roosevelt's exclusion of men from her press conferences forced news organizations that had a male-only policy to employ women. Ruby Black, Furman's main competitor, became the first woman hired by United Press (the predecessor of today's United Press International) only because the organization needed a woman to report on the first lady. In return, Black became one of Roosevelt's staunchest supporters, to the point of being considered her sycophant. She was the chief target of a *Harper's* article by a New York newspaperwoman accusing those in the press conference group of being Eleanor Roosevelt's "willing slaves."

Black, a stronger feminist than many of the other reporters, prompted Roosevelt at one of her first press conferences to make a statement opposing legislation intended to bar married women from federal employment if their husbands also were on the government payroll. When Roosevelt spoke against the measure, marking the first of many times that she violated her professed rule of not discussing political issues, her comments received relatively little news play: most of the women were not assigned to political news and had no reason to report it. Though Roosevelt's views on the retention of married women workers got little attention, however, the details of the annual White House egg-rolling event at Easter filled columns.

Even friendly reporters complained that the first lady meandered from topic to topic and avoided serious discussion. Furman commented on the schoolteacher-like tone with which she lectured to the women. Comparing Eleanor Roosevelt's press conferences with those of her husband, Furman wrote in an Associated Press feature: "At the President's press conference, all the world's a stage, at Mrs. Roosevelt's, all the world's a school. . . . Give Mrs. Roosevelt a roomful of newspaper women, and she conducts classes on scores of subjects, always seeing beyond her immediate hearers to the 'women of the country' with whom she would share the quickening thought-streams that pour over a President's wife." Before the 1936 election, Furman wrote in her diary, Roosevelt went off the record on three controversial subjects: birth control, accusations attacking her role in the Arthurdale project (a resettlement community for West Virginia miners that became mired in cost overruns), and charges by historian Mary Beard that men had robbed women of their history.

Yet the conferences did produce some news, which the reporters tended to accept on Roosevelt's own terms. When the first lady said she supported teaching about communism in public schools but not advocating it, Furman noted she herself had a "swell and profitable" story that she wrote in three versions for the Associated Press. After fighting broke out in Europe before World War II, the women reporters sought to find out whether the first lady advocated U.S. intervention, but they played down her hesitant statement that she supported repeal of the Neutrality Act, which was designed to keep the United States out of the conflict. In 1944, they reported her erroneous assurances that her husband's health was no bar to his candidacy for a fourth term. He died within six months of his reelection.

Acutely aware that the majority of the nation's daily newspapers opposed New Deal policies, the Roosevelts knew they needed to tread carefully where the press was concerned. In all four of his presidential campaigns, Franklin Roosevelt won editorial support from only a minority of newspaper publishers. Press conferences allowed both the president and the first lady to develop cordial relationships with individual journalists, who used their access to the White House to impress their superiors in spite of most publishers' hostility to the New Deal. Eleanor Roosevelt also invited Furman, Black, and some of the other women reporters to visit her at the family estate at Hyde Park, New York, and the Roosevelt summer home at Campobello in Canada.

Emma Bugbee of the solidly Republican *New York Herald Tribune*, for instance, regularly wrote favorable stories about the first lady in spite of her paper's editorial stand. Bugbee—along with Furman, Black, Dorothy Ducas (who represented the Hearst newspapers), and a male photographer—went with Eleanor Roosevelt on a trip to inspect Depression-era conditions in Puerto Rico and the Virgin Islands in 1934. Accompanied by Hickok in her capacity as a government investigator, Roosevelt toured slum areas and almost exhausted the reporters, who sent back stories on her tireless pace. The women barely mentioned the presence of Hickok, who some historians speculate may have had a lesbian relationship with Roosevelt. *Time* magazine, however, depicted the trip, which coincided with Hickok's forty-first birthday, as a boondoggle for Hickok. It characterized her as a "rotund lady with a husky voice" who had "gone around a lot with the first lady."

Obviously, sex-segregated news conferences would never pass muster today. Even at the time, they met some opposition, particularly since Franklin Roosevelt admitted women to his weekly press conferences, although very few covered the president. One who did was May Craig, a correspondent for Maine newspapers. Craig also attended the first lady's conferences and argued that it was unfair to exclude men when women were trying to make a case for equal opportunities, but she had little support. When Eleanor Roosevelt received an official, although unpaid, appointment as assistant director of the Office of Civil Defense in September 1941, her press relations changed. She was forced to hold press briefings at civil defense headquarters, where male as well as female reporters quizzed her about alleged inefficiency in administration and favoritism in hiring. Martha Strayer, a reporter for the *Washington Daily News,* noted that these conferences, unlike her others, put the first lady "on the defensive." In February 1942, Roosevelt resigned as the result of the scathing disapproval she received from the press for promoting the employment of friends in civil defense jobs and proposing that dancing be taught in bomb shelters as a form of physical fitness.

After her resignation, the press softened its condemnation, picturing her as a woman of good intentions, even if she was inept. Sidestepping the issue of her civil defense performance, Roosevelt portrayed herself as a victim of her position. She contended that the experience "convinced me being in the White House would prevent me from doing any real job in World War II."

Roosevelt quickly resumed her women-only press conferences. When a male reporter sought permission to attend, he was rebuffed. Roosevelt told the women, who had organized as her Press Conference Association, that they could admit him but that if they did, she probably would end the meetings. One association officer told her colleagues that Roosevelt considered the women-only meetings "precious." Men were allowed at one meeting in 1943 when Roosevelt reported on her trip to Pacific bases as a Red Cross representative, but they professed to be uncomfortable and turned out war-between-the-sexes features. "I felt like I had blundered into the powder room of an art gallery," one male reporter was quoted as saying. Males, however, freely attended Roosevelt's conferences when she was traveling.

Long before the celebrity-crazed culture of today, Roosevelt realized that the public had an almost insatiable appetite for tidbits about the lives of presidents and their families. Although some topics were off-limits, such as her children's divorces and her vacations with Hickok, Roosevelt capitalized on the eagerness of the news media to write human interest stories that reinforced the limitations of women's sphere in the early twentieth century. Furman wrote in her diary that Roosevelt would happily tell "when she gets up in the morning and what she eats for breakfast [but] she rules out controversial subjects, and won't be queried on anything in the province of the President." Nevertheless, many of the first lady's comments had a political dimension, although the women might or might not use them for their stories. Reporters paid little attention when she backed the appointment of an opponent of the proposed equal rights amendment (ERA) to the Inter-American Commission of Women. "Most of the leading gal reporters being equal rightsers [*sic*] this didn't get much of a rise," Furman noted.

Although the women reported Roosevelt's visits to segregated institutions and military units, racial issues were downplayed, perhaps reflecting the prejudices of the journalists themselves. For example, when Roosevelt said, in response to a question, that artists who performed for King George and Queen Elizabeth of England on their state visit in 1939 would have a chance to meet the monarchs, she made an important political statement. Since it was widely known that Marian Anderson, an African American, would be asked to sing, the first lady's comment showed that she and her husband accepted racial equality at social events in officially segregated Washington. Furman, apparently more eager to spare Roosevelt criticism than to write about civil rights, thought the question was asked "with malice."

Continuing with her own career as a writer, which she had launched before moving into the White House, Roosevelt wrote a daily syndicated newspaper column entitled "My Day," a diary of her activities; it started on December 30, 1935, and lasted almost until her death in 1962. By 1938, the column appeared in sixty-two newspapers, with a total circulation of 4,034,552. In addition, she continually appeared in news photographs and newsreels, sometimes at her husband's side but often by herself, and was continually on the go—traveling, making speeches, meeting the disadvantaged, inspecting New Deal projects, and supporting the World War II war effort. She also wrote for women's magazines and gave sponsored radio broadcasts as well as paid lectures. In 1937, she sold serialized rights to the first volume of her autobiography to the *Ladies' Home Journal* for $75,000, an amount equal to her husband's annual salary as president.

Caricatured for her appearance, marked in part by protruding teeth, Roosevelt did not like press photographs. Having arranged with a New York department store to give her new clothing at a reduced rate, she was obligated to wear the garments for fashion photographs. According to one photographer, she disliked posing and "never bothered to look at herself before her picture was taken." She endured being photographed as part of the public image-making necessary for a first lady.

In earning money while in the White House, Roosevelt upheld the right of a married woman to work at a time when only about one-fourth of the U.S. labor force was female. By giving much of what she made to charity, she tempered criticism about profiting from her position. She also benefited from the fact that the women who covered her raised few questions about her financial arrangements. They defused political criticism of her activities to a degree by picturing her as a wife who reported back to her husband on what she had learned during her travels.

Since the public knew that Franklin Roosevelt was impaired physically as a result of infantile paralysis (although many Americans were unaware that he actually could not walk), journalists showed relatively little skepticism about her frequent trips. Prior to the election of 1936, for example, Kathleen McLaughlin, a member of the press conference group, praised the first lady in the *New York Times* for acting as her husband's "eyes and ears." The president himself frequently quoted "my Missus" in cabinet meetings and said she "gets around a lot."

The newswomen first tolerated "My Day" as an amateur effort beneath their professional notice, but their opinions changed when Roosevelt used the column to break news stories that otherwise might have been saved for the press conferences. A prime example was her resignation from the Daughters of the American Revolution (DAR) in 1939, obliquely announced in her column, in protest against the organization's refusal to let Marian Anderson sing in its segregated Constitution Hall. According to Hornaday, "Mrs. Roosevelt was always looking for ways to earn money. We resented that when she wrote her column competing with us." Yet like most of the other women, Hornaday, the first president of Mrs. Roosevelt's Press Conference Association, remained on good terms with the first lady.

Since Roosevelt's day, the efforts of first ladies and their White House staffs to control their news coverage have expanded greatly. Far more than in the 1930s, we have become a celebrity-smitten culture. The line between hard and soft news has eroded as a twenty-four-hour cable news cycle has placed tremendous pressure on the news media to attract audiences by a succession of fresh sensations. The Internet allows instant communication of gossip and personal opinion without any check for accuracy. Politicians raise millions for advertising, often misleading, that attacks their opponents. Confronted by this media mix, first ladies are expected to hold their own in order to communicate effectively. Yet what kind of news can or should be expected from an individual who does not hold public office herself? In that regard, Roosevelt's example is still instructive. Positive portrayals of first ladies seem to stem from symbiotic relationships between them and the news media, cemented by personal contacts.

Motivated by both Hickok and Howe, Eleanor Roosevelt was able to establish warm friendships with reporters in a pre–Watergate era when journalists allowed presidents and their families to have more privacy than they do today. Because Howe "insisted that newspaper people were the most honorable group in the world," the first lady wrote, "I took it for granted that the women were as honorable as the men, and my confidence was very seldom betrayed." Recognizing that other women were interested in what she did simply because she was the president's wife, she supplied the press with a host of information, mainly innocuous, that was suited to the news conventions of her day.

By current standards, Roosevelt had no extraordinary message, although her press conferences elevated the status of women. While her topics touched on the predictable, such as the need for women to vote and take part in community life, she stressed the accomplishments of notable female figures, many of whom she introduced at her conferences. Her special guests included key women in the New Deal and others of achievement as well as official visitors such as the king and queen of England, who visited the United States in 1939, and Madame Chiang Kai-shek of China. Amelia Earhart, a friend of the first lady, was found curled up on a couch at one gathering. Though it was obvious that Roosevelt intended to offer only a sanitized view of White House life, the conferences enhanced the importance of her role. They gave women journalists direct entrée to the White House and clearly impacted the role of the first lady as a leader for American women.

Because the Twenty-fifth Amendment, added to the Constitution in 1951, set a two-term limit on the presidency, no first lady ever again will have as long a tenure in the White House as Eleanor Roosevelt did. During that tenure, she expanded horizons for her successors, establishing the right for presidents' wives to have a public presence as long as they did not openly disagree with their husbands' views. She also claimed the privilege of pursuing an independent career as a way of establishing individual autonomy and self-worth, although most of her successors, apart from Hillary Rodham Clinton, have not followed in this direction.

By revealing details of her personal life (albeit mainly insignificant ones), Roosevelt augmented the position of the first lady as a celebrity, making media-oriented relationships key to modernizing and expanding the concept of being first lady. The seemingly ubiquitous Roosevelt presented herself to the public through the mass media, which in turn fed on coverage of her extensive travels and voluminous pursuits.

Aided by her understanding of mass communications, she often had higher ratings than her husband; in 1938, for example, the Gallup Poll showed she had an approval rating of 67 percent compared to 58 percent for the president. While first ladies often but not always outrank their husbands, Roosevelt's rating was particularly impressive because critics regularly derided her activism and her perceived influence on New Deal policies. Able to project herself as a unique individual through the media of her day, she transformed the role of the first lady from genteel hostess into a national presence judged mainly by success or failure as a mass communicator. From a halting beginning, she established herself as one of the most revered women of the twentieth century. In the second volume of her autobiography, she wrote, "As I look back over the years, I think I have much for which to thank the newspaper women." They had helped make her what she became. Eleanor Roosevelt's lengthy presence in the White House still casts a long shadow over those who have followed her. Furthermore, it throws into relief our understanding of the women who preceded her as first lady of the nation.

TWO

EARLY FIRST LADIES AND THE
PUBLIC SPHERE

From the days of George Washington to the present, presidents' wives have found themselves in the public eye, subject to journalistic appraisal of their behavior. As the wife of the nation's first chief executive, Martha Washington was expected to fulfill the ceremonial role performed by royalty in European courts yet personify the simple dignity appropriate for a republican form of government. Presiding with her husband at state functions following his inauguration in 1789, she scripted a part played by each of her successors: hostess for the nation. While presidents' wives today extend their roles in various directions, official entertaining remains a prime responsibility. So does the presentation of a suitable image for their husbands' administrations.

A plantation mistress and one of the richest widows in the colonies at the time of her marriage to George Washington in 1750, Martha Washington took seriously her position as the president's partner but modestly described herself as "an old-fashioned Virginia house-keeper." While keeping a distance from politics, she knew that she and her husband would be carefully watched to see if they set a tone for the new government that would command respect from leaders of the older countries of the world. As Margaret Truman, the daughter of President Harry S Truman, put it, "The first first lady thus became a major player in bridging the murky gap between presidential dignity and democratic accessibility—a role other first ladies have continued with varying degrees of success to this day."

Becomingly dressed in white to denote simplicity rather than queenly elegance, Washington served as her husband's consort for staid dinners and receptions in New York, the first capital. Her presence, enhanced by two grandchildren who often accompanied her, brought public adulation and solidified her husband's image as a family man. Yet her position restricted her movements and made her a target for the political press of the day that attacked her husband.

There was uncertainty over her title. Should she be called "the presidentess," "Lady President," or even "Marquise"? Finally, officials settled on "Lady Washington," the name used by cheering crowds when she had traveled from Mount Vernon to join her husband. "Lady," however, conveyed visions of British nobility and was discarded by subsequent administrations. (The term emerged again in the nineteenth century when the designation "first lady" became accepted.)

In the presidential residence, Martha Washington complained, as many of her successors have done, of limitations on her personal freedom. She wrote in a letter in October 1789, "I never go to any public place, indeed I am more like a state prisoner than anything else. There [are] certain boundaries set for me which I must not depart from." In a letter two months later, she resolved to be happy in spite of the fact that "I, who had much rather be at home, should occupy a place [with] which a great many younger and gayer women would be prodigiously pleased."

When the capital moved to Philadelphia in 1790, her Friday night assemblies drew the attention of newspaper editors who usually ignored the activities of women. Unlike President Washington's receptions, which were limited to male officials, her "drawing rooms" presumably were private parties since women were invited, but the press considered them fair game for comment. According to contemporaries, she sat on a slightly raised platform and greeted women guests with a nod after each made "a most respectful curtsy." Guests were expected to sit silently as they waited for President Washington to make his rounds, saying a few words to each one. Supporters of George Washington's Federalist party lauded her conduct of a "Republican court" and praised her "unassuming" and "unaffected" personality.

In contrast, editors representing the anti–Federalist party led by Thomas Jefferson attacked her gatherings. Perhaps fearing the influence of women in politics, which he had witnessed disdainfully while a diplomat in Paris, Jefferson disliked Martha Washington's assemblies. The *National Gazette,* the mouthpiece of his Democratic-Republican party, placed her "levees," according to one writer, as "number two in the ten warning signs of creeping monarchy and aristocracy."

Political opponents also complained that she rode in a cream-colored coach that smacked of royalty; it had the Washington coat of arms and was drawn by six handsome horses and attended by liveried grooms. Anti-Federalists fumed when she sent out engravings titled "Lady Washington" that showed her wearing a high headdress called a "Queen's Nightcap." Apparently intended for the Federalist press, the engravings marked the start of what eventually would become common practice: the furnishing of an image of a president's wife to the media of her era. In response, Washington gave up plans for her correspondence to be marked with a coat-of-arms seal. This incident was the first of many times to come when a president's wife modified her behavior in the face of press disapproval. When George Washington made his precedent-setting decision to vacate the presidency after two terms, his wife happily returned with him to Mount Vernon.

Her successor, Abigail Adams, took a different approach to the role of being the president's spouse, acting as a political as well as a domestic and social partner to her husband. When John Adams was serving in the Continental Congress that drafted the Declaration of Independence, Abigail Adams, who had been left to run the family farm back in Massachusetts, urged him to support legal rights for women. She wrote, "Remember the Ladies, and be more generous and favourable to them than your ancestors. Do not put such unlimited power into the hands of the Husbands. Remember all Men would be tyrants if they could." Adams responded, partly in jest, "Depend on it, we know better than to repeal our masculine systems. . . . We have only the name of masters, and rather than give this up, which would completely subject us to the despotism of the petticoat, I hope George Washington and all our brave heroes would fight." She then countered, "I can not say that I think you very generous to the Ladies, for whilst you are proclaiming peace and good will to

Men, Emancipating all nations, you insist upon retaining absolute power over Wives."

Adams's opponents, however, questioned who wielded the power in the Adams household. Rather than "Lady Adams," they sarcastically called the wife "Mrs. President" or even "Her Majesty," marking the first but hardly the last time a president's spouse would be attacked for exercising influence over her husband. As Edith Mayo, a Smithsonian expert on first ladies, expressed it, "Such discomfort with a first lady's voice in the business of the nation has changed very little over most of the nearly two hundred years that followed."

Since John Adams had been vice president under Washington, Abigail Adams had witnessed Martha Washington's performance at close hand and doubted she had the "patience, prudence, [or] discretion" to follow her predecessor. Nevertheless, she served as an economical hostess who watched the family finances as well as an unofficial adviser who received numerous requests to recommend individuals for government jobs, which she contended she did not do. Both she and her husband encountered hostility from political opponents who found them more convenient targets than the revered Washingtons.

Stung by criticism, she took as personal affronts anti-Federalist newspaper stories that attacked her family as well as her husband, claiming that her children and in-laws had received favored treatment from the Federalists in power. In 1798, midway through her husband's sole term, she experienced a four-month-long mental and physical collapse. It hurt Abigail to see herself and John referred to in print as "Darby and Joan," the subjects of an English ballad about an elderly couple oblivious to the world around them. She could hardly believe that editors would call the president "old, querulous, Bald, blind, crippled Toothless Adams." As a surreptitious counterattack, she asked her circle of personal correspondents to send copies of documents supporting Adams to friendly newspapers.

The couple's political partnership was not always beneficial to the president himself as he set policy. As a sounding board and confidant, for example, Abigail Adams urged her husband to go to war with France, but he wisely ignored her advice, according to historians. The maintenance of U.S. neutrality in the conflict between France and England during Adams's administration is viewed as one of his biggest achievements.

Unfortunately, John Adams did side with his wife in support of the infamous Alien and Sedition Acts of 1798, which made it a crime for newspapers to print "false, scandalous or malicious writings" against members of Congress and the president. Although the law provided for truth as a defense, the press of the day mixed fact and opinion, and it was impossible to prove the truthfulness of opinions. The acts resulted in fines and imprisonment for Jeffersonian editors who criticized the Adams administration. Ignoring the First Amendment, Abigail Adams rejoiced when a congressman was sentenced to four months behind bars for opining that John Adams had an "unbounded thirst for ridiculous pomp."

With the presidential election of 1800 partly a referendum on the two acts, voters chose Thomas Jefferson and repudiated Adams's bid to stay in office. The acts expired, and anyone still imprisoned under them was pardoned. John and Abigail Adams returned to Massachusetts from the unfinished White House in Washington, where they had moved toward the end of their term and where she had hung her laundry in the East Room. Like Martha Washington, Abigail Adams helped define the position of the first lady, demonstrating that a president's wife could play a substantial role if her husband encouraged her to air her opinions.

Jefferson, a widower, invited the popular Dolley Madison, wife of his close friend and political ally Secretary of State James Madison, to serve as his hostess when his daughter was not available. Endowed with a warm and charming personality, the buxom Dolley Madison was seventeen years younger than her learned husband, who presented a wizened appearance and lacked the social acumen she displayed in behalf of his career. Jefferson considered her an example of Republican womanhood, a lively partner for the powerful but also, according to historian Catherine Allgor, "astute enough to appear politically null." No Abigail Adams in forthrightness, Dolley Madison exhibited a tactful manner and sunny disposition, conversing amiably with those of all political persuasions.

Nevertheless, her role at Jefferson's side was enough to cause scandalous rumors that found their way into print. Political opponents of Jefferson and Madison inferred that she was the president's mistress, in part because the Madisons initially had lived with Jefferson in the White House after moving to Washington. They attacked the morals of both James and Dolley Madison along with those of her sister and brother-in-law, claiming the husbands had used the wives as prostitutes to further their own careers. One congressman referred to the rumors in speeches, and innuendo about the purported scandal appeared in a Baltimore newspaper.

A Quaker widow in Philadelphia who had helped run

a boardinghouse before her marriage to Madison, Dolley was wounded by the accusations, but they had little effect on her husband's political career. Elected president in 1808 as the candidate of Jefferson's Democratic-Republican party, he was reelected four years later. His first opponent, Charles Pinckney, in a wry tribute to Dolley Madison's social graces, claimed he "was beaten by Mr. and Mrs. Madison."

As the first presidential wife to move into the White House at the beginning of her husband's term, Dolley Madison took full advantage of her opportunity to set the tone for the administration and to establish precedents for her successors. Two Madison scholars, David Mattern and Holly Shulman, commented, "Through her conduct she defined republican manners and created republican rituals that affirmed the political legitimacy of her husband." After persuading Congress to appropriate funds to renovate the run-down mansion, the "Lady Presidentress," as she was called, staged a lavish public reception each Wednesday night that drew so many guests it was called "Mrs. Madison's crush" or "squeeze." The center of attention in elegant outfits including trademark turbans ornamented with huge birds-of-paradise feathers, Dolley Madison, in the words of a nineteenth-century writer, "looked and moved like a queen." But with her snuffbox, engaging smile, and unassuming manners, she still conveyed democratic informality, making the White House a neutral public space where officials and nonofficials alike could maneuver for political advantage.

She soared further in public esteem when the British attacked Washington during the War of 1812 and burned the White House. Not leaving until the British were almost at her door, she made sure the Gilbert Stuart portrait of George

Washington and other documents of state were saved before fleeing herself. Upon returning to the capital, she was elected the "first directress" of the Washington City Orphans Asylum, the first of many formally organized projects of presidents' wives.

To a greater extent than Martha Washington and Abigail Adams, Dolley Madison became a celebrated public figure. The *National Intelligencer,* a Washington newspaper that was read throughout the young nation, mentioned her favorably. An early magazine used a woodcut engraving copied from her portrait as an illustration for its cover. This occasion was the first of many to come when the likeness of a president's wife was used, in the words of Carl Anthony, a biographer of first ladies, "to grace a publication." Leaving Washington in 1817, Dolley Madison moved back to the capital after her husband's death in 1836, living across the street from the White House and reigning as a grande dame.

At her death in 1849 when she was eighty-one, President Zachary Taylor stated, "She will never be forgotten because she was truly our First Lady for a half-century." Never before had the term *first lady* been used in public, but it was a fitting recognition of the way Madison had acted "to solidify an important role for the President's consort," as another historian of first ladies, Betty Caroli, put it. In her later years, Madison advised presidential families on White House entertaining, a tangible gesture of her influence. According to Caroli, the title of first lady, not used in Madison's lifetime, did not take firm hold with the public until 1911 when a play by that name based on the Madisons became popular. Robert P. Watson, another scholar of first ladies, pointed out there is no consensus on the origins of the title but instead "competing theories and arguments surrounding its development." In spite of the controversy, few would argue that Dolley Madison had not earned the title.

Not surprisingly, her successor found it difficult to follow her performance. President James Monroe's elegant and regal wife, Elizabeth Monroe, created an uproar by refusing to make visits to wives and daughters of members of Congress. The women of official Washington retaliated by boycotting the White House. Pleading ill health, Elizabeth Monroe stayed away from Washington when she could. Her attempt to hold informal White House receptions proved unsuccessful; a newspaper wrote of the disgusting nature of the people who attended, including "some whose heads a comb has never touched, half hid by dirty collars."

London-born Louisa Adams, the daughter of an American merchant, helped her husband, John Quincy Adams (a son of John and Abigail Adams), win the presidency in the disputed election of 1824, which was decided by the House of Representatives. She called on wives of congressmen, entertained frequently, and held a magnificent ball in honor of her husband's rival, Andrew Jackson. This mammoth event led *Harper's Bazaar* to declare, "Everybody who was any body was there." Yet once in the White House, John Quincy Adams was unable to push his program through Congress, and his administration failed, while his wife coped with depression.

Louisa Adams, who had endured twelve pregnancies and seven miscarriages between the ages of twenty-one and forty-two, became a virtual recluse. An accomplished singer and harpist, she spent time in the White House writing plays and sketches revealing the unhappiness of her earlier years, when she had said that "hanging and marriage were strongly assimilated." She was incensed when opposition newspapers printed charges that her husband had improperly spent government funds to buy a French billiard table for family use and that she had undemocratic ways due to her English birth. In self-defense, she wrote an unsigned biographical account of her life for a Washington newspaper, *Mrs. A. S. Colvin's Weekly Messenger.* Probably to her relief, her husband overwhelmingly lost his reelection bid to Andrew Jackson after a dirty campaign in which Adams's backers accused Jackson's wife, Rachel, of immorality.

Surprising to us today, when first ladies are perennial subjects for women's magazines, presidents' wives were not featured in the sex-segregated publications born in the decades before the Civil War. *Godey's Lady's Book,* the most important of the new women's magazines, and its imitators did not write about the men's world of politics or the women who claimed some part of it, at least not until after they were dead. To write about the living was seen as somewhat disrespectful in an era dominated by the "cult of true womanhood," which called on women to exemplify four virtues: piety, purity, submissiveness, and domesticity.

By contrast, during the Revolutionary War period, women such as Martha Washington and Abigail Adams had played key economic roles, managing family holdings while the men were away and acting as business partners with their husbands. As economic conditions improved in the new nation after the War of 1812, the situation changed dramatically. The ideal of the "lady" emerged, personified by wan females who did not work and were supported by male relatives. In the popular mind, ladies sat in parlors, dressed in elaborate outfits, and occupied themselves with genteel pursuits such as writing sentimental poetry and holding tea parties. Seen as passive and often in ill health due to childbearing, the lady was not expected to venture into the man's world of money-making and politics. Neither was she supposed to be exposed to the glare of public attention. According to nineteenth-century convention, a lady's name properly appeared in newspapers only three times: when she was born, in an announcement; when she was married, in a wedding story; and when she died, in an obituary. Women's magazines such as *Godey's,* although they published contributions from women, often shielded their writers from public notice by using initials or pen names to mask their identities.

Consequently, before the Civil War, news of presidents' wives remained relatively sparse in the newspapers and magazines, except for an occasional mention that found its way into print in the guise of political comment. After the vital presence of Dolley Madison, the role of the first lady was diminished for decades, with various female relatives of presidents frequently filling in for absent or ailing wives, since it was clear each president needed a hostess. With some exceptions, the first ladies and their stand-ins got relatively little attention.

Andrew Jackson's wife, Rachel, died before he took office, distressed by partisan attacks on her character for allegedly marrying Jackson before her divorce from her first husband was final. Jackson's successor, Martin Van Buren, another widower, escorted Dolley Madison to social events and gained an official hostess when Madison introduced her cousin Angelica Singleton to Van Buren's son Abraham. Within months, the two were married and Angelica Singleton was installed in the White House, where she copied

European royalty by dressing in white and assembling a group of women who resembled ladies-in-waiting to attend her. Her pretensions did not benefit her father-in-law, a Democrat, who was accused of behaving like a king. In the next election, he was replaced by an Indian-fighting Whig, Gen. William Henry Harrison, who died in 1841 only a month after his inauguration. Harrison's wife, Anna, never set foot in Washington.

When Vice President John Tyler, called "His Accidency," became president, his invalid wife, Letitia, "modestly shrank from all notoriety and evaded the public eye as much as possible," Carl Anthony noted. When she died in September 1841, the *National Intelligencer* printed the conventional praise accorded demure nineteenth-century ladies—that she had been "a Wife, a Mother, and a Christian."

In striking contrast, the second Mrs. Tyler, thirty years younger than her husband, did not subscribe to the cult of true womanhood and craved publicity before and during her White House years. At nineteen, Julia Gardiner, known as the "Rose of Long Island," had shocked her wealthy parents by posing in fashionable clothes for a lithographed handbill signed with a rose to advertise a New York clothing store. Within six months after the death of Tyler's first wife, the flirtatious belle had accepted the president's invitation to play cards at the White House, where he started a fervent courtship by chasing her around tables. The couple eloped in June 1844 after Gardiner's father and two members of Tyler's cabinet were killed in a shipboard explosion while on an excursion with the president.

The twenty-four-year-old Julia Tyler determinedly made a social splash in the eight months remaining in Tyler's term, taking advantage of the changing newspaper climate in the 1840s to actively draw attention to herself. After using Gardiner money to refurbish the White House, according to a contemporary report, she surrounded herself by "twelve maids of honor" and held receptions while seated "upon a raised platform wearing a headdress formed of bugles and resembling a crown." She also started the custom of having bands play "Hail to the Chief" to give the presidency a royal flourish.

Her White House performance was made to order for the new penny press of the day, which tried to attract readers with colorful human interest stories instead of partisan political comment. Tyler assiduously cultivated F. W. Thomas, the Washington correspondent for the *New York Herald* (the leading penny newspaper), who fawned over the "Lovely Lady Presidentress" in *Herald* stories that often were reprinted in other papers. He told readers she was superior to Queen Victoria and "the most accomplished woman of her age." Her brother Alexander also wrote rhapsodic newspaper accounts of her regal entertaining that served a political as well as a social aim: her parties helped push the annexation of Texas, the biggest accomplishment of John Tyler's undistinguished presidency.

The Tylers were followed by a different kind of couple, Sarah and James Polk—political partners in the tradition of John and Abigail Adams. Sarah Polk, who had no children, served as her husband's secretary and advised him on the conduct of the Mexican War. A devout Presbyterian, she banned hard liquor and dancing at the White House, but she dressed elegantly, entertained appropriately, avoided controversy, and won praise for her sweet and sincere manner. Determined not to be just a housekeeper, she declared before Polk's election in 1844, "If I get to the White House ... I will neither keep house nor make butter," a spirited response to a comment that the wife of Henry Clay, Polk's opponent, churned good butter and had a spotless house. Yet Sarah Polk was not an advocate of women's rights, distancing herself from the Seneca Falls convention in 1848 that launched the drive for woman suffrage.

Approving her religious decorum, a Nashville newspaper applauded her dignity and "salutary influence." On her departure from Washington in 1849, a national women's magazine, *Peterson's,* lauded her in a poem ending, "You are modest, yet all a queen should be." As Betty Caroli said, since magazines up to that time did not write about living women, "the singling out of Sarah Polk for such a gesture indicates that she had attained unusual prominence." Furthermore, the gesture was a harbinger of what was to come—increasing public attention to the position of first lady as new forms of printed products stimulated public curiosity about the appearances and activities of presidents' wives.

Sarah Polk's immediate successors, however, were throwbacks to the days of the first Mrs. Tyler. Margaret Taylor, the wife of Zachery Taylor, kept to herself in the upper rooms of the White House. She refused to sit for her portrait or even a "photograph" (a daguerreotype, an early form of photography). After President Taylor died in 1850, an engraver who was eager to sell depictions of the deathbed scene but did not know what Margaret Taylor looked like concealed her face with a large handkerchief.

The presidency fell to Vice President Millard Fillmore, whose wife, Abigail, had taught school before and even briefly after their marriage, making her the first president's wife to have held paid employment. She set up the White House library but had her daughter substitute for her as a hostess. Although in declining health, the bookish Abigail Fillmore could not totally avoid the spotlight, as her image became an item of commerce. Copies of her daguerreotype sold well, especially among women.

When Franklin Pierce was elected president in 1852, his wife, Jane, stayed upstairs in the White House for two years, mourning the death of her son in a train accident. After that time, she occasionally went out but continued to mourn. Her aunt took over as hostess. Victorian sentiment made it possible for Jane Pierce to avoid any duties without being criticized, just as it accepted delicate health as a rationale for other first ladies who avoided public lives. The cult of true womanhood allowed nineteenth-century presidents' wives to live in virtual seclusion if they did not seek social eminence. Women such as Jane Pierce, who abhorred her husband's political career, were offered a convenient personal escape from a male-oriented world.

By the time the nation was on the verge of the Civil War, the role of White House hostess took on new visibility with the advent of Harriet Lane, the niece of President James Buchanan, a bachelor. As his administration floundered, Lane tactfully organized seating arrangements at the White House to keep Northern and Southern enemies apart. Her likeness appeared in the pages of the new illustrated newspapers that were gaining favor with women readers and wide distribution by rail. In 1858, *Harper's Weekly* referred to Lane as "Our Lady of the White House," and two years later, *Frank Leslie's Illustrated Newspaper* printed her engraving and commented below it, "The subject of our illustration . . . may be justly termed the first lady in the land."

When Mary Todd Lincoln arrived in Washington in 1861, newspapers on both the East Coast and the West Coast called her simply "first lady." Her husband and others in the White House referred to her as "the Lady President" or "Mrs. President." Eager to show official Washington that she and her husband were not uncouth westerners, she purchased expensive gowns and set out to redecorate the White House. At first, *Leslie's* praised her "exquisite taste," admiring the "moulded [*sic*] shoulders and arms of our fair 'Republican Queen.'" Improved printing technology led to the use of engravings based on actual photographs, enabling readers to see her attire and demeanor. As Jennifer Fleischner, a recent biographer, put it, "She reveled in the creation of her image, born in the columns of the daily newspapers that rolled off the steam presses in unprecedented numbers, midwifed by the special correspondents who, reporting on Mrs. Lincoln's comings and goings, telegraphed their dispatches to papers throughout the land." A thirst for intimate details even led to false reports that she was pregnant.

Unfortunately, Mary Lincoln kept quiet about her visits to wounded soldiers and her assistance to freed slaves. Knowledge of her charity might have quelled talk of her alleged disloyalty, but she took no steps to make herself a sympathetic figure. Exploding over trifles and increasingly erratic, she disintegrated mentally following the death of her eleven-year-old son, Willie, in 1862. She could have taken refuge in mourning as Jane Pierce had done, but she instead chose to continue appearing in public as first lady.

She showed fortitude in the White House by insisting

on playing a visible, if misguided, part in the administration. After Abraham Lincoln's assassination in 1865, her bizarre behavior led her eldest son to have her committed to a mental institution, from which she won a battle for release. Although extremely unsuccessful, she had tried to enlarge the position of first lady, but history does not remember her kindly.

Eliza Johnson, the tubercular wife of Vice President Andrew Johnson who followed Lincoln as president, fell back into the pattern of the reclusive wife. She stayed upstairs at the White House and left entertaining to her daughters. Thus, the tradition continued of having youthful surrogates who fit the accepted definition of femininity stand in for a president's wife who desired to abdicate a public role.

The pattern changed dramatically in the person of Julia Grant, a self-confident woman with a zest for entertaining. She relished life in the White House when her husband, Gen. Ulysses S. Grant, the Civil War hero who had led the North to victory, was elected president in 1868 and reelected four years later. Cross-eyed and stout, the unpretentious Julia Grant liked attention, even though unflattering comments were printed about her looks, and she posed for photographers in profile to conceal her eye condition.

By Grant's era, a first lady's wardrobe, personal style, and social activities had become legitimate news. Presidents' wives and families were logical subject matter for enterprising women writers who, often using pen names to shield themselves from being considered unladylike, sent columns of human interest material from Washington to dozens of competing newspapers in big cities across the country. Among them was Emily Edson Briggs, who wrote as "Olivia" for the *Philadelphia Press*. Describing a White House reception for her readers, she called Julia Grant "fair, fat and forty."

Although her showy White House entertaining, which included twenty-nine-course dinners, rivaled or exceeded that of the maligned Mary Lincoln, Julia Grant experienced only muted press criticism. Mary Clemmer Ames, the Washington columnist for a prominent New York publication, *The Independent,* sniffed that Grant was "born without the natural gifts or graces which could have made her a leader óf other minds" but noted that her "good nature" went "far to take the place of higher and more positive characteristics." Since the social climate of the Gilded Age after the Civil War emphasized conspicuous consumption, there was no outcry when she ordered 587 pieces of new White House china in 1870 and added hundreds more for the resplendent 1874 wedding of her daughter, Nellie. The scandals of Ulysses Grant's second term, which included corruption among cabinet members, did not faze his wife, even though she was on close terms with some of those implicated. When she urged her husband to run for a third time and he refused before telling her so, she wrote in her autobiography, "I did feel deeply injured."

Lucy Hayes, Julia Grant's successor, brought a pious note to the White House. Known as "Lemonade Lucy," she refused to serve alcoholic beverages, wore no jewelry, and took pride in her Methodist religion, holding prayer meetings with her husband, President Rutherford Hayes, and singing hymns. Ames, who became a close friend, credited Hayes with "that tender light in the eyes which we have come to associate with the Madonna" and called her "the first lady of the land." Other correspondents followed suit.

The first president's wife who was a college graduate, Hayes was praised as a representative of the "new woman," a term then coming into use for educated women with broader interests than entertaining. She seemed a likely candidate to speak up for woman's rights, a cause often allied with the temperance movement, and women's education. When the first lady remained silent, Emily Briggs upbraided her in a column as being "so high and far away that you cannot hear the groans of the countless of our sex." Hayes geared her role in the White House to that of a traditional wife, but extensive press attention to her temperance stand expanded the concept of the influence of a president's wife. Journalists also raised the question of whether the first lady should be expected to exert influence on behalf of women's issues.

Hayes's strict policy against serving alcohol was overturned by the next first lady, Lucretia Garfield. She was in the White House for only six months before a disappointed office-seeker assassinated her husband, but she gave one press interview—in defense of the character of James Garfield's controversial secretary of state, James G. Blaine—that showed she had a surprising willingness to speak out politically. Ames wrote that Garfield had "a strength of unswerving absolute rectitude her husband has not and never will have."

The next two presidents, Chester A. Arthur, the vice president who succeeded Garfield, and Grover Cleveland, who was elected in 1884, had no wives when they took office. Arthur, a widower, tapped his sister to be his hostess. Cleveland, the only Democrat since the Civil War, was one of just two bachelors ever elected to the office (the other was Buchanan); he drafted his sister, Rose, a college teacher who passed the boredom of receiving lines by mentally conjugating Greek verbs. When Cleveland entertained a widow, Emma Folsom, and her twenty-one-year-old daughter, Frances, in 1885, newspapers speculated he was planning to marry. So he was, but the bride was not the widow as expected but the daughter, a recent college graduate twenty-one years his junior.

When they wed in a private White House ceremony in 1886, pictures of the virginal-looking bride in newspapers and magazines entranced the public. Riding a wave of sensationalism called "new journalism" that was led by Joseph Pulitzer in New York, reporters camped around the Clevelands' honeymoon cottage in western Maryland and spied on the couple with binoculars. The gruff president accused them of "making American journalism contemptible" in a letter to the *New York Evening Post,* although the bride, nicknamed "Frankie," appeared unfazed by the attention. As a writer of the period put it, if she were royalty, "she could not bear with greater ease, tact and graceful dignity the burden of social leadership which has fallen upon her."

As industrialization lifted middle-class living standards in the late nineteenth century, women as readers and consumers became increasingly important to publishers. Newspapers started women's and society pages featuring department store advertising aimed at women. A new base of national advertising for standardized food products led to the establishment of profitable women's magazines such as *Ladies' Home Journal* and *Good Housekeeping.* Readers of both newspapers and magazines avidly perused stories on first ladies and their families, who were glorified as idealized representations of the American spirit.

In addition, the widespread use of photography created

a visual popular culture in which images of the first ladies were used, without their permission, on items as varied as dinner plates, campaign posters, buttons, and souvenirs. A picture of Lucy Hayes was used to advertise an iron, and advertisers seized on Frances Cleveland's name and likeness to sell soap, perfume, candy, and other products in fraudulent testimonials. To protect her, legislation was introduced in Congress forbidding the unauthorized use of a woman's likeness or representation, but it did not pass.

Public enthusiasm for Frances Cleveland initially helped defuse criticism of her husband's private life, which had become a factor in the 1884 campaign when Cleveland acknowledged that he might have been the father of an illegitimate child born to a widow with whom he and others had had relations eleven years earlier. During his reelection bid in 1888, opponents circulated stories that he mistreated his wife. In response, Frances Cleveland, who tried to keep aloof from politics, authorized publication of a letter in which she expressed the wish that all American women had husbands "as kind, attentive, considerate and affectionate as mine."

Although Cleveland lost that election to Republican Benjamin Harrison, he regained the presidency in 1892; his campaign posters featured pictures of Frances Cleveland placed above and between images of himself and his running mate. On her return to Washington, Frances tried to keep her children (three by the end of the second term) apart from the public and press after tourists on the White House grounds almost smothered the oldest with kisses. Her efforts gave rise to ugly rumors that the children were deformed. Seeking privacy, the Clevelands rented a house several miles away and spent family time together there.

Benjamin Harrison's wife, Caroline, died shortly before the end of his presidential term. Despite ill health, she had overseen the renovation of the White House, modernizing the kitchen and adding electric lights and private bathrooms. In addition, she was the first president-general of the Daughters of the American Revolution, and she agreed to raise funds for the Johns Hopkins Medical School only on the condition that it be a coeducational institution. With a keen sense of public relations, she arranged for publicity pictures of her grandson, "Baby McKee," who became the most photographed child in the United States. She received more recognition for starting the White House china collection, however, than for her interest in women's organizations, and she was lauded for her domesticity.

By the end of the nineteenth century, the president's wife had become a national public figure, whether or not she sought to be one, as improved communications media wiped out distances across the country. Americans insisted on seeing photographs of their first lady. Yet she was not necessarily expected to demonstrate personal capability. Even if incapacitated, first ladies could be used as political props, Caroli concluded, and they were praised for "sweetness and docility over independence."

This fact was illustrated in the case of Ida McKinley, a probable sufferer of epilepsy who demanded constant attention from her husband, William McKinley, elected president in 1896 and reelected in 1900. She appeared in formal, posed photographs, wearing lace and diamonds that gave her a doll-like appearance. To counter rumors that she was insane, she was featured in the first campaign biography of a presidential candidate's wife. The president's devotion to his infirm spouse won him admirers, and the country readily accepted an invalid first lady, just as it had accepted surrogates for much of the century.

Expectations for first ladies changed dramatically during the twentieth century as the United States became a world force. U.S. presidents played key parts on a global stage, closely watched by news media that became increasingly powerful. Presidential wives emerged as vital aspects of the presidency itself, although the individuals holding the title of first lady defined their roles differently.

As the first president to take office in the twentieth century, Theodore Roosevelt brought new energy to the position, which he assumed in 1901 after McKinley died from an assassin's bullet. Roosevelt and his wife, Edith, along with their six high-spirited children and innumerable pets, shook the White House to its rafters, yet they still maintained a social schedule with an aristocratic flavor. Recognizing the growing importance of the Washington press corps, the president instituted regular press briefings. Edith Roosevelt hired the first person to handle publicity for the first lady, a move that helped establish the president's wife as an official figure and laid the foundations for her paid staff.

Social secretary Belle Hagner systematized the release of social news and monitored the coverage and images of the Roosevelt family that appeared in newspapers and magazines. Edith Roosevelt endeavored to limit direct contact with members of the public while still satisfying their curiosity. Her picture appeared alongside her husband's, but she maintained her personal privacy. "I haven't talked to the press, not in seventy-one years, and it's too late to begin now," she snapped at a reporter late in her life.

Her ambitious successor, Helen Herron Taft, had prodded William Howard Taft to run for president and loved living in the White House, where she saved $100,000 of her husband's salary by instituting household economies. She made no secret of her influence. In 1909, readers of the *Ladies' Home Journal* found out that "had it not been for his wife, Mr. Taft would never have entered the Presidential race." Unhappily, the first lady suffered a stroke that curtailed her activities two months after the inauguration. Reporters were not told about the stroke and did not raise questions, operating under an unspoken agreement, in effect for at least the first decades of the twentieth century, to separate the first lady's public role and private life.

Two women served as first lady during Woodrow Wilson's tenure as president from 1913 to 1920, gaining public attention in vastly different ways. Wilson's first wife, Ellen Axson Wilson, a talented artist whose paintings had been reprinted in women's magazines, was stricken with Bright's disease while backing a campaign to rid Washington of unsanitary alley dwellings occupied by African Americans. She died on August 6, 1914, after telling her husband that if the alley improvement bill was passed, she would "go away more cheerfully." In her honor, Congress passed the legislation, but no provision was made to provide housing for the displaced.

Seven months after her death, Wilson, a man accustomed to drawing strength from supportive women, was introduced to Edith Bolling Galt, the widow of a well-to-do Washington jewelry store owner. A passionate courtship ensued, leading to their marriage on December 18, 1915, despite press criticism that an appropriate period of mourning had not passed. The new first lady, who came from impoverished southern gentry and had little formal education, devoted herself entirely to her husband. She served as his confidant during the reelection campaign of 1916 and U.S. entry into World War I the following year and accompanied Wilson to the Paris peace talks in 1918.

When the president suffered a stroke in October 1919 and was incapacitated for the rest of his term, Edith Wilson became his chief aide, engaging in a cover-up of his true condition rather than urging him to resign. She decided who and what he should see and attempted to act as a go-between with Senate leaders in an unsuccessful effort to get the United States to accept the Treaty of Versailles and join the League of Nations. With the presidency functioning poorly, newspapers revealed her extraordinary power; the *London Daily Mail,* for example, on February 22, 1920, disclosed the "startling" news that "the wife of President Wilson has for months past been acting President of the United States."

In her autobiography, Edith Wilson explained naively, "I, myself, never made a single decision regarding the disposition of public affairs. The only decision that was mine was what was important [to refer to the invalid president] and what was not, and the very important decision of when to present matters to my husband." A recent biographer, drawing on newly disclosed medical reports, concluded that Woodrow Wilson was totally unfit to continue in office and that his wife persisted in "sustained inventions that were consequential for all the world."

According to Lewis Gould, a scholar of first ladies, Edith Wilson still is seen as an example of the dangers that could arise if a presidential wife seeks real power. It is not likely that any first lady ever again could shield an ill husband and hold the reins of the presidency, for the Twenty-fifth Amendment to the Constitution calls for a clear succession of power in case the president is incapacitated. But the case of Edith Wilson continues to provide a rationale for journalists to keep a watchful, and somewhat suspicious, eye on the first lady.

Women finally got the vote in 1920, making the publicity-conscious Florence Harding, wife of Warren G. Harding, the first president's spouse to be able to vote for her husband. Heavily involved in his political career, she felt an affinity for journalists because she had long served as the manager of Harding's newspaper in Marion, Ohio. Mary Randolph, White House social secretary during the 1920s, commented, "I am sure the Presidency meant more to her than it ever did to Mr. Harding. . . . I have it on good authority that when the [Republican] Convention nominated him, she said: 'Well, Warren Harding, I have got you the Presidency; what are you going to do with it?'"

In Washington, Florence Harding showed a special fondness for members of the Women's National Press Club, founded in 1919 by women who had covered the suffrage movement; for them, instituting the new club was a way of combating hostility from male journalists who would not admit women to the National Press Club. Inviting the group for a cruise on the presidential yacht, the first lady astounded the women by slapping the dignified club president, Cora Rigby of the *Christian Science Monitor,* on the back and exclaiming, "Well here we are, all girls together." Opening the White House grounds to visitors, the "Duchess," as the sixty-one-year-old Harding was called, posed for numerous pictures, including those for newsreels shown in movie theaters. To try to appear more youthful, she made liberal use of cosmetics, which were just then becoming generally accepted.

Careful of her public image, she did not serve alcoholic beverages openly in the White House, consistent with Prohibition, which was then the law of the land. But she privately mixed drinks for Harding and his associates and socialized with the flamboyant Evalyn Walsh McLean, owner of the Hope diamond. As a key adviser to her husband on politics and patronage, Florence Harding took a particular interest in World War I veterans and felt betrayed when a personal friend who was put in charge of the Veterans Bureau turned out to be corrupt, like a number of other Harding cronies given high offices.

In spite of her policy of not permitting interviews and direct quotations, she invited women journalists to tea and, according to her biographer, Carl Anthony, "proceeded to 'chat' for attribution." Recovering from a near-fatal illness and heavily made up, she greeted women journalists in the White House living quarters in 1923, wearing a rose-colored velvet negligee. She answered questions about her health and social matters, giving so many details about her illness that it "revolted" one reporter. A contemporary reporter, Ishbel Ross, found the excitable Duchess uneven in her press contacts, initially refusing, for example, to tell reporters what she would wear to the inauguration, though she later tried "for some rapprochement" but failed to "carry it far." For the most part, Harding received favorable press treatment, which depicted her as a housewife who helped her husband in business and politics.

After President Harding died unexpectedly in 1923, the

Duchess took most of his and her private papers out of the White House and destroyed them. The move was an apparent attempt to conceal the widespread corruption of Harding's administration, which produced the Teapot Dome scandal, involving the illegal sale of government oil reserves, and other instances of malfeasance. Her actions also may have been intended to conceal Harding's numerous sexual dalliances.

Grace Coolidge, who followed Florence Harding, had tended to overshadow the Duchess even as the wife of the dour vice president, Calvin Coolidge. Younger and considered more charming and attractive than her predecessor, Coolidge was portrayed as another Dolley Madison when she became first lady after Warren Harding's death. Press enthusiasm only heightened after the taciturn and curt Calvin Coolidge won the presidency in his own right in 1924. His slender, vivacious wife humanized the administration. Ishbel Ross, her biographer, said, "From her first day as mistress of the White House she presented a picture of dignity and warmth." She willingly posed for numerous photographs that showed her in the fashionable flat-chested, low-waisted outfits of the day, many of which were picked out by her husband. Her picture appeared in all types of publications, including the new tabloid newspapers, which were aimed at big-city readers, as well as mass-circulation magazines. When one of her two sons died of blood poisoning in 1924, she received an outpouring of sympathy and affection.

A graduate of the University of Vermont and a former teacher of the deaf, Grace Coolidge managed to make the Jazz Age compatible with the image of a reticent New England housewife. She smoked cigarettes, then considered daring for a woman, but only in private. The public relished details of her frequent appearances at ceremonial events and her precedent-setting invitations to stars of stage, screen, and radio to visit the White House. Journalists praised the first lady's sparkling wit, even though she said very little. Calvin Coolidge refused to let her give interviews or make speeches, and he forbade her to ride horses, drive a car, fly in an airplane, bob her hair, "wear culottes for country hiking, or express her views on politics, or in any way step out of character as wife and mother," Ross continued. "Not that she showed any disposition to do so, and whatever views she may have had she kept to herself," Ross added. Reporters for women's and society pages eagerly sought descriptions of her gowns, entertaining, busy schedule, and appealing manners, although the Coolidges were not always forthcoming even with innocuous items. As Randolph, the social secretary, explained, "How difficult my own position was it would be impossible to describe to any but a sympathetic tight-rope walker. If I withheld information, I was 'in wrong' with the Press. . . . Had I given it, I wouldn't have been of the slightest value to the President and his wife." One political observer said Grace Coolidge was "worth one million dollars a year to the Republican Party."

Calvin Coolidge's decision not to seek reelection in 1928 cleared the way for Herbert Hoover and his intellectual wife, Lou Henry Hoover, called "The Lady," to move into the White House. The reserved Lou Hoover took little interest in her wardrobe and lacked the flair for public appearances that had been Grace Coolidge's strong suit. Unlike her successor, Eleanor Roosevelt, Hoover "failed to win the country's approval or its interest," according to Betty Caroli.

Yet the cosmopolitan Lou Hoover possessed an extraordinary background. The first woman in the United States to earn a degree in geology, she was a graduate of Stanford University, where she met Herbert Hoover, a mining engineer. With their two sons, the couple lived all over the world before Herbert Hoover became secretary of commerce under Harding. Fluent in five languages (including Chinese), Lou Henry Hoover had joined her husband in translating a Latin manuscript on mining into English and organized relief committees in Europe during World War I. As national president of the Girl Scouts and head of the Women's Division of the National Amateur Athletic Federation, she had promoted women's fitness, although she opposed women's participation in the Olympics as unhealthy.

Hoover was the first president's wife to speak over the radio, addressing various groups, including Girls Scouts and 4-H Club members, and urging women to volunteer to aid the unemployed. Nevertheless, she had little public rapport, giving out stiff photographs of herself and refusing to permit pictures to be taken of her grandchildren. Her insistence that the White House staff stay out of sight in the halls and respond to hand signals instead of speech while serving meals was in line with the reticence that made some observers consider her aloof.

Ross noted that Hoover refused to give interviews and was "a problem for the press." She and her husband entertained extensively, but they issued last-minute invitations, and reporters could not get lists of White House guests in time to meet deadlines. Ross recalled Hoover was "at her best" when she led women reporters on an outing at the presidential retreat, Camp Rapidan, where they "almost felt that they were welcome."

When the Depression hit in 1929, the first lady, long known for her benevolence, did not publicize her numerous charitable efforts. Her distrust of the press heightened after southern newspapers lambasted her for inviting the wife of an African American congressman to tea at the White House in 1930. As one biographical sketch put it, the first lady "became increasingly suspicious of what she saw as an ever-present, intruding press corps that often did not place a priority on accuracy." When Herbert Hoover overwhelmingly lost his reelection bid to Franklin D. Roosevelt in 1932, she left Washington with bitterness, convinced the Democratic party had smeared her husband in the campaign.

After Hoover, Eleanor Roosevelt seemed a godsend to Washington women reporters because her press relations "were founded on mutual trust," Ross explained. True, Roosevelt relied on affable relations with journalists. But she also built on solid underpinnings based on the development of the institution of the first lady, which, by 1933, was instrumental in setting the tone for presidential administrations. During her twelve years of media contact as the president's wife, Roosevelt readily grasped the growing demand for news from the White House to feed the appetite of the expanding mass media, eager for pictures, stories, and sounds to attract an audience.

Roosevelt realized that the job of first lady required development of a public persona separate from the actual person who had the title. By holding press conferences, giving interviews, posing for photographers, and welcoming coverage of her ceaseless rounds of travel and activity, as well as through her close friendships with select women reporters and her general availability to journalists, Roosevelt helped generate the news that journalists needed to do their jobs. In return, reporters generally pictured her favorably, although some remained alert to news conventions that emphasized conflict and controversy in her era, just as they do today.

Roosevelt had the advantage of working with news media that allowed her to separate her public role from segments of her personal life. By giving most of what she made to charity, she was able to continue her own career, earning money from her newspaper column, magazine articles, radio broadcasts, and lectures. In public, she discounted her involvement in administration policy and patronage matters, possibly to downplay the criticism heaped on previous presidents' wives who were believed to hold power.

In private, as Caroli pointed out, "Eleanor peppered her letters to friends with references to her attempts to influence both legislation and appointments." She was part of the first network of activists to promote women's political advancement, marked in the Roosevelt administration by the appointment of Frances Perkins, the first female cabinet member, as secretary of labor. For example, Eleanor Roosevelt held garden parties in the 1930s at the White House to facilitate networking among professional women living in Washington. Whether she emphasized or downplayed her activities, perhaps her most striking accomplishment as first lady was, in Caroli's words, her "resolve to use the press, rather than let it use her." She succeeded so well that presidents' wives after her have reacted to her example of activism, either by emulating it or by distancing themselves from it. Sarah McClendon, a journalist who covered the White House for a half century, observed, "[Eleanor Roosevelt] set a standard that all the first ladies who have followed her must measure themselves against."

THREE

JACKIE KENNEDY AND THE
CONSTRUCTION OF CAMELOT

From the time that Eleanor Roosevelt left the White House
in 1945 to the time that Jackie Kennedy entered it in 1961,
American society underwent a dramatic transformation.
Roosevelt's tenure as first lady had been marked by two cat-
aclysmic events: the Depression and World War II, when the
nation desperately sought first to stave off economic collapse
and then to win the greatest war in history. Eleanor Roosevelt's multifaceted approach to the role of first lady and the
voluminous news coverage she generated fit an era of extraordinary events.

In sharp contrast, her immediate successors, Bess Truman and Mamie Eisenhower, offered no challenge to journalistic conventions that confined women to stereotypical
activities. They represented their times and provided a frame
for the emergence of the glamorous Jackie Kennedy. Coverage of Truman and Eisenhower emphasized that they were
traditional wives and mothers, and the public accepted them
on those terms as the post–World War II generation moved
to the suburbs and sought to glorify family life.

Bess Truman was greatly distressed when Franklin D. Roosevelt's sudden death catapulted Vice President Harry S Truman into the presidency in 1945. Fearing press disclosure of the suicide of her father many years earlier, Bess Truman, in the words of her daughter, Margaret, "underwent a terrific inner struggle to overcome her deep aversion to becoming first lady." Truman preferred living in Independence, Missouri, to living in the White House, which she and her husband called the "Great White Jail." The story of her father's suicide never became public in her lifetime. Journalists of the era, in line with popular views on good manners, were disinclined to probe into the personal lives of White House occupants.

In the wake of Eleanor Roosevelt, Bess Truman first announced she would hold a press conference for women reporters and then canceled it, realizing there was no requirement that she imitate her predecessor. Her attitude, journalist Marianne Means noted, was, "I'm not the one who is elected. I have nothing to say to the public." When press women asked how they would "get to know you," she retorted, "You don't need to know me. I'm only the President's wife and the mother of his daughter."

Press reaction was split, with some columnists upholding her right to her privacy. According to Gil Troy, a scholar of first ladies, "Unwittingly, Bess Truman had tapped into a broad public frustration with Eleanor Roosevelt and with an expanding definition of news that celebrated personality and trivia over politics and substance." Yet in the middle of the twentieth century, it was impossible for a first lady to totally avoid the press, as Truman soon learned.

Advised by her husband's press secretary, Charles Ross,

to maintain a minimal relationship with women journalists, she invited them to tea and attended events sponsored by women's press groups but said little of substance. Edith Helm, her social secretary, and Reathel Odum, a personal aide, both of whom were terrified of saying the wrong thing, were told to see reporters and relay their questions to her. At their first meeting with reporters, Helm wrote later, "Miss Odum and I felt and looked like condemned criminals." Helm handed out mimeographed copies of Truman's social engagements, marking the first use of press releases to record a first lady's comings and goings.

Bess Truman's calendar produced little news. A women's page reporter desperate for any item would be reduced to such inquiries as "What will Mrs. Truman wear to the tea for the United Council of Church Women today?" When this kind of question was relayed to the first lady, she was likely to snap, "It's none of her damn business," leaving her secretary to politely inform the reporter that "Mrs. Truman hasn't quite made up her mind."

A stout matron frequently photographed in a dark suit with a white blouse and gloves, Bess Truman took little interest in fashions. When reporters hinted that she presented a dowdy appearance, her husband retorted, "She looks just like a woman ought to look who's been happily married for a quarter of a century." While passing a billboard advertising the musical *Gentlemen Prefer Blondes,* the president told a columnist that "real gentlemen prefer gray."

His affection for his wife clouded his judgment during what Margaret Truman called "one of the nastiest political crossfires of the Truman presidency," which she blamed on her mother's inability to realize "that she too was a public figure as much as the President." After Bess Truman agreed to attend a Daughters of the American Revolution (DAR) tea at Constitution Hall, the building where Marian Anderson had been banned from singing because of her race, Adam Clayton Powell, an African American congressman, telegraphed her to decline. He said the DAR also had refused to let his wife, pianist Hazel Scott, perform there. The first lady wired Powell back that "acceptance of the hospitality extended is not related to the merits of the issue." President Truman sent a telegram supporting her, even though, according to Margaret Truman, he was inclined to "condemn the DAR."

When Bess Truman went to the tea and remained a DAR member herself, Powell publicized the telegrams and called her "the last lady." The incident, which invited invidious comparisons with Eleanor Roosevelt's resignation from the DAR in support of Anderson, embarrassed the Truman administration, which backed civil rights. Bess Truman long had served as an informal political adviser to her husband, but the Powell episode, Margaret Truman wrote, temporarily damaged the "Truman partnership."

After the Powell incident, the first lady showed better political judgment by truncating the normal White House social season, since the ending of World War II had led to soaring prices and food shortages for average Americans. Instead of elaborate dinners, she staged a more informal series of teas and luncheons, and she shook thousands of hands at receptions. Reflecting the middle-class social values of the day, newspapers and magazines gave favorable treatment to her women's Spanish class at the White House and a four-day visit from members of her Independence bridge club. In

1946, Bess Furman, who was then the chief woman reporter in the *New York Times* Washington bureau, described the first lady to *Times* readers as the "Independent Lady from Independence," determined to remain herself and not "give a hoot for the whole goldfish bowl business." Journalist Sarah McClendon, a veteran Washington journalist, pointed out that Bess Truman spent months in Independence but that her husband consulted her, in person or by phone, "whenever he had a decision to make."

When Harry Truman confounded the experts by winning the 1948 presidential election, Bess and Margaret Truman received some of the credit for the victory. Key participants in his whistle-stop campaign tour, they silently smiled and waved when Truman introduced his wife as "the Boss" and his daughter, who was launching a professional singing career, as "the Boss's boss," presenting, as Troy put it, a family scene that "resurrected Americans' idealized past." Marianne Means said the term *boss,* as used in the semirural parts of the United States, was "a good-natured admission that while a man's wife rarely had an opinion in public, she didn't hesitate to push her point of view with her husband in private." Newspaper readers were told that Bess Truman insisted her husband curb his salty language and watch his manners in public.

As the Korean War dragged on, Truman decided not to run in 1952, to his wife's relief. His presidency ended with applause for her performance. As Troy noted, in the tradition of "Republican Motherhood," the term bestowed on exemplary mothers in the era of the founding fathers, Bess Truman had appeared "decent, dignified, and dutiful." The liberal *St. Louis Post Dispatch* proclaimed, "The contrast between

Bess and Eleanor is easy on the eyes, easy on the ears, and easy on the nerve centers." In the middle of the twentieth century, large segments of the press and public still preferred a first lady who had little to say in public, but it was increasingly obvious that a first lady could not escape attention from journalists.

Mamie Eisenhower, first lady from 1953 to 1960, liked living in the White House far more than Bess Truman did, although she had been lukewarm to the prospect initially. As the wife of "Ike," Gen. Dwight D. Eisenhower, the supreme commander of the Allied forces in World War II, Mamie Eisenhower long had been the subject of gossip. Her granddaughter-in-law, Julie Nixon Eisenhower, noted, "When in 1952, Ike chose a way of life that would mean permanent fame and entail constant press attention . . . Mamie was not enthusiastic." Fortunately for the first lady, the mainstream press of the day did not consider it in good taste to print persistent gossip that she was an alcoholic or that Ike had wanted to divorce her after the war to marry Kay Summersby, who had been his wartime driver in Europe.

Only after her husband's death in 1969 did Mamie Eisenhower publicly address these rumors. In 1973, she told Barbara Walters in a television interview that there was no truth to what people had thought for years: that she was "a dipsomaniac." She explained she suffered from Ménière's disease, an inner-ear disorder that affected her balance. Six years later in another television interview with Walters, she discounted the Summersby story, declaring there was "no romance." But during the 1950s, these rumors had circulated by word of mouth rather than by repetition in the media, as they would today.

The press of the 1950s praised Mamie Eisenhower, with her heart-shaped face and friendly manner, as a model wife. When Dwight Eisenhower became the Republican standard-bearer in 1952, she was turned into a campaign asset in part because the Democratic candidate, Adlai Stevenson, was divorced. Eisenhower's supporters, in an effort to court women voters, passed out "I Like Mamie" buttons, and two songs were dedicated to her. The *New York Times* said she was worth "50 electoral votes." Unlike Bess Truman, she enjoyed having her picture taken on the campaign train, even restaging a photo of herself to accommodate photographers who had missed snapping their shutters when she greeted an early morning crowd in her bathrobe and hair curlers.

Described by Means as "extremely feminine, in a rather sweet, clinging-vine way," the grandmother of four was said to adore "flowered hats, colored gloves, full-skirted, fluffy dresses and anything done up in pink." She made no pretense of either advising her husband or being interested in women's issues. She even avoided mention of Oveta Culp Hobby, the former head of the Women's Army Corps whom Eisenhower appointed to the cabinet post of secretary of health, education, and welfare, because, according to daughter-in-law Barbara Eisenhower, she "thought that women who had jobs like that were very unfeminine."

Wearing a pink bed jacket, Mamie Eisenhower stayed in bed until noon in her pink bedroom, which she used as a personal command center for White House management. With years of experience as a military wife, she gave detailed orders to the staff, spent money cautiously, and symbolized Middle America in her cultural and clothing tastes. Journalists could have pictured her as a ruling matriarch; instead, they portrayed her as the prototype of a congenial suburban housewife.

Less than two months after the inauguration, Mamie Eisenhower held her first and only press conference. It was attended by thirty-seven women reporters and forty-one men reporters, with the Secret Service requiring the men to let the women precede them into the room. Only one of the men asked a question. Video cameras recorded the event for possible showing on the new media of television, but little news resulted from the first lady's reading of her schedule, listing what one reporter called "tea by inexorable tea." Other press conferences were vetoed by Jim Hagerty, President Eisenhower's press secretary, who feared she would be asked controversial questions she could not answer.

Mary Jane McCaffree Monroe, Mamie Eisenhower's secretary, said the first lady did not enjoy her press conference and, moreover, had been warned by her mother, a frequent White House guest, that it was unladylike to be a public figure apart from her husband. Mamie Eisenhower maintained cordial relationships with women journalists by attending their social events, and she cooperated with the impersonation of the president at a Women's National Press Club stunt party by lending Ike's golf apparel for costume needs. Still, press contacts were curtailed, with the first lady's secretary giving out news, Isabelle Shelton of the *Washington Evening Star* said, "as sort of a catch-as-catch-can thing in which you had to ask the right questions or lose the game."

According to Maxine Cheshire, a *Washington Post* reporter, "no first lady was ever as gently treated in print as Mamie Eisenhower," due to what Cheshire called the 1950s' "Emily Post approach to reporting about the occupants of the White House." Cheshire said her biggest *Post* "scoop" was to find out where the first lady bought discounted evening slippers to dye to match her gowns. Both Cheshire and Jack Anderson, who assisted Drew Pearson in writing a Washington investigative column, faulted the press for failing to raise questions about Mamie Eisenhower's acceptance of gifts from foreign governments. Anderson noted, "When Drew made so bold as to tweak Mamie Eisenhower for latching on to a diamond necklace so heavy she could hardly carry it around, the stories died the quick death of press neglect."

In general, Mamie Eisenhower enjoyed excellent media coverage because her appearance and values resonated with those of Middle America. With her trademark bangs, pearl chokers, charm bracelets, and pink evening gowns that resembled strapless dresses worn at senior proms, the first lady set the style for fashion in the 1950s. It was, Betty Caroli contended, fashion that emphasized a folksy separation of spheres for men and women and encouraged women to value a youthful appearance more than their intelligence. Eisenhower's celebrated shirtwaist outfits—featuring flared skirts, pleats, and ruffles topped off with mink coats and eye-catching hats—put her on the annual lists of the world's best-dressed women. She and Pat Nixon, the wife of Vice President Richard Nixon, were photographed together attending the popular charity luncheon fashion shows that the first lady liked.

In an as-told-to article for *Today's Woman* magazine, Mamie Eisenhower made short work of feminism, declaring, "Being a wife is the best career that life has to offer a woman." She said she had "only one career, and his name is Ike." Advertisers capitalized on her popularity. Macy's sold copies of her tight-fitting headwear, and a chocolate manufacturer featured the recipe for "Mamie's Million Dollar Fudge." Mass-circulation magazines publicized the first lady's pursuits. Millions learned that she loved to play canasta and that the Eisenhowers, like many other Americans, sometimes ate dinner on tray tables in front of the television set, a staple in a growing number of American homes.

When President Eisenhower suffered a heart attack in 1955, the public was fully informed on his medical condition. But in Mamie Eisenhower's case, details of her physical condition were not released even when she had to have a hysterectomy, which the White House referred to vaguely as a problem of older women. A more forthright description of her health might have forestalled some comments in the *Washington Post* and other quarters that she was not sufficiently active as first lady. Her physical condition, which also included a heart ailment and asthma, somewhat curtailed her role as a hostess.

In Eisenhower's reelection campaign of 1956, Mamie Eisenhower made history as the first president's wife to appear on television to support her husband in campaign ads. A month before the election, she joined Ike for a televised "chat" with seven women voters, remarking that on voter registration rolls, she listed her occupation as "First Lady." For the most part during the campaign, she merely posed by her husband's side and lent her name to magazine articles written for her, such as one in *Good Housekeeping* that called on women to "vote for my husband" or for his opponent, Adlai Stevenson, but "please vote."

During Eisenhower's second term, she drew some criticism for taking trips partially subsidized by taxpayers to a Phoenix spa to lose weight. The rumors of her drinking finally found their way into print when a columnist charged that the purpose of one Phoenix trip had been to "dry out." The White House did not dignify the story by denying it, and it faded from the public agenda.

When it was time for the Eisenhowers to vacate the White House in 1961, Mamie Eisenhower, more than other presidents' wives, "hated to leave," according to J. B. West, the head usher. Perhaps, at the age of sixty-four, she sensed an eclipse of her own performance as first lady by a youthful successor whose sophisticated ideas on both fashion and interior decorating would soon impel journalists to sneer at what Cheshire called Mamie's Eisenhower's "smalltown dowdiness." By that time, modern mass communications had made the personal style of the president's wife an object of intense media scrutiny.

The statuesque Jacqueline "Jackie" Bouvier Kennedy, known for her chic wardrobe and good looks, was only thirty-one years old and had a small daughter and a baby on the way when her husband, John F. Kennedy, narrowly defeated Richard Nixon for the presidency in 1960. After he was assassinated on November 22, 1963, she presented a picture of regal dignity. It was she who persuaded journalist Theodore H. White to eulogize the Kennedy years in *Life* magazine with the term *Camelot,* which captured her own—and the nation's—belief in an elite administration of eloquent heroes who attempted noble deeds. She wanted her husband's presidency to be remembered as a time when the White House attracted the brilliant and the best to bring a new vigor—a "New Frontier," as Kennedy called it—to the American dream of democratic glory. Subsequent disclosures of John Kennedy's insatiable appetite for sexual conquests, other tragedies involving the Kennedy family, and her own strained second marriage to Greek shipping magnate Aristotle Onassis tarnished that bright image. Yet Jackie Kennedy, shown on television throughout the world as a majestic widow grieving at her husband's funeral, cemented her place in history as a first lady who understood the importance of ceremony and the consolations of ritual. In addition, by restoring the White House to its original early nineteenth-century appearance, she left the legacy of a living museum to the American people.

Neither the reality of the Kennedy political world, based in Boston's Irish Catholic machine, nor the large, competitive Kennedy family itself initially appealed to the aristocratic Jackie Kennedy. Perhaps to exercise personal independence, she constructed her own media presence. While pregnancy kept her from having a very active role in the 1960 campaign, she was photographed in trendsetting maternity clothes, which emphasized her expanding figure rather than hiding it. Like her wardrobe in general, her maternity outfits drew raves from fashion writers and the public, who applauded her bright pink slacks and oversized T-shirts.

Playing the role of a supportive spouse, she met with reporters and gave interviews, although her primary media activity was writing an informal column that appeared in newspapers. Jackie Kennedy's "Campaign Wife," an Eleanor Roosevelt–type of daily column released by the Democratic National Committee in 1960, predictably urged women to vote for "my husband" and declared that "Jack has always believed that women are vital to a campaign." Long on chitchat and short on issues, the column gave her latitude to respond to criticism of her fondness for high fashion. "All the talk

over what I wear and how I fix my hair has amused and puz-
zled me," she wrote. "What does my hairdo have to do with
my husband's ability to be President?"

When *Women's Wear Daily* claimed she spent $30,000 a
year on her clothes and bought them in Paris, she retorted, "I
couldn't spend that much unless I wore sable underwear." Instead of giving exact figures, she snidely remarked, "I'm sure
I spend less than Mrs. Nixon on clothes." Jack Kennedy, who
feared adverse political fallout, did not share her enormous
pleasure when her name topped the list of the world's twelve
best-dressed women shortly before his inauguration in 1961.
To abate criticism of her thirst for French couturiers, her social secretary, Letitia Baldrige, announced that the first lady
had selected an American designer, Oleg Cassini; intended to
avoid "extravagance"; and planned to buy outfits "made in
America."

In actuality, Jackie Kennedy spent more than $40,000 a
year on her wardrobe while in the White House, and contrary to a statement that the public would see her in the same
clothes repeatedly, she was, according to one journalist,
"never photographed wearing the same outfit twice." Her
total personal expenditures, which included charges for food,
liquor, furnishings, art objects, and other items as well as her
clothing, came to more than the president's annual salary of
$100,000. In 1962, she spent $121,461.61. Information of
this type was not reported until years later.

In an apparent effort to identify with Middle American voters, Jackie Kennedy downplayed the Kennedy wealth
in public statements during the 1960 presidential campaign.
One way she did this was to minimize the presence of the
employees who assisted her. In a preelection picture spread,

Life, then an influential weekly magazine with a huge circulation, showed her answering 225 daily letters to her husband at her Georgetown home while lamenting the lack of a full-time secretary. Another shot showed her tucking her daughter in for a nap because she "does not have a nurse for Caroline." Yet Jackie Kennedy actually had both a live-in nurse for Caroline and a personal secretary, Mary Gallagher, who said in a memoir that her days "couldn't possibly have been more full-time."

As it turned out, President Kennedy had no need to worry about the public response to his photogenic wife. "Yes, a tremendous amount of money was spent on her wardrobe," Baldrige said, "but the public loved it. If she had been dowdy or disinterested in fashion, JFK's place in history would never have been so secure."

In fact, the public could not get enough of her, as the new first lady's image was turned into salable commodities. Women rushed to adopt Jackie Kennedy's bouffant hairstyles, pillbox hats, and low-heeled shoes and to buy sleeveless, off-the-rack dresses with simple lines and brilliant colors that resembled her designer originals. Waterskiing became popular because she did it. Her photograph on magazine covers boosted the sale of both high- and lowbrow publications and captivated millions of admirers. Fan magazines featured her alongside celebrities such as Elizabeth Taylor, equating the first lady with Hollywood superstars. Photographs focused on her arresting features and perfect posture; although she chain-smoked, no picture showing her doing so ever was printed.

Just as Jackie Kennedy wished to wear beautiful clothes, she wanted to live in a historical mansion full of beautiful objects. Taking the traditional preinauguration tour of the White House with the outgoing first lady, Mamie Eisenhower, she had been appalled at its shabby, hodgepodge look. Clark Clifford, a Washington insider and adviser to her husband, said she told him, "'I wish to make the White House into the First House in the land'—from the standpoint of its furnishings, its painting, the rugs on the floor.... Nobody had ever approached it that way before. At that time it was really pretty drab."

Although he feared the restoration would backfire politically, Clifford set up the White House Fine Arts Committee to track down historical objects and raise money for their purchase. Jackie Kennedy did not hesitate to spend liberally to achieve her goal, obtaining funds through private donations and the sale of White House guidebooks published by the newly formed White House Historical Association. When Maxine Cheshire of the *Washington Post* wrote an investigative series on the restoration, pointing out that some newly purchased items were fake antiques, the first lady became incensed.

Fears that the public would not approve died down, however, after she presented the fruits of the restoration to a record audience of forty-six million Americans who watched a special color television program on Valentine's Day in 1962. Speaking in her whispery, Marilyn Monroe–like voice, she took CBS viewers on an hour-long tour of the White House, describing its recently acquired historical treasures. The president appeared briefly at the end of the program. Norman Mailer did not like the show, comparing Jackie Kennedy's voice to that of a breathless weather girl. Critics noted that she sidestepped questions about federal policy toward the arts as too "complicated" to answer. But most viewers loved the program.

Both Jack and Jackie Kennedy, who moved so gracefully in the midst of Cold War tensions, seemed made for television. The audience had no idea of the president's recurrent back pain and other ailments or of his wife's frustrations with his philandering. Gil Troy noted, "Good-looking couples like the Kennedys, who emphasized vague appearances rather than specific accomplishments or passionate commitments, prospered in America's cool, TV-oriented culture." Television projected style, if not substance, and the Kennedys excelled in style.

Any lingering doubt that Jack Kennedy may have had about his wife's political appeal had been laid to rest the previous year when she accompanied him on official trips abroad. At high-level meetings in Europe in the early summer of 1961, she created a sensation. Looking like a queen in a white satin gown, she dazzled dignitaries, including the contentious French president Charles de Gaulle, who was impressed with her knowledge of his language and culture. President Kennedy wryly told a crowd of journalists, "I do not feel it inappropriate for me to introduce myself. I am the man who accompanied Jacqueline Kennedy to Paris."

In Vienna, her breeding and good manners won praise. She insisted the overlooked Nina Khrushchev, wife of the Soviet Communist leader Nikita Khrushchev, stand beside her and wave to a huge crowd, prompting the people to shift from chanting "Jac-kie" to "Jac-kie—Ni-na." Beguiling Nikita Khrushchev himself with her wit at a state dinner, Jackie Kennedy outshone her husband's lackluster performance at his first superpower summit.

A few weeks earlier, she had been a hit in Canada when the Kennedys paid their first state visit, with local crowds shouting, "Jack-ie, Jack-ie." On trips to South America in late 1961 and to Mexico the following summer, she excited audiences when she spoke in Spanish.

Subsequent trips abroad without her husband also brought extensive press coverage and widened precedents for first ladies to travel independently. Following the summit in 1961, she went on a vacation to Greece with her sister, Lee Radziwill. The two women backed off from an official schedule featuring Greek history, drama, and art to cruise surreptitiously on a yacht. Nevertheless, a shot of the tanned first lady watching a Greek tragedy "was the leading international photograph of the summer." The following summer, Italian photographers—the aggressive paparazzi—rushed to the Italian Riviera when she vacationed there with four-year-old Caroline. Press photographs of the first lady swimming with Gianni Agnelli, the wealthy head of Fiat, led her husband, conscious of his administration's image in the 1962 elections, to send her a pointed telegram: "A LITTLE MORE CAROLINE AND LESS AGNELLI."

A month after the successful television tour of the White House in 1962, she went with her sister on a semi-official trip to India and Pakistan, with a stop in Rome for an audience with the pope. Some one hundred journalists covered her arrival in New Delhi as the guest of Prime Minister Jawaharlal Nehru. The *New York Times* reported in a front-page story her "gay and glowing welcome" punctuated "with a splash of Asian splendor." Picture magazines showed her riding on a spangled elephant in India and viewing the shimmering Taj Mahal. Stopping in Pakistan to show U.S.

neutrality in the rivalry between the two countries, she eagerly accepted a valuable gelding that was trained for the foxhunting she loved to pursue (over objections from animal rights activists) in the Virginia countryside.

The *Times* reported that on her way back to the United States, she was "greeted with cheers and wolf whistles when she drove to Buckingham Palace for lunch with Queen Elizabeth II." Having said little of note to the journalists who accompanied her, she issued a discreet statement when she returned to Washington, saying simply, "I have missed my family and have no desire to be a public personality on my own." It was obvious to most, however, that she was.

Not all press coverage was positive. The socially conscious members of the media complained that "illiterate masses" had been overlooked due to her misplaced emphasis on visits with "maharajas and titular leaders." A Republican congressman claimed the cost of a documentary on the trip made by the U.S. Information Agency was "exorbitant." His protest had little impact. Eventually shown all over the globe, the documentary provided the opportunity for millions to vicariously experience her exotic itinerary and marvel at her colorful outfits. The film also accustomed the public to seeing a president's wife as a diplomatic presence in her own right—a Cold War symbol of the success of American capitalism as contrasted with Communist society.

Long before she moved into the White House, Jackie Kennedy had become acquainted with the media spotlight. Her picture had appeared in newspapers when she bowed to society as "debutante of the year" in 1947. When she became the bride of the rich, handsome, and up-and-coming Senator Kennedy of Massachusetts in 1953, a bevy of news photographers recorded the lavish wedding that united two of the nation's most eligible Roman Catholics. Before her marriage, she worked as an inquiring photographer for the *Washington Times-Herald,* posing different questions each day to randomly chosen individuals and publishing their answers along with their pictures. Most questions were innocuous ("Do you think a wife should pick out her husband's suits for him?"), but on November 7, 1952, she had asked Tricia Nixon what she thought of her father's election as vice president, leaving the six-year-old to respond, "He's always away. If he's so famous, why can't he stay home?"

By the time Kennedy was inaugurated as president, his wife had developed a strong resentment against any effort to publicize her own children except by releasing photographs of her choosing. She battled repeatedly with Pierre Salinger, President Kennedy's press secretary, to limit press access to Caroline and baby John-John, wanting them to grow up as unaffected as possible by the limelight surrounding them. According to a White House photographer, "The President understood the political advantages of having the children photographed, whereas Jackie saw it as an invasion of their privacy. Pierre would schedule photo sessions for the children when Jackie was out of town, then blame the President when Jackie went after him."

Baldrige saw the issue as part of an ongoing battle of the sexes between the West Wing, where the president's advisers were, and the East Wing, which housed the first lady's staff. When the West Wing gave orders affecting the first lady without consulting her, Baldrige fought back. She recalled, "If Pierre went against the specific instructions of JBK [Jacqueline Kennedy] I would get hell from Jackie, I'd tattle on Pierre to the President, and the President went to bat for me against Pierre. Jackie, in other words, had great power in ceremonial matters and press coverage of the family." Such reprimands on Kennedy's part may well have been disingenuous. His wife's first cousin, John Davis, said the president had no hesitancy in using the media to create an appealing political image by exploiting his family with merciless calculation.

Slim, elegant, and somewhat shy, the first lady, who spoke in a very soft, childlike voice, adhered to what *Newsweek* said seemed to be "a silent and private oath of her own." The magazine reported she apparently had resolved the following: "(1) I shall be seen and not heard, at least not heard much; (2) I shall discourage fashion stories in every way except by the clothes I wear; (3) I shall restore the White House, to the way it ought to have been." She also had vowed, *Newsweek* continued, to entertain "distinguished artists," to bring up "my children myself, in privacy," and to carry out only "projects I have time for, but I shall get very involved in those." Her silent manifesto revealed her ambivalence toward the role she was expected to play.

Educated at Vassar and the Sorbonne, the product of a broken, upper-class marriage, Jackie Kennedy long had traveled in elite circles as the stepdaughter of a wealthy stockbroker. As first lady, she showed little interest in women's causes, including her husband's Commission on the Status of Women, or in meeting large groups from women's organizations. Carrying out many of the routine social duties traditionally performed by presidents' wives bored her, so she called on Lady Bird Johnson, wife of Vice President Lyndon Johnson, to take her place more than fifty times. President

Kennedy's mother, Rose, and his sisters also filled in when the first lady canceled "because of sudden ill health." Her disinclination to appear led to embarrassing situations. For example, when she gave what she called a "PBO" (polite brushoff) to the president of a South American nation because she preferred to go waterskiing with astronaut John Glenn, a State Department representative was forced into an awkward conversation with the aggrieved head of state in a stumbling effort to explain the situation.

"The one thing I do not want to be called is first lady," she told an aide after the inauguration. "It sounds like a saddle horse." Unable to keep the term from being used, she finally gave up efforts to be known simply as Mrs. Kennedy and accepted the title. She sought to stay at arm's length from her admiring public, treating it, one biographer said, like an "admiring escort at a Princeton prom: politely, pleasantly, aloofly." The air of mystery only added to her appeal; the more remote she seemed, the more the public wanted to know about her.

The administration "fed the ravenous journalists gallons of hogwash," Davis contended, picturing her as "the most beautiful, the most charming, the most brilliant, the most aristocratic, the most adoring wife and mother who ever lived." Much of the press willingly accepted her on those terms. However, her stardom denigrated her immediate predecessors, who seemed old and frumpy by comparison, and created an unrealistic media expectation for first ladies that would challenge her successors.

The first president's wife to name a press secretary, Jackie Kennedy selected an inexperienced young woman, Pamela Turnure, rumored to have been one of Jack

Kennedy's romantic interests. Helen Thomas, the veteran White House reporter for United Press International, said Turnure had "about as much business being press secretary as I would have directing the Space Agency." Baldrige said Turnure was instructed to tell reporters "nothing ever, except for occasional spoon-fed bits of information when she was given the signal." In a memo, the first lady informed Turnure, "My press relations will be minimum information given with maximum politeness."

With news organizations still limiting most White House assignments for women reporters to those involving the first lady, Jackie Kennedy was a godsend to the female Washington press corps. Her travels, her elaborate White House entertaining and redecorating, her fashions, her children and their pets, her nursery school for Caroline, her jet-set lifestyle, her boating and horseback riding, and her visits to Kennedy homes at Hyannis Point, Massachusetts, and Palm Beach all made news—and not necessarily just for the women's pages.

Thomas recalled, "The irony is that Jackie Kennedy unwittingly gave a tremendous lift to me and many other women reporters in Washington by escalating our beat . . . to instantaneous front-page news." Eleanor Roosevelt's concern for liberal causes had put her on the front page, too, but the public, conditioned by the middle of the twentieth century to idolize celebrities, had an even more unquenchable thirst for news about the glamorous Jackie Kennedy twenty-four hours a day. Thomas said, "One biting quip from Jackie or a spill from a horse could launch a thousand headlines."

Unlike her witty and eloquent husband, who enjoyed a humorous give-and-take with journalists, Jackie Kennedy had relatively little interaction with reporters. Her press corps, which called itself the "Jackie watch" or the "diaper detail" in reference to her children, would not be daunted. If reporters could not interview her, they interviewed those she did business with—shopkeepers, hairdressers, caterers, even the owner of the diaper service the family used.

Experienced White House social reporters such as Winzola McLendon of the *Washington Post* found that Jackie Kennedy's "attitude toward the press ran hot and cold." McLendon nevertheless credited the first lady for making the White House such a magnet for female journalists that "a lot of women started going there every day learning on the job what to do." Thomas observed that when Jackie Kennedy "was creating the image of a concerned first lady, she wanted press coverage. When she was flying off on her Friday-to-Tuesday weekend trips, she wanted to pull the velvet curtain closed."

In private memos, Jackie Kennedy referred to female reporters as "harpies." She looked down on women journalists as unstylish, unmannerly, and intrusive, trying unsuccessfully to limit their access to White House dinners and suggesting that they "be kept out of sight behind the pillars and potted palms." The president was much more receptive to the journalists. According to columnist Esther Van Wagoner Tufty, when he watched his wife give "dirty looks" to women reporters, "he took hold of her very hard" and told her to "'say hello to the girls, darling,'" leaving "the imprint of his hand in her flesh." Tufty saw a memo in which the first lady facetiously suggested "keeping the harpies at bay by stationing a couple of guards with bayonets near them."

Jackie Kennedy was particularly irritated by Helen

Thomas and by Fran Lewine of the Associated Press, whose assignments called for keeping close watch on the first lady's activities. One Sunday when the two correspondents stood outside a church she attended, Jackie Kennedy retaliated by reporting to the Secret Service that she was being followed by "two strange Spanish-looking women." As a result, the journalists were promptly but briefly arrested. Thomas called the incident "a brilliant carom shot since Fran is Jewish and I'm of Arab descent."

The confrontation was an attack on two of the most outstanding Washington women journalists, both of whom served as president of the Women's National Press Club, a leading organization for Washington newswomen in the mid-twentieth century. Thomas parodied Jackie Kennedy's travels in 1961 at the newswomen's annual show spoofing politicians; Vice President Johnson was on hand for the event, but the first lady declined to attend. Both Thomas and Lewine profited professionally from turning out reams of copy about the first lady. Each moved up the wire service ladder and became one of the first women reporters to cover the president as well as his wife.

Jackie Kennedy's dislike of the press stemmed from an inability to come to terms with the intense public interest in her and her family because they lived in the White House. She considered herself treated unjustly as women journalists watched her through their long-range binoculars as she vacationed outside Washington; she watched them back through her own. When journalists asked what she planned to feed a new puppy, she shot back, "Reporters."

The press corps did not think the first lady's attitude was justified. Lewine, who covered Jackie Kennedy on her trips at home and abroad and even followed her on a press yacht when she cruised in the Aegean Sea, had no qualms about a possible invasion of privacy. In an oral history interview, Lewine said, "If she went out in public, then we figured that was fair game. And if she didn't want that covered, she should have stayed home." She added that the first lady could have avoided some of her difficulties by having a more professional press relations staff so that the press "wouldn't have been quite as intrusive as it became."

Lem Billings, a close friend of John Kennedy, said it was understandable that the first lady disliked the press because "no matter what she did it crucified her." He listed news stories that reported such things as "using a government helicopter to fly to Glen Ora [the Kennedy weekend home in Virginia], swimming in shark-infested waters off Florida . . . dancing the twist . . . subverting White House tradition by doing away with tails and top hats at formal banquets." Yet, he said, the first lady "exceeded permissible bounds" to escape press censure because she refused to attend events such as a congressional wives' luncheon in her honor at the White House, instead ducking out to go to a ballet in New York. Her husband, unwilling to offend the wives of key legislators, showed up instead, marking the first time a president attended an official event as the first lady's representative.

Jackie Kennedy projected herself as a regal wife and mother intent on rearing her children while bringing culture, refinement, and American antiques to the president's mansion. Determined to make the White House a showcase for American civilization, she hired a French chef and planned dinners that epitomized elegant sophistication, inviting performances from classical musicians such as cellist

Pablo Casals and enthralling André Malraux, the French minister of culture, with her knowledge of art and literature. In April 1962, the Kennedys hosted a White House dinner party for Nobel Prize winners, prompting the president to say, "I think this is the most extraordinary collection of talent, of human knowledge, that has ever been gathered together at the White House, with the possible exception of when Thomas Jefferson dined alone." All of this material made marvelous copy for women reporters.

On August 7, 1963, Jackie Kennedy gave birth prematurely to a third child, Patrick Bouvier, who lived less than two days. Two months later, she went back to Greece for a vacation without her husband. She cruised to Turkey on Aristotle Onassis's yacht, *The Christina,* where she was photographed dining and dancing late at night, and she also visited Morocco before returning to Washington. This time, *Newsweek* said her "immunity" from political criticism had worn off, as Republicans raised questions about her acceptance of hospitality from Onassis (whose business practices had figured in two congressional inquiries) and "all-night parties in foreign lands." The Kennedys did not respond to attacks on the trip, but a columnist for the Republican-leaning *New York Daily News* defended the first lady on grounds the death of her baby entitled her to "a change of scene."

Only a month after her return from Greece, Jackie Kennedy went with her husband on the ill-fated political fence-mending trip to Texas that resulted in his assassination on November 22, 1963. Troy speculated she agreed to go to repair her marriage as well as her reputation. After the assassin's bullet abruptly ended John Kennedy's life, her poise and dignity as she planned his funeral left an enduring mark on American history. Her private grief was expressed in a media-rich spectacle that lingered in a nation's collective memory. Even at her husband's funeral, she was the director and stage manager, perhaps the last of the first ladies to do what she wanted without reliance on professional image-makers. She had orchestrated her own Camelot. After her, the position of the first lady would be a more scripted entity.

FOUR

FIRST LADIES AS POLITICAL HELPMATES: LADY BIRD JOHNSON AND PAT NIXON

Jackie Kennedy was followed as first lady by two presidents' wives who personified what Meg Greenfield, the Pulitzer Prize–winning editorial page editor of the *Washington Post,* called the capital's "prevailing wife culture," which "sought to segregate and trivialize them [the wives] as a species." Both Claudia "Lady Bird" Johnson, first lady from 1963 until 1969, and Patricia "Pat" Ryan Nixon, first lady from 1969 to 1974, had played the role expected of political wives long before their husbands were elected president. In the White House, each functioned as a political helpmate, but Lady Bird Johnson ended her stay with lasting recognition for her accomplishments, whereas Pat Nixon departed as a tragic, misunderstood figure. Lady Bird Johnson managed to overcome what Greenfield called the "prevailing inhibitions" against women in Washington to live a life of self-respect and influence. In doing so, she maximized her contacts with the media of her era. Pat Nixon's performance betrayed an inability to pursue the same course. Yet each woman was totally devoted to a difficult, demanding husband and worked hard on projects that had voter appeal but still seemed safely within the realm of activities deemed suitable for genteel women. Their personal experiences testified to both the opportunities and the limitations that faced the wives of presidents in the late twentieth century and illustrated the growing importance of the media.

LADY BIRD JOHNSON

There was no doubt that Lady Bird Johnson centered her life around her husband, Lyndon B. Johnson, but her interest in environmental causes, politely masked under the feminine name of "beautification," gave her a personal identity during her tenure in the White House. Shocked like the rest of the nation at the assassination of President John F. Kennedy in Dallas, she told Jackie Kennedy on the plane bringing the president's body back to Washington, "Mrs. Kennedy, you know we never even wanted to be Vice President and now, dear God, it's come to this." She said she felt like a participant in a Greek tragedy, watching "a noble protagonist overtaken by an inevitable doom." Modest and reserved, Lady Bird Johnson saw herself facing a daunting task in the White House, once remarking to a friend, "I feel as if I am suddenly on stage for a part I never rehearsed."

In fact, the role was one for which she was very well prepared. True, she had not been enthusiastic about Johnson running as vice president with Kennedy in 1960, but that was because her husband had hoped to be the presidential candidate himself. Certainly, she had not expected to become the president's wife due to an assassin's bullet, but she had filled in for an absent Jackie Kennedy on so many occasions that she had mastered the ceremonial aspects of the first lady's position. She also had a capable staff in place, with Elizabeth "Liz" Carpenter, an experienced Washington newspaperwoman and former aide to Johnson himself, as her press secretary. Carpenter, who became her chief of staff as well as her press secretary in the White House, employed an assistant, Simone Poulain, the first staff member with a television background to work for a president's wife.

It had not been easy for Lady Bird Johnson, a middle-aged woman who spoke with a southern accent and was not particularly photogenic, to stand in the shadow of the sophisticated Jackie Kennedy. As the vice president's wife, Helen Thomas recalled, "Mrs. Johnson took a back seat and was very retiring. In fact, when Kennedy died and Mrs. Johnson became the first lady . . . I think she said that a big shadow had lifted. I think she always felt that way." In her published diary, Lady Bird Johnson wrote that the "shadow" did not lift until after Jackie Kennedy's marriage to Aristotle Onassis in 1968, revealing that it hovered over her for most of the Johnson presidency.

As Lady Bird Johnson assumed her new role, the press characterized her as being "politically attuned." The *New York Times* pictured her as gracious, hardworking, disciplined, and devoted to her husband: "Married to an emotional, complicated, often flamboyant man, she has never publicly lost her composure, not even when spat upon in a Dallas hotel during the 1960 campaign."

In a profile for the *Saturday Evening Post,* then an influential weekly magazine, Nan Robertson called her a "consummate politician" and said that "some people describe her with adjectives like 'corny,' 'calculating' and 'cold-eyed.'"

The profile pointed out that the camera "is not kind to the first lady as it was to her predecessor. . . . Her warm amber eyes, on television and in photographs, look black and often hard. The charming smile occasionally seems forced, her animation sometimes appears exaggerated. It is a pity." Ending on a laudatory note, the article commended the first lady for being "accessible" to the press and praised her "open heart."

While most coverage was favorable, *Time* magazine treated her somewhat unkindly in a cover story before the 1964 election, when Johnson won the presidency in his own right. Comparing her to Jackie Kennedy, *Time* declared Lady Bird Johnson fit in the "club woman, rather than the Queenly mold" and noted that "she is no glamor girl. Her nose is a bit too long, her mouth a bit too wide, her ankles a bit less than trim, and she is not outstanding at clotheshorse-manship." *Time* also asked "if she is a sort of self-created Galatea, playing the role of a politician's perfect wife, the possessor of a flawless mediocrity that generates warm admiration but no scorching envy."

On the plus side, though it sneered at her "twanging drawl," the magazine praised her as a tireless campaigner for the Kennedy-Johnson ticket in 1960 and quoted Robert Kennedy as saying "chivalrously" that "Lady Bird carried Texas for us." The story pointed out that she had traveled widely since Johnson's unexpected inauguration to boost the administration's War on Poverty program and to promote interest in conservation.

As first lady, Lady Bird Johnson expanded her horizons and developed her own abilities, just as she had been doing for years, but always in the context of putting her husband and two daughters first. In the 1964 race, she became the first

president's wife in history to conduct a whistle-stop campaign on her own. She toured the South by train in an effort
to bolster the Democratic party, which was shaken by widespread opposition to her husband's support for civil rights
legislation. She covered 1,682 miles in four days, making 47
stops in 8 states and drawing 250 reporters whose news organizations paid for them to go on the campaign train.

When picketers appeared to protest Johnson's push for
equal rights, according to Carpenter, Lady Bird Johnson
"controlled them" by putting up her hand and saying, "'My
friends, this is a country of free speech, and I have a respect
for your viewpoint. But this is my time to give mine.' And to
our amazement, they were quiet." Carpenter said the chief
political value of the trip stemmed from its being shown for
four nights on television network newscasts. "You had five
minutes every night—time you can't buy or afford to buy in
a campaign. And we were on it [television] every night because it was unique that a woman was doing it."

After Johnson's landslide election in 1964, Lady Bird
Johnson launched her beautification campaign, a logical
outgrowth of her previous trips to the West with Secretary of
the Interior Stewart Udall, a champion of preserving natural
resources. The campaign built on references to preserving
natural beauty in Johnson's 1965 State of the Union address,
which included plans for a White House conference on the
subject, and in his subsequent message to Congress devoted
to "creative conservation" to promote "the values of beauty."
The beautification effort was aimed at enhancing the environment of urban areas and preserving natural beauty
throughout the nation, in part by regulating billboards along
interstate highways.

Lady Bird Johnson and her staff thought long and hard before deciding on beautification as her special interest. Bess Abell, her social secretary, said, "She wanted to have a project so that her time wasn't just posing for publicity pictures and shaking hands and giving tea parties. She wanted to have a project, something that she could identify with ... that would be involved in some way in the President's program."

Beautification supported Lyndon Johnson's effort to build what he called the Great Society, a continuation of Democratic initiatives under Roosevelt's New Deal to expand the federal government to attack social, economic, and environmental problems. By no means was beautification Lady Bird Johnson's sole activity. She also served as honorary chair of the Head Start program to give educational opportunities to disadvantaged preschool children, continued Jackie Kennedy's historical restoration of the White House, and maintained a full schedule of social and ceremonial events along with overseeing the marriages of her two daughters. But beautification was her premier cause.

Lady Bird Johnson did not engage in the same type of outspoken activism as Eleanor Roosevelt, with whom she often was compared. She never gave press conferences, nor did she write a syndicated newspaper column like Roosevelt had, although she kept a diary of her White House years that became a best seller when it was published in 1970. In that diary, she wrote that when she held a tea in January 1964 for women members of the White House press corps, then numbering about sixty-five, she hoped she would never "have to be afraid of them." She tried to make sure she had no reason to be. Under her direction, Carpenter ran a sophisticated, efficient press operation for the East Wing of the White House, taking care of news related to the president's wife and family, while the president's press secretaries handled news from the Oval Office in the West Wing.

Carpenter explained the difference between Eleanor Roosevelt and Lady Bird Johnson in terms of their concepts of wifehood: "Mrs. Roosevelt was an instigator, an innovator, willing to air a cause even without her husband's endorsement. Mrs. Johnson was an implementer and translator of her husband and his purposes." She might also have added that Lady Bird Johnson was far more dependent on staff support than Eleanor Roosevelt, who had only one assistant, her secretary.

Lady Bird Johnson realized that the word *beautification* carried unfortunate connotations that could easily discredit her efforts. She recognized that "it sounds cosmetic and trivial and it's prissy." Yet no better term could be found, Carpenter said, since "the alternatives were stodgy and they didn't sound like anything new. Conservation. Environmental beauty. Nothing." Besides, Carpenter added, newspapers "condensed it more."

The obvious way to make the term work in a headline was to shorten it to *beauty*. Stories dealing with ladies and beauty logically fit in newspaper women's sections of the day. (For example, the *Washington Evening Star* headlined one typical news story about the campaign "A PLEA FOR U.S. BEAUTY" and placed it on the front page of its society/home section, using the headline "FIRST LADY DISCUSSES BEAUTY" for the continuation of the story on an inside page.) In the 1960s, women's sections, soon to be changed by most newspapers into lifestyle sections, were under attack by feminists on grounds they trivialized women's activities. Placement of stories on the beautification campaign in these sections tended to lessen the importance of the effort and to discount it in the minds of some feminists.

Lewis Gould, a historian of the beautification effort, concluded, "There was always an undeserved tone of apology and supplication about what Lady Bird Johnson did for the environment; this arose from the label beautification." Contending the campaign showed the constraints on women in public life in the 1960s, he said Lady Bird Johnson had no real choice except to tacitly accept the "attribution of inferiority toward women that the word beautification implied." In reality, the beautification effort went far beyond a garden club approach to planting flowers.

The campaign called for partnerships between the public and private sectors to provide funds needed to improve the environment. According to Carpenter, Udall proposed that the beautification effort initially center on the nation's capital to complement the Johnson administration's plan to clean up the Potomac River. With Lady Bird Johnson working to improve her "hometown" of Washington, the administration hoped that women in other areas would follow her example and organize efforts to beautify their own towns.

Katharine Graham, owner of the *Washington Post,* was an influential member of the First Lady's Committee for a More Beautiful National Capital, the group set up by Lady Bird Johnson to spearhead the campaign. Graham speculated that Carpenter played a major role in developing the program in order to enhance Lady Bird Johnson's role in the administration. Graham said, "Liz Carpenter told me that she was thinking up something to replace Jackie's White House [restoration], and I think it was conceived by Liz as a program which she [Lady Bird] could do as the first lady that would give her some significance. Now although it was thought up as perhaps an idea of Liz's that would be good for her, I think it meant a great deal to her in the end."

Initially, Graham was skeptical of beautification in light of Washington's pressing needs. She said she feared "people would even resent it and not give money to it because when we are all being asked for money for ghetto problems, education problems, school problems, health problems, you just felt embarrassed going to people and saying, 'Will you give a garden' . . . at moments it got silly." She changed her mind when she found the campaign resulted in new parks, playgrounds, and flower beds paid for by "outside money and outside resources that [otherwise] the city would not have had."

The flower- and tree-planting projects that resulted continue to add to the ambience of the capital today. Plantings included some two million daffodil bulbs, new groves of cherry trees, 83,000 flowering plants, thousands of annuals, and 25,000 trees. To Lady Bird Johnson's credit, the beautification effort attempted to improve the rundown inner city as well as the areas surrounding national monuments. The campaign had a much more lasting impact on the tourist areas of the capital than the cleanup efforts, rat-eradication programs, and other poorly funded endeavors directed at blighted sections. Nevertheless, Lady Bird Johnson tried to raise public awareness of the link between poverty and lack of natural beauty.

Interest in beautification produced a countless array of news stories for the women who covered the first lady's side of the White House. The ebullient Carpenter helped stage event after event and trip after trip to spotlight the first lady's activities, planning tours of national parks, wilderness refuges, and historical houses that appealed to her press corps. Helen Thomas recalled: "Climbing mountains pursued by gnats, riding Snake River rapids in Wyoming, watching from the beaches as she—not I—snorkeled in the barracuda-filled Caribbean, bobbing in a flotilla of rubber rafts down the Rio Grande . . . no newswoman wanted to be left behind when Lady Bird set out on her adventures."

In total, Lady Bird Johnson made forty trips covering 200,000 miles in promoting beautification and the environment, education including the popular Head Start program for disadvantaged preschool children, antipoverty efforts, historical preservation, and other administration initiatives. She flew in the same chartered plane with representatives of her press corps, which numbered about eighty-five by the end of the Johnson years. In fact, she could not have taken the trips without reporters being present because no public funding went into her travels and the news organizations that were represented were charged for the cost of the planes.

To publicize the need to protect natural resources, Lady Bird Johnson led her press corps on trips that turned into wilderness excursions. Journalists covering her visit to the Grand Tetons in 1965 took a thirty-mile trip in a rubber raft. The *Washington Evening Star* described the experience under the headline "RAIN-PELTED NEWS REPORTERS CHALLENGE SNAKE RIVER" and said it tested the journalists' "frontier mettle." The next year, seventy reporters joined Johnson for a raft trip down the Rio Grande in Texas.

Carpenter considered the trips extremely successful except for the presence of anti–Vietnam War pickets as opposition to President Johnson's Vietnam policies grew. She said, "Newspaperwomen want an activist first lady. . . . The fact that she would get out and be a set of eyes and ears for the President thrilled them. It also improved their beat . . . they had a better play on their stories." Women journalists also traveled with the first lady on trips to the family ranch in Texas.

Katie Louchheim, a State Department official and Democratic activist, said that President Johnson "both admired and resented [her] activities." She noted that "many of us had heard him speak caustically of her meetings with talkative conservationists that interfered with his taking a nap; or of her absence when he wanted her: 'She's out planting a tree somewhere.'"

The first lady's most enduring legacy was the passage of the Highway Beautification Act of 1965. This compromise measure to regulate billboards pleased neither the billboard industry nor conservationists and their allies. Lady Bird Johnson took the unprecedented step for a president's wife of involving herself directly in pressing for the legislation. In a six-column headline, the *Washington Star* writers asked in surprise, "DID THE FIRST LADY 'LOBBY' FOR BEAUTIFICA-TION?" They answered the question by saying, "The White House shies away from any suggestion that Mrs. Johnson was actually lobbying. But there really isn't any other word that accurately describes her activities." Yet the article appeared in the society/home section, a placement that served to under-cut its message of a woman taking a substantive political role.

In an attempt to embarrass President Johnson by infer-ring he was giving in to a woman, opponents attacked the bill on grounds it was being pushed by his wife. In Montana, a billboard called for Lady Bird to be impeached. In an unusual personal attack, Representative Robert Dole, a Kansas Republican, proposed an amendment to delete references to the "Secretary of Commerce" whenever they appeared in the bill and to substitute the words "Lady Bird."

Lady Bird Johnson's response to finding herself involved in public controversy was, in Gould's word, "guarded." While she did not give up her beautification efforts, she decided to be "more careful and less visible." She long had been familiar with the need for wives to stay behind the scenes in the male-dominated world of politics.

In 1963, while still the wife of the vice president, she had said in a speech: "I would say that the life of any congressional wife revolves around three things: husband, children, and home . . . as wives of busy men whose daily business is the nation's business, our best chance to find the significant is to help our husbands achieve their own legislative aims." Abigail McCarthy, wife of Senator Eugene McCarthy, the Minnesota Democrat who challenged President Johnson over conduct of the Vietnam War, called the comments an excellent description of the "vocation" of "political wives." Lady Bird Johnson's own life presented an example that was hard to emulate. As a political wife, she facilitated Lyndon Johnson's rise from a depressed agricultural hamlet in central Texas to the powerful position of Senate majority leader and then on to the White House. In the process, she developed sharp business skills that made the family extremely wealthy.

She did not have an easy life as the wife of a towering figure who dominated those around him. Crude and cutting at times, Lyndon Johnson mastered the art of politics and

dreamed of building a more just nation, but he was a philandering husband who demanded total devotion from his wife.
He received it, regardless of his behavior. Describing the
"showy affection" between the two, *Time* noted that Johnson
"has been known to swat Lady Bird so hard on the behind
that her feet nearly leave the floor."

Her loyalty was not always admired. Jackie Kennedy,
who scorned the political wife culture, was said to have observed acidly, "Lady Bird would crawl down Pennsylvania Avenue over splintered glass for Lyndon." Helen Thomas said
Lady Bird Johnson tried to protect her husband from the
consequences of his actions: "She soothed friends he had rode
roughshod over and shielded him when he was boorish."

At least one White House reporter disliked the first
lady's style as a political wife. Muriel Dobbins, a correspondent for the *Baltimore Sun,* remarked, "When Mrs. Johnson
first came in, I followed her on about three of those beautification trips, and she made those sugar-coated speeches until
the *Sun* said they weren't going to spend anymore money
having me watch her plant azaleas." Dobbins said the first
lady lacked spontaneity in her speeches.

A rare exception came in 1968 when she answered an
anti–Vietnam War outburst from singer Eartha Kitt at one of
a series of White House luncheons set up to recognize
women of achievement. Dobbins commented, "It was the
first time I ever heard her say anything she hadn't thought
out thoroughly first or that Liz Carpenter hadn't written for
her." The first lady told Kitt she prayed for "a just and honorable peace" but that until it occurred, Americans needed
to "work on bettering the things in this country that we can
better."

Along with holding luncheons for women "doers," Lady Bird Johnson staged the first fashion show ever held at the White House. A committee of fashion writers assisted in planning the 1968 event, which they then covered for their newspapers. Although she carefully watched her expenditures on clothing in spite of her wealth, Lady Bird Johnson long had shown an interest in improving her wardrobe and appearance as her husband rose in Washington. Abigail McCarthy said that, as a senator's wife, she admired Lady Bird Johnson's self-discipline and determination to present herself well. "Through the years," McCarthy said, "I saw her progress from the motherly and slightly plump mother of small children to the chic, slim, and well-dressed woman she was when her husband became vice president."

Lyndon Johnson appreciated his wife's strength of character, sought her advice, liked to buy her clothes, and missed her when she was away, but observers witnessed his failure to respect her on numerous occasions. Katharine Graham became incensed on a visit to the Johnson ranch during the 1964 presidential campaign when Johnson grumbled that he had to attend a barbecue in his honor because "Lady Bird had gotten him into it." Graham recalled in her autobiography, "He was so savage about her that I . . . spontaneously said, 'She also got you where you are today.'" This angered Johnson further, and he continued "blaming her and complaining," Graham wrote, "until I finally heard myself saying, 'Oh, shut up, er . . . Mr. President.'" A brief silence followed, she added, broken by Hubert Humphrey, Johnson's vice presidential running mate, "making some comment that alleviated the tension."

Graham also recalled an instance following a White

House dinner when Johnson, angered by a story in the *Washington Post,* called her into his bedroom. He yelled at her, leaving her "frozen with dismay" and thinking "this can't be me being bawled out by the President of the United States while he is undressing." Finally, she wrote, "he bellowed 'turn around'" while he continued "with his angry monologue until I turned back at his command to find him in his pajamas." Such incidents did not find their way into Graham's newspaper, which at that period differentiated sharply between the public and private lives of presidents and their families. For the most part, private lives were left alone.

Although the Washington press corps ignored rumors of Johnson's amorous pursuits just as it had overlooked similar stories concerning President Kennedy, it had no compunctions about attacking Johnson in general and grew increasingly unfriendly during his administration. In addition to faulting his Vietnam policies, journalists accused him of refusing to tell them the truth, behaving erratically, and showing little consideration for their profession by scheduling trips and press briefings with no advance warning. These criticisms may have been justified, but attacks on Johnson because of his background were not, according to Nancy Dickerson, the first woman CBS television correspondent and later a longtime White House NBC network correspondent. She said that the press unfairly "ridiculed Johnson for his Texas origins, for the cut of his pants, for the way he tweaked his big ears, and for his lack of what they considered 'style.'"

Very little of this animosity spilled over to Lady Bird Johnson, although she perceived that she was looked down on as a southerner. Graham recalled calling Carpenter to compliment her on the first lady's performance on an ABC television program on beautification. She was surprised to find out Carpenter was keenly interested in whether Lady Bird Johnson's "Southern accent was noticeable at all."

Born in tiny Karnack, Texas, the daughter of a well-to-do merchant and landowner, the future first lady was cared for by a maiden aunt after the death of her mother when she was five years old. Alone a good deal, she remembered years later, she "grew up listening to the wind in the pine trees of the East Texas woods." A love of nature lay behind her selection of beautification for her special interest. Her nickname, Lady Bird, which took the place of her given name, Claudia, was related to her childhood environment. She said it came from her African American nurse, who compared her to dotted ladybird beetles and said she was as "purty as a ladybird."

She and Lyndon Johnson met in 1934 shortly after her graduation from the University of Texas at Austin, and they soon eloped. It was a precipitous action for a serious young woman who had earned two bachelor's degrees with honors. She had followed her arts degree with one in journalism because she thought that newspaper people, in contrast to others, "went more places and met more interesting people, and had more exciting things happen to them." So shy that she had been delighted when she narrowly missed being the valedictorian of her high school class and consequently did not have to give a commencement speech, she did not immediately seek a job following college. She went home to remodel her father's house.

After the petite Lady Bird was introduced to Johnson, a towering six feet three inches tall with an oversized ego to match, he proposed during their first day together. She declined, but Johnson pressed his suit by letter and phone from

Washington, where he was working as an aide to a congressman. In their correspondence, she told him she would hate for him to seek a career in politics, although she said she loved him. Ten weeks after they had met, he returned to Karnack, determined they would wed, saying, "We either do it now or we never will." She did it and accompanied him back to Washington.

As a novice political wife, she soon discovered her husband, the product of the depressed Texas Hill Country who had worked his way through San Marcos State Teachers College, had lofty ambitions and exacting expectations. Promises to take her to museums and cultural activities faded as Johnson urged her to learn the names of the constituents of his employer. She had to master cooking and the art of entertaining his political associates at a moment's notice on a slim budget. He insisted that she perform his personal chores—bring him coffee in bed, lay out his clothes, fill his cigarette lighter, shine his shoes—and she did. She developed a positive attitude, explaining: "He early announced, 'I'd like to have coffee in bed,' and I thought, 'What!?!? Me?!?!' But I soon realized it's less trouble serving someone that way than by setting the table and all."

When a Texas congressman died in 1937, leaving a vacant seat, she borrowed $10,000 from her father against her inheritance to help finance Johnson's campaign. Her father donated $25,000 more. Johnson won on a platform of supporting Franklin D. Roosevelt and the New Deal, the first of his six successful campaigns to win election to the House of Representatives. In 1942, Lady Bird Johnson ran her husband's congressional office for eight months while he served in the armed forces during World War II. Answering constituent mail and making political decisions, she received no pay but got invaluable training in politics and management skills that she would put to good use.

In 1943, Lady Bird Johnson bought a small radio station, KTBC, in Austin for $17,000, using money remaining from her mother's estate of $63,000 plus landholdings. The debt-ridden station became the basis for the Johnson family's multimillion-dollar media empire. Through his political contacts with the Federal Communications Commission, Johnson was instrumental in securing permission for the station to expand into a television operation that monopolized the Austin market. A shrewd businesswoman, Lady Bird Johnson kept a close eye on the station's bottom line and bought interests in other media properties and in real estate. She kept up her business and political interests after the birth of two daughters, Lynda Bird in 1944 and Lucy Baines in 1947. During the time Johnson was president, *Life* magazine estimated her fortune, then in a family trust, at $9 million.

She overcame her shyness sufficiently to campaign for Johnson during his winning race for the U.S. Senate in 1948. After he suffered a major heart attack in 1955, she insisted he follow a healthier lifestyle so he could continue his career. She also took a public-speaking course to prepare herself for more campaigning. By the time she became first lady, she was an effective speaker who used folksy southern sayings and colloquial phrases such as "y'all" to relate to audiences. Reluctant to use the word *I,* in order to emphasize that she and her husband were a political team, she often made comments such as "We went and made a speech."

Over the years, she also learned how to cope with her husband's unfaithfulness, which included overtures to women journalists. Nancy Dickerson stated, "[Johnson] propositioned me once." On that occasion, she wrote in her autobiography, Lady Bird Johnson dispatched Bill Moyers, her husband's press secretary, to persuade Johnson to leave Dickerson's room. Dickerson explained, "Lady Bird was secure in the knowledge that LBJ's love for her superseded any sexual desire, or even sexual relationship. In her realm she had no peer; she knew it, he knew it, and so did everybody else."

As the holder of a journalism degree, Lady Bird Johnson understood the way the press operated, and she wanted to please reporters as well as her husband. Carpenter said, "She knew the five W's [the journalist's who, what, when, where, and why] and the H [how], and she knew the difference between the A.M. [morning newspaper deadline] and the P.M.[evening deadline]." Describing Lady Bird Johnson as "a saint to work for," Carpenter added, "I could call any time of the day and say, 'Fran [Lewine] and Helen [Thomas]—the AP and UP girls—have this problem and have got this question.'" Even if the question could not be answered, Lady Bird Johnson would give her enough information so she could return the reporters' telephone calls.

Working with Carpenter, reporters received a never-ending supply of news that presented the first lady doing far more than simply pouring tea. The material was made to order for newspaper women's pages as they were being transformed into cultural/lifestyle sections, as well as for women's magazines. Editors featured stories on the first lady's beautification project and her other activities apart from being a hostess. But they also ran traditional stories and pictures on White House social events and employed widely read society columnists who reported on Washington parties and official entertaining.

Betty Beale, a syndicated columnist who worked for the *Washington Evening Star,* said the Johnsons were unfairly compared to the Kennedys in terms of social style and grace. Consequently, she noted, they "were daily subjected to printed putdowns." Beale wrote about the Johnson era bringing the frug, the watusi, and the jerk, "free-wheeling gyrations to rock music," to White House parties, prompting additional music at social functions and more liveliness than previously. Yet the public remembered the elegance of the Kennedys, with Jackie Kennedy (until her marriage to Onassis in 1968) annually outranking Lady Bird Johnson in the Gallup Poll's "Most Admired Women" survey.

The biggest society stories were the weddings of the Johnson daughters, Lynda Bird and Lucy Baines, both of whom were married while Johnson was president. Lucy, who changed her name to Luci, had a wedding in 1966 at the National Shrine of the Immaculate Conception, attended by seven hundred guests. Her sister was married in a candlelight service at the White House shortly before Christmas in 1967.

Stories on her daughters and their plans did not always please Lady Bird Johnson. When Helen Thomas reported that eighteen-year-old Luci planned to marry Pat Nugent before her father knew it, Lady Bird Johnson, like her husband, was "seething." Similarly, when *Women's Wear Daily* published a description of Luci's wedding gown in advance of the official release date, the first lady and her family were irate. In retaliation, the White House barred all reporters for that publication from the wedding. But these incidents were exceptions to the generally warm relationships between Lady

Bird Johnson and the media. She invited the newswomen to White House events, thanked them for stories she liked, and gave them lots to write about.

Lyndon Johnson made his bombshell announcement on March 31, 1968, that he would not seek a second term as president due to tensions arising from the Vietnam War. Lady Bird Johnson, who herself had been booed on two campuses because of Vietnam, was relieved. She feared his health would give way if he stayed in office. One of her last acts as first lady was to entertain her press corps at a White House Christmas party. She modestly confided to her diary, "I like this crowd. I've gotten better from them than I deserve, by and large."

Considering the dominating nature of her husband and the stereotypical expectations for women of her era, Lady Bird Johnson raised the role of political wife to a new level. She had a direct impact on legislation and energized the un-defined position of the first lady, carrying on the tradition of Eleanor Roosevelt. Helen Thomas said Johnson grew as a person while serving as first lady: "She made up her mind to be a 'doer' herself and to make her own interests a cause. She left the White House more poised, confident and happy." In Texas, she continued her beautification efforts by creating the National Wildflower Research Center.

PAT NIXON

In contrast, her successor, Thelma Ryan Nixon, known as Pat because she was born close to St. Patrick's Day, did not pro-mote any specific project apart from the vague one of volun-teerism and rarely expressed herself on public issues, al-though she backed the equal rights amendment. She also urged her husband to nominate a woman to the U.S. Supreme Court, but he did not. Her daughter, Julie Nixon Eisenhower, commented that "she kind of lost faith that journalists would interpret things as they really are, and just didn't want to reveal herself at all."

In fact, Pat Nixon was such a private person that her two daughters, Julie and Tricia, did not even know her real name was Thelma until their father, Richard M. Nixon, unsuccessfully ran as the Republican candidate for president in 1960. With the slogan "Pat for First Lady" a part of the campaign and her homemaking abilities widely publicized, Pat Nixon appeared personally humiliated by the outcome, as cameras captured her tear-streaked face when her husband conceded to Kennedy. By the time he won his 1968 presidential bid, she had become privately disillusioned with politics, but along with her daughters, she campaigned as she always had. Television, a medium in which she was never comfortable, showed her loyally standing by his side even when Nixon himself seemed almost oblivious to her presence.

As a consequence, journalists and other observers looked at her pasted-on smile in public appearances, first obvious during the years when Nixon was vice president, and called her "plastic Pat" and "Pat the robot." In private, she presented a different picture. One woman reporter wrote: "The tense guarded campaign wife with the rehearsed smile was in relaxed moments a warm and peppy person." Her personal warmth failed to carry over to public forums, however. Helen Thomas noted, "She had come up through a stoic school for Presidential wives and she may have been the last one to think it necessary to hide her feelings completely."

Her reticence to display emotion in public stemmed from several factors, including: a childhood of hard work, poverty, and caring for ill parents that had taught her to carry on in spite of adversity; a dislike of the personal revelations increasingly expected of candidates in a media-dominated world; a perceived need to conform to the image of women as cheerleaders and supporters for males; and tension between her husband's advisers and her own staff. These factors diminished her ability to carry out the public communication increasingly needed to perform the role of first lady effectively. Underlying them all was the issue of her relationship with her husband, which appeared increasingly distant to the journalists who covered her. As newspapers were forced to provide more human interest material to compete with television, reporters looked more closely than before at the personal styles and interactions of public figures.

In the case of Richard Nixon, what they saw was a disturbing lack of attention to his wife. Not necessarily the stuff of news stories, their observations nevertheless did little to portray the president as a likable individual. Recalled Kandy Stroud, a reporter for *Women's Wear Daily,* "I rode in the limousine with them, the first time I was alone with them together. He did all the talking, she did none. She just sat there . . . like a staff member . . . the entire ride and he didn't refer to her, or defer to her."

A *Washington Post* reporter, Donnie Radcliffe, told author Kati Marton, "Nixon seemed to forget about her in big moments. He didn't want her to upstage or embarrass him." Since there was no evidence that she ever had done so, he apparently had no need to worry, but his staff, headed by H. R. Haldeman, considered her a potential threat. According to Betty Caroli, one of Pat Nixon's aides said, "You wouldn't believe the sexist attitude of some of those guys, and Haldeman was the worst of the lot." Far more than either Kennedy or Johnson, Richard Nixon refused to acknowledge the potential of his wife to take a substantive role in his administration, although he needed her as a visible supporting player. Hugh Sidey, of *Time* magazine, concluded, "She kind of followed along with him, and he used her in campaigns, but once he got in the White House that was the end of it."

From his first unexpectedly successful foray into politics as a candidate for Congress in 1946 to his triumphant election to the presidency in 1968, Nixon had appealed to voters through his wife and family. With campaign literature stressing the team of "Pat and Dick," Nixon, a Navy veteran of World War II, personified a generation of leadership that called on women to play an active but always subordinate role in political image-making. Pictures of the trim, photogenic Pat Nixon and their two blonde little girls helped humanize Nixon when he ran for the Senate in 1950 as a hard-hitting anti-Communist. By calling attention to his family in his famous "Checkers speech" (Checkers was a dog given to his daughters) on television, he got off the hook in 1952 for accepting secret funds for office and travel expenses and stayed on Eisenhower's ticket, winning election as vice president for two terms. Pat Nixon, however, was embarrassed as she gazed intently at her husband while he discussed their personal finances during the broadcast. He stressed that she had no mink coat but only "a respectable Republican cloth coat and I always tell her she looks good in anything." Even in the White House, Nixon celebrated the anniversary of the celebrated speech, but his wife refused to talk about it.

In Nixon's losing bid for the presidency in 1960 against John F. Kennedy, Pat Nixon campaigned much harder than the reluctant Jackie Kennedy. According to Lester David, her biographer, she declined to give overt political speeches, but she became "the most active and visible wife of a presidential candidate in American political history" up to that point. When Nixon decided to run again for the presidency in 1968, after entering the race for governor of California over her objections and losing that election, Pat Nixon again hit the campaign trail like a good soldier obeying orders. Some campaigning, however, was delegated to her daughters, both of whom presented traditional feminine appearances in opposition to those of the long-haired hippies protesting the continuation of the Vietnam War.

It was apparent to journalist Helen Thomas that Pat Nixon "was clearly not gung ho about campaigning," while Nixon's high-powered public relations men, who had little regard for women, "did not seem to care whether she was around or not." By then, the women's liberation movement combined with the social upheavals stemming from the Vietnam War had made Pat Nixon's determined pleasantness and refusal to voice her own opinions seem old-fashioned and suspect to many of the journalists who covered her, a fact of which she was well aware. Like her husband, she resented what she saw as the liberal media that represented an elitist world.

One journalist who managed to break through her reserve was Gloria Steinem, the feminist leader who wrote for *New York* magazine. When Steinem pressed her on what woman she most admired in history, Pat Nixon replied indignantly: "I never had time to think about things like that—

who I wanted to be or who I admired, or to have ideas . . . I've never had it easy. I'm not like all you . . . all those people who had it easy." Four years later, she expressed relief when Nixon was reelected for a second term, telling her staff, "I'm going to relax in these last four years." She could not foresee what lay ahead.

The only president to resign his position, Nixon was forced out on August 9, 1974, after tapes of conversations in the Oval Office revealed that he was a party to efforts at political sabotage, including the cover-up of a burglary at the headquarters of the Democratic National Committee in the Watergate apartments. Pat Nixon had not known of the existence of the tapes; when they materialized, she said they should be burned, but her husband did not seek her advice. In an emotional farewell to the nation, Nixon praised his mother but failed to mention his wife or his daughters loyally standing nearby. It was a commentary on a strained marriage in which the principals did not show affection to each other in public, as well as on a failed presidency. Lester David quoted a friend of Pat Nixon as saying, "She gave so much and got so little of what was really meaningful to a woman—attention, companionship, consideration."

Pat Nixon represented both an American success story and an American tragedy. She was the attractive, bright daughter of a poor miner turned small farmer and worked her way through the University of Southern California. A popular high school teacher, she had married Nixon, an ambitious young lawyer in Whittier, California, and stayed at his side as he overcame political defeats, rebuilt his support in the Republican party, and finally made it to the White House. Yet she was a woman locked up inside herself who resented the demands that politics made on her marriage and her children, telling a friend shortly before her husband was nominated for president in 1960, "I gave up everything I've ever loved." As first lady, she worked hard but received relatively little credit for her endeavors, which did not make much of an impression on the media.

In actuality, Pat Nixon hosted thousands of people at the White House, opening the grounds and offering tours for the disabled. She made the mansion more accessible to the public by providing more printed information and historical displays for tourists. She carried out an extensive campaign to complete Jackie Kennedy's restoration of the mansion by locating actual antiques instead of reproductions and adding to the collection of portraits of presidents and their wives. She religiously spent four to five hours a day on her mail, responding to requests from those she called "the little guys." Yet in part because she did not spotlight a concrete cause or program of her own, her detractors, whose hostility toward her husband both politically and personally carried over to her, sneered at what they considered her misplaced martyrdom.

Soon after arriving in the White House, Pat Nixon found that media expectations for the first lady had changed since the 1950s when she was the wife of the vice president under Dwight D. Eisenhower. As Julie Nixon Eisenhower put it, "For eight years the newspaper coverage of Mamie Eisenhower [who became Julie's grandmother-in-law after her marriage to Mamie's grandson, David] was no more weighty than what she wore, her menus, and the stir she caused when she decided to receive guests with her right glove off." But, Eisenhower continued, the newswomen covering her mother "wanted a First Lady 'project' and a newsmaker in her own right." Pat Nixon, unfortunately, did not move confidently in those directions.

Projects appealed to Pat Nixon less than "personal diplomacy," which she told Thomas was her "only claim to fame both at home and abroad." As the wife of the vice president, she had traveled repeatedly across the United States and visited fifty-three nations as well. By the time she left the White House, she had gone to seventy-eight countries, including war-torn Vietnam, and crisscrossed the United States, often encountering antiwar protestors. She had become the most widely traveled first lady in history up to that point.

Observers said her personal warmth was most obvious when she traveled without her husband. In 1970, accompanied by a group of reporters, she delivered nine tons of relief supplies on a hazardous flight deep into the snow-covered Andes Mountains in Peru after a disastrous earthquake there. Fran Lewine of the Associated Press recalled, "It was a wonderful trip because we did something for a change instead of just [fulfilling] this role of a first lady being out there to shop and tour. . . . [There] was a mission to this and therefore it had much more significance than the usual trip of a first lady." In the 1972 election campaign, Pat Nixon, a popular figure with Republican women, took the unusual step of making a campaign tour on her own, as did each of her daughters, with the family assuming surrogate roles for Richard Nixon himself. His political strategy called for him to appear to be busy with nonpartisan activities.

Initially, Nixon did not plan to take his wife on his historic trip to open relations with China in 1972, but he changed his mind after she made a successful solo visit to

Africa and represented the United States at the inauguration of a new president of Liberia. Still, Nixon reportedly said, if she were to go to China, she would go "solely as a prop." And she apparently agreed, telling journalists, "I wouldn't say anything to spoil the good work Dick has done."

A hesitancy to speak her mind for fear of hurting her husband marked Pat Nixon's media relations in general. Just after the presidential election in 1968, Betty Beale of the *Washington Star* published an open letter to the new first lady with pointers on what she should do. Beale called for a continuation of the kind of press operation in place under Liz Carpenter and ended with the hope the White House would be a "vibrant, warm music-filled home." To the detriment of both the first lady and the journalists who covered her, Beale's recommendations were only partially carried out. Pat Nixon turned the lights back on at the White House, after the frugal Lyndon Johnson had ordered them shut off, and made plans for formal entertaining, but her media relations floundered.

In contrast to the effective press operation under Carpenter, reporters assigned to Pat Nixon said they initially dealt with what *Newsweek* termed a "Closed Door Policy" of "choking off information, giving out releases late ... and favoring certain reporters over others." In an effort to take charge of the situation by making the first lady a public relations arm of the presidency, Nixon's key advisers, H. R. Haldeman and John Ehrlichman, expanded the Office of the First Lady in 1969. The reorganization gave the office thirty employees and a budget and combined the positions of staff director and press secretary. The new post went to Constance Stuart, whose husband worked for Ehrlichman, in a move seen as lessening the role of the first lady in directing her own affairs.

Stuart, a public relations professional, expressed a desire to work out any difficulty between the president's men and the first lady's staff before "it got to the husband and wife level." (Curiously, the division of responsibilities between the president's staff in the West Wing and the first lady's staff in the East Wing led to a series of communications by formal memos between Nixon and his wife. On one occasion, for example, "The President" requested "Mrs. Nixon" to outfit his bedroom with a "bigger table on which he can work at night.")

Stuart set up what Maria Smith of the *Washington Post* called the "largest, most expensive press or public relations staff ever assembled to promote the public image of a President's wife," estimating its cost at $150,000 a year. Some reporters liked Stuart's brisk energy, but others objected to what they saw as her Madison Avenue "snow-job" technique. She held biweekly press briefings and incurred the wrath of society reporters by unsuccessfully trying to ban notebooks at White House parties.

Although Pat Nixon eventually was linked to volunteerism, her efforts were diffused. According to Gil Troy, the first lady "scurried about, helping poor kids here, elderly widows there, dabbling in literacy crusades, urban planning, postal academies for inner city education, and environmentalism." Stuart was forced to decline a $100,000 donation from a Nixon supporter to support the first lady's projects, since they had not "gotten off the ground."

In terms of social news, although White House entertainment was lively and varied, the Nixons themselves left

dinners early and almost never stayed to dance, affording little opportunity for reporters to glean feature material on
them. The biggest society story was the televised White
House wedding of Tricia Nixon and Edward Cox on June
12, 1971, a royal-like event at which the Nixons actually
danced together, solidifying an image of what the president
called "America's first family you can be proud of." Another
successful broadcast in 1971 was an hour-long ABC special,
A Visit with the First Lady, based on Pat Nixon's trip to new
national park sites as well as her management of the White
House.

Unhappily, preludes to the disaster that lay ahead soon
filled news columns. The story on the marriage shared space
on the front page of the *New York Times* with the first install-
ment of the Pentagon papers. This publication of a leaked
government archive on the history of the Vietnam War set the
parameters for political sabotage that ended with Watergate
and Nixon's downfall.

By the time of Tricia Nixon's wedding, the president's
aides had lost confidence in Stuart and designated one of
their own, Alexander Butterfield, to oversee handling of
"events and publicity." Stuart left after Nixon was reelected
in 1972 and was replaced by Helen Smith, whom Helen
Thomas praised because she "never lied." Pat Nixon pared
down her staff and served as her own staff director, but her
press relations remained a problem to the administration.
Richard Nixon himself instructed his press secretary, Ron
Ziegler, to improve the situation, complaining that "despite
an unprecedented effort on the part of Mrs. Nixon to handle all sorts of visiting delegations, foreign diplomats, etc.,
over the past four years we have been unable to break

through in terms of getting some kind of coverage in the press." He blamed the situation on antagonism from the women's press corps toward his presidency, but according to Carl Anthony, the reporters did not perceive her activities as substantive copy.

Laudatory news did appear, such as a story in the *New York Times* on February 15, 1973, that the first lady received three thousand letters a week and personally answered every one of them. A *Washington Post* article a week earlier was more critical. On February 8, the newspaper reported on Pat Nixon's resignation as honorary chair of the Day Care Council of America, following the group's criticism of President Nixon's veto of a day care bill. The story quoted a council representative as saying that "after her initial two days of visiting day care centers and being photographed she never did anything else."

At times, reporters found her determined to present a public front that seemed to be a smokescreen for reality. When Beale interviewed her prior to Nixon's reelection as president in 1972, for instance, she spoke of her husband, not herself, saying, "I think being a partner to a great man is about the top experience." In a subsequent interview on "the real Richard Nixon," she praised her husband as "considerate, kind and gentle," dismaying Beale, who hoped that for the sake of credibility, "she would find some fault with him."

Reporters also detected false notes in her public conduct. Pat Nixon claimed she did not smoke or drink, for example, but she actually was a heavy smoker who died of lung cancer. She also drank on occasion, although her family vigorously denied allegations of heavy drinking during the Watergate episode. They were made by Bob Woodward and Carl

Bernstein, the *Washington Post* reporters credited with uncovering the scandal.

Thomas recounted an incident when the first lady reached out for a glass of sherry from a tray, then pulled her hand back when she observed newswomen watching her. Thomas wanted to tell her to go ahead and take it, but she realized that Pat Nixon "had been brought up in the old school that first ladies have NO 'bad habits.'" Her life might have been happier had she not been. In 1958, a British journalist said, "She chatters, answers questions, smiles and smiles, all with a doll's terrifying poise. . . . One grey hair, one hint of fear, one golden tea-cup overturned on the Persian carpet and one could have loved her."

After the former first lady's death in 1993, Bonnie Angelo, who had covered her for *Time* magazine, wrote, "Somehow Pat Nixon never quite captured the fancy of the American public. The cameras that caught the angular planes of her face missed the soft contours of her heart." Angelo believed this "was because Pat Nixon stood by her man [and] her man could not shake the visceral distrust of the public and the media." In 1999, Helen Thomas remembered Pat Nixon as warm and lively and recalled how she had staged a surprise celebration of Thomas's engagement, concluding, "She was probably the most underrated first lady I've covered."

FIVE

FIRST LADIES AND FEMINISM: BETTY FORD AND ROSALYNN CARTER

To some degree, all first ladies have been viewed in the light of the political developments of their eras involving women, but this was particularly true in the cases of Betty Ford and Rosalynn Carter, the two presidents' wives who presided over the White House following the departure of the Nixons. Both women tried to use their influence to promote feminist causes, particularly passage of the equal rights amendment (ERA). Although they were unsuccessful in that regard, they drew widespread media attention that highlighted the use of their position as a platform to push specific legislation and to promote women's issues. While they had different styles, both women encountered considerable hostility from segments of the public that were not attuned to feminism and thought each first lady was overstepping her bounds.

Yet in terms of their White House performances, both have been ranked higher by scholars than their husbands. Historian Robert Watson found that President Gerald Ford was ranked thirty-second in one poll and twenty-fourth in another, whereas his wife ranked much higher—fourth and ninth—in a comparison of rankings of presidents and presidential spouses. President Jimmy Carter was ranked twenty-fifth in two polls, but his wife ranked twentieth in one poll and fifth in another. In each case, however, the husband failed in his bid to stay in the White House, a warning, perhaps, that activism by first ladies does not necessarily translate into votes at the polls and may even suggest public rejection of nontraditional presidential couples or partners. Adding to the complexity of the picture, Betty Ford apparently gained more in public esteem for her willingness to speak openly about her breast cancer than for her political stance. Nevertheless, both Betty Ford and Rosalynn Carter enhanced the significance of the position of the first lady in terms of the media by attempting to make it a more vital political symbol than it had been since the days of Eleanor Roosevelt.

BETTY FORD

When Betty Ford moved into the White House following the departure of Richard Nixon in 1972, she was an unknown quantity to most Americans. Her husband, Gerald Ford, a well-liked, conservative Republican congressman from Michigan, had become president under unprecedented circumstances on August 9, 1972, following Nixon's resignation in the face of impeachment proceedings. In his inaugural address, Ford pronounced an end to the "long national nightmare" of Watergate and promised to run an open administration, contending "truth is the glue that holds the government together." In sharp contrast to Nixon's failure to acknowledge his wife, Ford declared he was beholden to "no man and to only one woman, my dear wife, Betty." This statement marked the first time in history that a presidential inaugural speech included a reference to a first lady.

Minority leader of the House of Representatives, Ford had been selected as vice president only eight months before by President Nixon, after Spiro T. Agnew, a former governor, had resigned from the post due to allegations of corruption during his political career in Maryland. A former professional dancer and the mother of four children, Betty Ford stood with a big smile beside her husband when he was sworn in as vice president on December 6, 1973. In her autobiography, she commented, "If I had known what was coming, I think I would have sat right down and cried."

Reporters flocked to the Fords' suburban home in Alexandria, Virginia. Nancy Dickerson, then working for PBS and one of the first journalists to interview Betty Ford, found her determined to maintain "life as always." The unpretentious Ford told Dickerson that when Nixon phoned to offer the vice presidency to her husband, she had been cooking his favorite pot roast.

Although she may have appeared poised and in command of herself, Betty Ford described her initial interview experiences, even with ground rules worked out by her staff, as "terrifying." She agreed to appear on television with Barbara Walters only on the understanding that she did not want to talk about political issues, but when Walters asked for her position on abortion, Ford answered frankly. She said that she agreed with the Supreme Court's ruling in *Roe v. Wade* and "that it was time to bring abortion out of the backwoods and put it in the hospitals where it belonged." She received piles of angry mail, but her reputation for candor was established.

Betty Ford wrote in her autobiography that in the next few months, as the events leading up to Nixon's resignation were fully reported, the possibility of becoming first lady so frightened her that she "was blocking it out." After the inauguration, she created a stir when she said that she and the president were going to take their own bed to the White House and that they would not have separate bedrooms like their predecessors. Playing up interest in the private lives of presidents as a partial response to Watergate disclosures, the press pointed out that the Fords were the first presidential couple who did not have individual bedrooms since the Coolidges. This fact titillated the public, although, as Helen Thomas pointed out, in itself it revealed little about presidents' intimate lives.

Betty Ford's comment on White House sleeping arrangements led to accusations that she "was disgraceful and immoral." She later told Sheila Rabb Weidenfeld, her press secretary, that, to her great surprise, "people have written me objecting to the idea of a President of the United States sleeping with his wife." Subsequently, in an interview with journalist Myra MacPherson, Betty Ford said that she had been asked everything except how often she slept with her husband and joked in response to MacPherson's inquiry that if asked such a question, she would answer "as often as possible." Her spontaneous remarks, which seemed like those of a woman next door, offended some clergy and those of a puritanical stripe. However, journalists and the general public applauded her levity, as well as the genial, low-key manner of her husband, and they found the Ford administration a welcome antidote to the Nixon administration and its attempt to make the presidency imperial.

According to Thomas, Betty Ford "enchanted reporters from the outset with her frankness and strong stands on controversial subjects." She broke taboos, Thomas noted: "She took a drink in public, picked up a cigarette, admitted to having taken tranquilizers for years, and to being a divorcee." She also said that she had undergone psychotherapy when she became depressed while her husband was traveling around the country making political speeches and that she had to raise her children virtually alone.

What was not known at the time was the extent of Betty Ford's use of alcohol and prescription drugs. For years, she had been taking a combination of painkillers to mask the pain of a pinched nerve and arthritis as well as tranquilizers to enable her to deal with her stressful life, washing it all down, as Kati Marton put it, with alcohol. She frequently was late for appointments and canceled appearances, and she spoke haltingly on occasion; according to Ford aide Stuart Spencer, while dining out she "would get bombed," making it "tough on her husband [who] really didn't know what to do." No one, including her staff, physicians, or reporters, apparently looked closely into the situation. Her addiction was not acknowledged publicly until 1978, more than a year after she left the White House, when her condition worsened to the point that the Ford family insisted she enter a rehabilitation facility. Thereafter, she became the guiding force in establishing the Betty Ford Center to help people with alcohol and drug abuse problems.

Although her forthright manner provided a well-publicized change from the bland platitudes of traditional first ladies, it did not suit the president's advisers. One aide, with an eye on forthcoming elections, drafted a memo pointing out the need to demarcate a sharp line between the conservative president and the liberal first lady on the issue of abortion. Rivalries broke out between her staff and the president's as each group sought to promote the interests of the person it served.

Drawn in part by curiosity, about 150 reporters, both male and female, attended Betty Ford's initial press conference, held within weeks after she became first lady. Handling questions well in spite of some nervousness, she said that she did not want to commit herself on whether she would encourage her husband to run for president in his own right. She announced her own focus as first lady would be on promoting the arts and programs to help deprived and retarded children as well as passage of the equal rights amendment. But before she could begin her efforts, two events took place that shaped the Ford administration.

Without advance warning, President Ford pardoned Richard Nixon on September 8, 1974. Betty Ford, who had been consulted about the decision, backed his action as a compassionate gesture, but large segments of the press and public were outraged that the former president had not been forced to confess and/or brought to trial. The Gallup Poll showed that Ford's public approval dropped overnight from 70 percent to 50 percent, and press approval, which had been nearly unanimous, plummeted to near zero. In common with some historians, both Betty Ford and her husband have said the pardon may well have cost Ford his bid to be elected president in the 1976 election.

Less than three weeks later, on September 28, Betty Ford was operated on for breast cancer, and her right breast was removed. In the past, little or no public announcement had been made of first ladies' medical conditions. The Ford White House broke that precedent, releasing complete details of her mastectomy. The operation had been performed only a day after she had carried on with her regular schedule, including a tea for Lady Bird Johnson and her daughters in connection with the dedication of a memorial grove on the Potomac River to Lyndon Johnson.

As a result of Betty Ford's disclosure, the disease of breast cancer, which once had been only whispered about, received widespread media attention that encouraged other women to go to their doctors for examinations. Checkups increased by 300 to 400 percent. Among those seeking mammograms was Happy Rockefeller, the wife of Vice President Nelson Rockefeller, who subsequently lost both breasts to cancer. In a 1994 interview, Betty Ford said her willingness to publicize her cancer, which was detected on a routine examination suggested by Nancy Howe, her personal assistant, had more impact than anything else she had done as first lady.

During her recuperation period, she received more than fifty thousand cards, letters, and messages as well as thousands of dollars, which she donated to the American Cancer Society. As a result of a cruel disease, Betty Ford became a beacon of courage to other women and illustrated the potential of the first lady to serve as a role model. The *New York Times Magazine* declared that if she "achieved nothing else during her husband's administration, the light her trouble has shed on a dark subject would be contribution enough."

Betty Ford's background, which included admiration for Eleanor Roosevelt and a love of performing for an audience, prepared her to be the most outspoken first lady since

Roosevelt's time. Even as a child in Grand Rapids, Michigan, she had admired Roosevelt. She explained, "I really liked the idea that a woman was finally speaking out and expressing herself rather than just expressing the views of her husband." As a loyal political wife, Betty Ford had had little opportunity to speak out until she unexpectedly found herself first lady. She called the position "an opportunity that came at the right time for me . . . it gave me a career that filled in that gap with children having reached the age of independence." At the time the Fords moved into the White House, their three sons were working or attending college, and their youngest child, Susan, was in her last year of high school.

In her youth, Betty Ford had not been shy of the spotlight. In high school, she dreamed of becoming a dancer and put on shows for hospitalized children. She studied dancing for two summers at Bennington College in Vermont, where she met Martha Graham, the leading exponent of modern dance. Not selected for Graham's main troupe, she still made it to Carnegie Hall, performing in Graham's auxiliary group, and she was a fashion model in New York before returning home and teaching modern dance in Grand Rapids. She also worked as a fashion coordinator at a leading department store. A four-year marriage to an insurance salesman ended in divorce when she was twenty-nine years old.

In 1948, she and Gerald R. Ford, a Grand Rapids lawyer, were married in the middle of his first election campaign for Congress, and she soon learned that being married to an ambitious politician meant being without a husband much of the time. Living in a Washington suburb, she did what was expected of a political wife of her era. She cared for her children, took her husband's constituents sightseeing and helped in his office, taught Sunday school in an Episcopal church, served as a den mother for Cub Scouts, and became active in the Congressional Club, an organization of wives of public officials. In 1964, a pinched nerve in her neck led to permanent pain, exacerbated by arthritis, and resulted in her use of prescription painkillers. Although the Fords had a happy marriage, her physical misery was compounded by emotional stress heightened by her husband's frequent absences to speak on behalf of fellow Republicans. When she came close to a nervous breakdown, Gerald Ford backed her in seeking psychiatric help—a bold step for the wife of a political figure in the 1960s.

Faced with the likelihood that he would never attain his dream of becoming Speaker of the House, since Democrats seemed solidly in control, Ford promised his wife that he would step down from his position in Congress after the election of 1976, and the couple was looking forward to retirement when he was chosen to be vice president. When fate propelled her into the White House, however, Betty Ford, who had become a staunch supporter of the equal rights amendment, believed that she had an obligation to become visible and active. As Carl Anthony put it, "By 1974 the role of women in American society was shifting, and she perfectly mirrored it." In common with other women of the period influenced by the women's liberation movement, she had worked before marriage, devoted years to raising a family, and now sought to be considered a person in her own right rather than an appendage to her husband.

By the time the Fords entered the White House, the demands on the first lady had become so complex that a support staff of about twenty-eight people had been assembled in the East Wing. Although Betty Ford kept many of the same staff members, she replaced Helen Smith, Pat Nixon's press secretary, with Sheila Weidenfeld, signifying that she sought to make her press operation different from that of her predecessor. Weidenfeld, a television producer and the first broadcaster to serve as a first lady's press secretary, had some familiarity with the White House, since her father had been the secretary of Dwight Eisenhower's cabinet.

Betty Ford decided on the change after Smith had let reporters cluster around her when she nervously flew to Chicago to make her first major speech at a fund-raiser. Smith had promised to keep reporters away until the event was over, but when they appeared, Ford recalled, "I had to talk to them or seem surly." She had no particular directions for Weidenfeld: "When I asked 'what do you want me to do?'" Weidenfeld said, "she laughed and said, 'Well, hold on, I don't know what I'm supposed to do.'"

As she took hold of the job, Weidenfeld decided that it was important to make the first lady feel comfortable with the media because "I always with all my talk shows wanted people to come across well because that's what television is all about." She knew the first lady "couldn't do all those [requested television] interviews." Consequently, she looked for a venue that would be a good fit for Betty Ford's personal style, recognizing that "she's not the type to face the nation. She is the type to chat with it." When Weidenfeld agreed to let her be interviewed by the genial Morley Safer on the CBS show *Sixty Minutes,* she never expected the program, which aired on August 10, 1975, to create the storm of controversy that ensued.

Weidenfeld explained, "Nobody in the White House

except me wanted the first lady to do that program. She didn't want to do it herself. . . . 'Sixty Minutes,' in my opinion, is the only program of its type that shows people as they are. I felt the public should see Mrs. Ford as she is, that she was ready for it, and that's why I pressed her to do the show." The problem, as it turned out, was that a sizable segment of the public was not ready for a first lady to frankly address changing patterns of conduct.

In the interview, Betty Ford repeated her prochoice stand. She also said, as she had before, that she wouldn't be surprised if her children had tried marijuana, adding, "It's the type of thing that the young people have to experience, like your first beer or your first cigarette." Asked if she thought it was immoral for young people to live together without marriage, Betty Ford responded that young people were doing so and that it might even limit the divorce rate.

But Safer's bombshell question was this: "What if Susan Ford came to you and said, 'Mother, I'm having an affair'?" Ford answered, "Well, I wouldn't be surprised. I think she's a perfectly normal human being like all young girls, if she wanted to continue and I would certainly counsel and advise her on the subject, and I'd want to know pretty much about the young man that she was planning to have the affair with; whether it was a worthwhile encounter or whether it was going to be one of those. . . . She's pretty young to start affairs."

Safer then said, "But nevertheless, old enough," and Ford agreed, "Oh, yes, she's a big girl." Newspaper headlines the next day picked up the sensational aspects of the interview. "SUSAN'S A BIG GIRL, AFFAIR WON'T JOLT MRS. FORD," blared the *Los Angeles Times.* The newspapers missed the point that Betty Ford was calling for open communication even if children's values differed from their parents' own. A public outcry followed. Thousands of letters attacking the first lady as an immoral disgrace were sent to the White House. Betty Ford was terrified that she had become a "real political liability to Jerry."

The Ford administration tried to make light of the situation. President Ford, in a jocular manner, told the press that when he heard what his wife had said, he figured he had just lost ten million votes, but when he read the newspapers, he raised his guess to twenty million. His press secretary, Ron Nesson, with whom Weidenfeld said she had to battle to get the same treatment given male members of the president's press staff, issued a statement that the president had "long ceased to be perturbed by his wife's remarks." According to Nancy Dickerson, Ford's staff honestly thought that Betty Ford was an albatross. Ford himself wrote later, "I was under no illusion as to what the reaction to her remarks would be [but] I had admired her candor from the moment we met and had always encouraged her to speak her mind."

Seeking to control the political damage, the White House sent a letter of explanation from Betty Ford to those who wrote inquiring about her remarks. Given by a recipient to the Associated Press, which published it, the letter spoke of the need for better communication with young people and assured correspondents that the Fords were faithful marriage partners. In the letter, Betty Ford stated, "I do not believe in premarital relations, but I realize that many in today's generation do not share my views."

By October 15, the White House mail was less one-sided in opposition. A total of 10,463 letters had been tallied in favor of Ford's comments, compared to 23,232 against. As

time passed, more favorable opinion appeared in the press. A
Harris Poll three months after the episode showed 60 percent
of the respondents accepted her answer to the question about
her daughter and only 27 percent disapproved, leaving the
pollsters to conclude that Betty Ford was a "solid asset" to her
husband.

In November 1975, the *Ladies' Home Journal* asked
seven well-known mothers of teenage children and two
hundred readers in eight cities across the country to give
their views regarding Betty Ford's comment on the possibility of her daughter having an affair. The magazine found that
less than a third (30 percent) "expressed disapproval of Mrs.
Ford's answer." Fifty-three percent approved, and the remaining 17 percent were neutral. Of the seven celebrity mothers,
only one was critical. Phyllis Schlafly, leading opponent of
the equal rights amendment, said, "It is no justification for
Mrs. Ford to say her daughter is a 'big girl' and 'a normal
human being.' To approve sin because other people are doing
it was the moral sickness of Watergate."

Schlafly tangled repeatedly with the first lady over her
enthusiasm for feminist causes. Betty Ford had encouraged
her husband to designate 1975 as International Women's Year
as a way of pushing for the ERA, which was, at the time, five
states short of ratification to become part of the Constitution. She sent letters and called state legislators urging them
to support the hotly debated amendment. She also urged her
husband to appoint women to high offices and gloried in the
appointment of Carla Hills to the cabinet as secretary of
housing and urban development and Anne Armstrong as ambassador to England. To make her case to her husband, Betty
Ford said she resorted to "pillow talk." In a *McCall's* interview

written by Myra MacPherson, which ran just after the Safer contretemps, she said, "If he doesn't get it in the office during the day, he gets it in the ribs at night."

Her ERA stand, publicized by frequent photographs of the first lady wearing a large "Ratify ERA in 1975" button, enraged some opponents. They accused her of abusing her position and using taxpayers' dollars for long-distance pro-ERA calls. When pickets gathered outside the White House proclaiming "BETTY FORD IS TRYING TO PRESS A SECOND-RATE MANHOOD ON AMERICN WOMEN," she became, according to Carl Anthony, the first president's wife to be picketed for her own political stance.

Less openly, she also became linked to another "first," one with tragic overtones: the first East Wing scandal to rock Washington. Maxine Cheshire, an investigative reporter for the *Washington Post,* discovered in the spring of 1975 that Nancy Howe, Betty Ford's assistant who was often referred to as her best friend, and husband Ed Howe had accepted a free vacation from a controversial Korean lobbyist. As a federal employee, Howe apparently had violated conflict-of-interest laws. Informed that the *Post* planned to print the story, Ed Howe died of what police called "a self-inflicted gunshot wound." Nancy Howe soon left the White House. Betty Ford was accused in print of firing her, but she denied doing so in her autobiography, saying, "When I was told she had to leave, I cried."

In addition to breaking precedents, Betty Ford took part in traditional first lady activities. She publicized the Hospital for Sick Children, a little-known Washington nursing home for chronically ill and abused children. She accompanied the president on a trip to China and, as captured in a memorable photograph, danced with students, stealing "the diplomatic show from her husband on his otherwise forgettable Chinese journey," the *New York Daily News* reported. To back her husband's campaign against inflation, she cut down on White House expenses and bought relatively inexpensive clothes from American designers. She also brought a more casual note to White House entertaining after the rigid formality of the Nixon years, promoting American arts and crafts and borrowing American artifacts from museums to use as centerpieces.

In short, Betty Ford scored as an outstanding first lady in the eyes of the media. *Time* magazine made her one of its twelve "Women of the Year" in 1976. Her husband, however, was not named "Man of the Year." Beset by fallout from the Nixon pardon, inflation, the fall of Saigon in the Vietnam War, a lackluster record, and a perception of being accident prone after stumbling in public, Gerald Ford found his political star had dimmed. Ronald Reagan emerged as a strong challenger for the 1976 Republican nomination. Ford ended up as the candidate, although, in Troy's view, he was less suited than his wife to the growing emphasis on both personality-based politics and personality-based journalism. Troy saw this trend illustrated by the spectacular success of *People* magazine, "a weekly founded in 1974 to focus on 'individuals rather than issues,' which was already selling more than a million copies an issue."

Campaign buttons urged voters to "ELECT BETTY'S HUSBAND" and "KEEP BETTY IN THE WHITE HOUSE." The first lady herself campaigned vigorously, avoiding more controversial remarks. She won praise for her dignity at a Jewish National Fund dinner in June 1976 when the organization's head succumbed to a heart attack while introducing her. She took control of the chaotic situation and led the three thousand diners in prayer while efforts were made to revive the stricken rabbi. She later wrote, "An inner strength takes over, and you don't know where it come from, and you can't take credit for it . . . no matter how scared I am, I seem to be able to carry on."

Gerald Ford lost the November election by a close margin to Democrat Jimmy Carter, who promised to bring a fresh perspective to Washington. When he was unable to give his concession speech because his voice had given out, Betty Ford read it for him. It was a remarkable end to a remarkable period in which a woman with a drinking and drug addiction problem had influenced the course of U.S. politics by merging the personal and the political. Was she actually a help or a hindrance to her husband—an asset or a liability? Perhaps there is no right answer. Liberals who liked Betty Ford were unlikely to vote for her conservative husband, while conservatives who disliked her might also have not wanted to vote for the opposing candidate. An example of a polarizing figure who came across as simply herself in the news media, Betty Ford stood out as the most significant feminist first lady between Eleanor Roosevelt and Hillary Rodham Clinton. As she fought against her own personal demons, she pushed back the boundaries surrounding the position of first lady.

ROSALYNN CARTER

Feminist causes also struck a strong chord with Rosalynn Carter, Betty Ford's successor. The determined wife and business partner of President Jimmy Carter, the little-known

former Georgia governor who won the presidency in a surprisingly successful campaign, Rosalynn Carter considered
herself a working woman. She pressed for passage of the
equal rights amendment and appeared at the Houston Conference for International Women's Year in 1977 with two of
her predecessors, Lady Bird Johnson and Betty Ford, to
show her support for it. When the ERA failed to be ratified
during the Carter administration, she expressed great
disappointment.

As first lady, Rosalynn Carter gave women's rights high
priority. She successfully urged her husband to appoint
women to high positions, and a record number of three
served in the Carter cabinet. She also pushed for better mental health programs, help for the aged and the retarded, and
childhood immunizations, and, like Pat Nixon, she promoted
volunteerism, among other concerns.

Of greater significance to the media than her causes,
however, was her relationship to her husband as a confidential adviser and political partner. The Carters made little secret of the fact that she knew about and did not hesitate to
approve or disapprove almost all the actions of the president,
although he did not always follow her advice. He sent her to
Central and South America shortly after his inauguration in
1977 to present the administration's approaches to foreign
policy. She played a role in setting up the Camp David talks
on bringing peace to the Middle East in 1978, taking detailed
notes on the conference. She advised her husband prior to his
major "crisis of confidence" speech in 1979, which addressed
national worry over inflation and energy and led to a cabinet
shakeup. That year, she also made a humanitarian trip to Thailand that resulted in more international aid for Cambodian

refugees seeking to escape slaughter by a hostile government in their own country.

Summarizing her activities during the first fourteen months that Jimmy Carter was in office, the *Washington Star* gave the following countdown: visited 18 nations and 27 American cities; held 259 private and 50 public meetings; made 15 major speeches; held 22 press conferences; gave 32 interviews; attended 83 official receptions; and held 25 meetings with special groups in the White House. Clearly, few other presidents' wives had maintained so hectic a pace in an endeavor to counsel their husbands, carry out traditional responsibilities, and accomplish their own personal goals as first ladies. When a reporter exclaimed that Rosalynn Carter was "trying to take on all the problems we have," her press secretary, Mary Finch Hoyt, retorted, "And what's wrong with that?"

Perhaps the answer to that question was that her efforts did not necessarily translate into positive news coverage of the Carters. Journalists did not always view the activities of Rosalynn Carter favorably in an increasingly complex media world in which news of first ladies, like that of other prominent wives, no longer had an assigned place in the genteel columns of women's and society sections. As these sections were being phased out, news of women in the public eye now appeared on the front pages of newspapers or in new feature sections often devoted to opinionated pieces on celebrities and lifestyles. Conflict, controversy, criticism, gossip, use of unnamed sources—all the news elements employed for stories about political intrigue now were being applied to first ladies, too.

Reporters questioned Rosalynn Carter's disciplined

style, her interest in policymaking, and her right to play a substantive role in the Carter administration, although she was neither an elected nor an appointed official. She had been dubbed "the steel magnolia" during the 1976 campaign by reporters who intimated she concealed ambition behind a facade of southern femininity. Subsequently, she declared in her autobiography, the issue of her image became an "annoyance that just wouldn't go away."

She said, "The 'steel magnolia' is in print forever. And by the end of our first year in Washington I found myself described as being 'fuzzy'—which is better than having a bad image, but not as good as a good one." According to Hoyt, the "fuzzy" tag came from Sally Quinn, a writer for the *Washington Post* who initially dismissed Rosalynn Carter's divergent interests and wondered, "Why doesn't she do one thing like Lady Bird Johnson and the environment?" "Fuzzy" soon was cast aside, Rosalynn Carter recalled, because "by virtue of a piece of gossip here or there I had gone from having a 'fuzzy' image to being 'most powerful.'" Wielding power was perceived as suspect for a first lady in the late 1970s because it appeared to undermine her husband's leadership. Hoyt said Rosalynn Carter then faced a situation in which "now I'm supposed to be so powerful I'm being muzzled by the President's men and I'm not doing anything differently!"

Rosalynn Carter's difficulties with the press stemmed, in part, from the Carters' lack of acquaintance with the Washington journalistic scene. In his campaign, Jimmy Carter, described as a "born-again Christian," ran as an outsider who had pledged to restore honesty and moral values to a capital mired in questionable post-Watergate politics and government extravagance. Determined to show himself as a man of the people, Carter, a Baptist Sunday school teacher, carried his own suitcase and wore cardigan sweaters to highlight heat conservation. Betty Beale, the *Washington Star* society columnist, noted that Carter set out to oppose "a Washington which he did not know, which did not know him, and which I am not sure he really ever understood." It was a Washington that could be unkind to those who violated its political and social mores, as Jimmy and Rosalynn Carter soon learned.

The Carters first showed their determination to alter the Washington scene by making changes in the interest of economy and informality. Rosalynn Carter wore the same dress for the presidential inaugural ball that she had worn for the inaugural ball in Georgia after her husband had been sworn in as governor. The president ordered staff cutbacks and pay reductions at the White House. He directed that thermostats be turned down to save energy as well as lower heating bills. He sold the presidential yacht and eliminated a portion of the fleet of presidential limousines. The Carters stopped holding annual events for ambassadors from other countries, which led to a decline in diplomatic entertaining. They cut down on glitter by initially eliminating dancing as well as hard liquor at White House dinners, substituted English for French menus, and replaced celebrity guests with average Americans.

Social reporters complained that the fun was gone from White House functions. Rather than being seen as decent, hardworking, and God-fearing people, the Carters were considered by some Washingtonians as narrow and penny-pinching, Hoyt noted, "so tasteless" and "so raw." The harshest criticism came when the Carters allowed their nine-year-old daughter, Amy, to attend a state dinner, sit with the guests of honor, and read a book during most of the meal. Beale said, "Washington was shocked." Such unortho-dox behavior did little to get the Carters off to a good start with representatives of the sophisticated Washington press corps.

When the Carters chose not to participate in the pri-vate parties that then marked the pinnacle of Washington social life, they offended important hostesses with ties to the media. Jody Powell, Carter's press secretary, told an inter-viewer after Carter lost the election of 1980 that he himself had made a major mistake in not facilitating contact between the first couple and the "leading female adherents of the Georgetown power elite." Nancy Dickerson agreed: "The Carters never bothered to embrace the mainstays of the Washington establishment. . . . They scorned Washington so-ciety. They alienated the press. They created a great deal of resentment." The most significant Georgetown hostess, however, Katharine Graham of the *Washington Post,* bore no grudges. Her newspaper endorsed Carter, not his opponent, Republican Ronald Reagan, although Reagan's wife, Nancy, made Graham her unofficial media adviser.

The Carters, owners of a family peanut business in the hamlet of Plains, Georgia, did not appear comfortable with the White House press corps. Helen Thomas, who covered the Carters on trips back home as well as in Washington, said that in Plains, the Carters were "genial hosts, though we al-ways had the feeling they did not suffer us gladly." When the Carters decided to send their daughter to the public school near the White House, Thomas recalled, Amy looked at the reporters lined up to watch her leave for the first day of class and asked, "Mom, do we still have to be nice to them?" Eager for Amy to be at home in the White House, the Carters allowed her to roller-skate in the East Room. Thomas said the Carters were very hurt after Jimmy Carter's defeat when a *Time* magazine columnist commented, "Now at last we're going to have some class in the White House."

Veteran Washington reporter Sarah McClendon complained that Rosalynn Carter "depended a great deal upon her public relations advisors." McClendon said, "The first time I saw her she was hesitant to talk to the press. She was always trying to keep her remarks off the record. . . . She turned to her public relations person to ask her if she could speak." McClendon insisted that she wanted to know what the first lady, not her adviser, thought but added, "I didn't have success with that approach because Mrs. Carter remained very, very cautious."

The new first lady displayed what one biographer called a "controlled manner, which allowed for few gaffes and fewer intimate revelations" than the style of her predecessor. Unhappily for Rosalynn Carter, that manner made her seem less open to the press than the popular Betty Ford. It was Jimmy Carter, not his wife, who made one of the most celebrated personal disclosures in U.S. politics. In an effort to appeal to voters who presumably decried his religiosity, Carter gave a preelection interview to *Playboy* magazine in which he confessed that he "had committed adultery in my heart many times."

The resulting furor, which quadrupled the usual circulation for *Playboy,* according to Gil Troy, outdid "Mrs. Ford's '60 Minutes' flap" and made Carter, with his conservative country background, into "a liberal political husband with an astonishingly political wife." Certainly, Rosalynn Carter, when asked by a television reporter if she had ever committed adultery, gave a politic reply. She answered the reporter firmly, "If I had, I wouldn't tell you!" Referring to the *Playboy* interview, she simply said, "Jimmy talks too much, but at least people know he's honest and doesn't mind answering questions."

After Carter won the 1976 election, journalists pressed to know Rosalynn Carter's views on administration policy because it was widely reported that she was one of her husband's most trusted advisers, if not his chief one. Zbigniew Brzezinski, Carter's genial national security chief, confided to Beale that "Rosalynn is the President's No. 1 adviser." Beale said Rosalynn herself acknowledged her importance when she told one thousand Democratic women, "Jimmy and I need your help." Her predecessors had not equated themselves with their husbands in such a fashion, saying instead, "The President needs your help."

In her autobiography, Rosalynn Carter said criticism of her influence "began to mount, when in the second year of Jimmy's presidency, I started attending Cabinet meetings." She thus was the first president's wife in history to sit in on the meetings. She said she did not participate but used them as a source of information for discussions with her husband.

"I never considered not attending them because of the criticism," she said; "I had already learned from more than a decade of political life that I was going to be criticized no matter what I did, so I might as well be criticized for something I wanted to do." In addition, Rosalynn Carter scheduled a weekly working lunch with her husband, arming herself with papers so she could refer to various subjects. After figuring prominently in Carter's campaign, she said she continued to present issues for his consideration, often acting as a "sounding board for him."

In Washington, the Carters were viewed as loners without large networks of personal friends, making them dependent on each other for close companionship. Having both grown up in Plains, their lives had been linked for years through the bonds of background, marriage, family, church affiliation, and business and political interests. By the time Carter became president, there was no doubt about their intense relationship, which sparked media debate over the extent of her influence. To Rosalynn Carter, there was nothing mysterious or unusual about it: "In the White House my relationship with Jimmy was the same as it always had been. We discussed business and strategy when we were working together in the warehouse, or campaigning, and when he was serving as governor, the way most husbands and wives do when they take an interest in each other's work."

Some Washington journalists found this relationship difficult to understand. Rosalynn Carter, unlike her four immediate predecessors—Betty Ford, Pat Nixon, Lady Bird Johnson, and Jackie Kennedy—was a complete stranger to the capital. Betty Caroli speculated, "Had she trained at the center of national politics, she might have formed a loyal support system among reporters and other old timers." Without one, she still made a positive impact as first lady, but her media relations were rocky.

An experienced journalist and press secretary who had worked for Eleanor McGovern when her husband, George McGovern, ran for president against Richard Nixon in 1972, Mary Hoyt blamed some reporters for an inability to rise above "insider" biases when covering the Carter White House. To her, "Mrs. Carter was unfairly criticized because she came in as a Washington outsider." If so, the situation demonstrated the failure of an elite group to recognize the motivation and orientation of a woman whose life had the makings of a Cinderella tale.

The daughter of a seamstress and an auto mechanic who died when she was thirteen years old, Rosalynn Carter, the oldest of four children, worked in a beauty shop to earn money as a teenager. After two years at Georgia Southwestern College, she was married, at the age of eighteen, to Jimmy Carter—the son of the most prominent family in Plains, the brother of her best friend, Ruth Carter, and her first and only sweetheart. Their wedding followed his graduation from the U.S. Naval Academy in 1946 and commission as a naval officer. Happy to be away from the inbred world of Plains, Rosalynn Carter enjoyed her independence as a peripatetic navy wife, giving birth to three sons in five years and taking care of her children while Carter was at sea.

Over her vigorous objections, Jimmy Carter, who believed the husband should be the head of the family, insisted on leaving the navy and going back home in 1953 when his father died to take over the family peanut warehouse. One concern was her relationship with her husband's formidable mother, the tart-tongued "Miss Lillian," with whom the Carters first lived after returning to Plains. Rosalynn Carter's attitude toward residing in Plains improved dramatically when she discovered an outlet for her abilities beyond housekeeping. She became a full-fledged partner in the peanut business, mastering management skills, keeping the books, and running the operation while her husband served in the

Georgia legislature. After giving birth to Amy in 1967, she overcame her fear of public speaking and campaigned on her own for Carter when he ran for governor successfully in 1970.

In the governor's mansion, she gained confidence in her social and administrative abilities, finding the move from Plains to the state capital at Atlanta an even greater transition than the move to the White House later. When Carter won the Democratic nomination for president and scored a narrow victory over Gerald Ford in 1976, she found it hard to believe she was the wife of the president of the United States. After walking hand in hand with her husband along Pennsylvania Avenue from the Capitol to the White House on Inauguration Day to symbolize that the Carters wanted to "be close to the people," the new first lady reminded herself, "We are first and foremost Rosalynn and Jimmy Carter from Plains, Georgia."

Although the Carters chose to remain a husband-and-wife team working together in a joint enterprise, as was common in the South, making the presidency a mom-and-pop operation did not sit well with segments of the press corps. Rosalynn Carter's journalistic treatment on the national stage raised numerous questions about women, power, and presidential marriages. Journalists were divided over the propriety of the personal closeness of the president and his wife in terms of its effect on governmental policy. When Carter was elected, was she elected, too? If so, to do what? Did her involvement in government make him look inadequate? Did she have the right to speak for her husband?

Arguments regarding the role of the first lady raged on. In the *Washington Post,* Abigail McCarthy presented the issue as one of attitude toward political wives. McCarthy said she herself fell back on the old analogy of the "'mom and pop' store, the family farm," only to be put down by another woman journalist who said "the difference is that the store and the farm belonged to the family; the White House doesn't." Yet McCarthy concluded that she was not sure this was true: "In a way the American voter does elect the family."

In her actions, Rosalynn Carter took this position when she went on her precedent-breaking trip to Central and South America. She prepared carefully by taking lessons in Spanish, which she had been studying for years, and participating in official briefings. In each of the seven countries she visited, she made a concentrated effort to find out special concerns leaders had about U.S. policy. "I was determined to be taken seriously," she said, even though she encountered "a little discomfort in the State Department and on [Capitol] Hill."

Some members of Congress opposed the trip, leading her to respond that their objections were based on sexist ideas "because I was a woman going into very male territory." The heads of the countries she visited reportedly were confused about the purpose of her trip. A Brazilian newspaper editorialized, "No matter how well informed she may be, Mrs. Carter will lack the indispensable experience to negotiate with GOB [government of Brazil] authorities who have a tradition of negotiators [sic] which dates back to imperial times."

Newsweek pointed out that the "mission, in contrast to the usual goodwill-mongering assigned to the wives of presidents, was billed at [President] Carter's own request as substantive—scouting the hemisphere's heads of state for him and interpreting his sometimes gauzy policies to them."

Although, the newsmagazine continued, there were "sniffish remarks" that foreign policy was not properly a first lady's line of work, "this iron-willed first lady put the complaints briskly behind her . . . , remarking undeniably that she is 'the person closest to the President of the United States.'" Still, questions persisted about her right to speak as the president's surrogate, with women journalists among her sharpest critics. Meg Greenfield contended in a *Newsweek* column titled "Mrs. President" that Rosalynn Carter should not engage in diplomacy unless some way was found to hold her accountable for her actions. The *New York Times* said the question should be "not just who she is, but how well-equipped to handle a Presidential errand."

On her return, she reported to the Senate Foreign Relations Committee what she had seen and heard. Betty Beale said no one ever questioned the first lady's mental capabilities: "From the first she came across as a no-nonsense woman." There were those who thought she would have been more successful had she been less serious. "She wanted to be covered the way any member of her husband's administration would be covered," *Washington Post* reporter Donnie Radcliffe told Kati Marton. "She didn't want to be identified with tea parties and fashion stories . . . Rosalynn's lack of a light touch as much as anything may have been one of her weaknesses. She didn't have much humor. If she could have loosened up a bit and shown us her playful side."

Her homecoming was featured positively on CBS's *Evening News,* with a correspondent saying on June 12, 1977: "What started as a rather doubtful mission has apparently ended successfully." The next night, the program showed her husband telling reporters "she has succeeded almost to per-

fection." Lee Thornton, the CBS correspondent who covered Rosalynn Carter, had no patience with those who contended the first lady deserved sympathetic treatment because
she was subject to many pressures. Thornton told a journalist that the first lady was a "tough cookie" who "wanted the
job, ran for office," and "knew what it was all about," adding
that "the women who get into the White House actually
want it ... more than almost anything."

Rosalynn Carter took no more diplomatic trips of the
South American type, on which she said she had been sent
because the president was too busy to go. She contended later
this was because her husband was "able to go himself." Her
subsequent trip to Thailand was in keeping with the efforts
of previous first ladies to ameliorate distress caused by wars.
She focused media attention on the grave situation facing
Cambodian refugees as she discussed their plight on NBC's
Today show and assisted in the organization of relief efforts.

In addition to serving as her husband's adviser, Rosalynn Carter had her own projects. Within a month following the inauguration, she held a press conference to announce
the formation of the President's Commission on Mental
Health. She had developed a strong interest in mental health
issues while her husband had been governor of Georgia,
where she had been a member of a commission that over-
hauled the state's entire mental health system. Although she
could not serve as the actual chair of the national commission
because of legal problems, she accepted an honorary title and
spoke on the subject repeatedly in the United States as well
as in Canada and in Europe.

The first lady described herself as "crushed" when the
Washington Post did not cover the story of the commission's

formation, although the *New York Times* had a "good, substantive article." Instead of writing about the mental health commission, the *Post* focused on the Carters' decision to ban hard liquor at state dinners. The first lady said the decision was based on economy—she had been told "we might save one million dollars by serving only wine and ending our state dinners before midnight so we wouldn't have to pay overtime to the staff."

The press treated the story differently, comparing Rosalynn Carter to nineteenth-century first ladies who had instituted "dry" polices—"Sahara Sarah" Polk and "Lemonade Lucy" Hayes. She indignantly retorted, "They make me sound like a real prude. I'm not a prude." In her autobiography, she said the "wine story created a major flap, much to our chagrin." She complained that journalists did not see the mental health commission as news: "I was told by the press it was not a 'sexy' issue—but 'no booze in the White House' obviously was." She stated she could understand that it is "much more entertaining for people to read about the glamour and excitement of beautiful clothes and celebrities and personal problems and 'no booze' than it is to read about the number of people in the country who need help with mental health problems, but it didn't seem right."

Rosalynn Carter devoted much effort to her mental health campaign, overseeing the issuing of a report in 1978 containing 117 recommendations that she personally presented to the public by appearing on two television news broadcasts, ABC's *Good Morning America* and PBS's *MacNeil/Lehrer Report*. She was distressed when Joseph Califano, the secretary of health and human services, appeared to be dragging his feet on implementing recommendations that were eventually included in a bill submitted to Congress in May 1979, called the Mental Health Systems Act.

A month earlier, she had testified personally before a subcommittee of the Senate Human Resources Committee in support of the recommendations, making her the first president's wife since Eleanor Roosevelt to testify before Congress. The bill was passed and funded by Congress, signed into law as the Mental Health Systems Act by President Carter in October 1980, but his administration was almost finished at this point. His successor, Ronald Reagan, cut most of the funding needed to implement the act, although expansion of the National Institute of Mental Health was carried out.

As first lady, Rosalynn Carter became the first president's wife to maintain her own working space in the East Wing of the White House, now officially called the Office of the First Lady, rather than in the family quarters. She reorganized and upgraded the functions and pay for her staff, which numbered about eighteen persons, but the effort generated some unfavorable publicity. Mary Hoyt said in her memoir that when it was reported her salary was $47,500 annually, considerably more than that of past press secretaries, the public complained "that we're being paid at all." Hoyt said she realized that "the public and the press had little understanding of the pressures of scope and dimension of the first lady's job."

A firestorm arose in 1979 when Edith J. Dobelle, former chief of protocol at the State Department, was selected for the new position of chief of staff for the first lady and paid $56,000, the same amount as the president's top aides. President Carter himself defended the appointment, designed to make the East Wing operation more efficient and better coordinated with what went on in the West Wing, saying the first lady needed "someone competent" to supervise her offices. Feminists might have been expected to view the equalization of East Wing and West Wing salaries as a step forward for women, but the press did not picture it this way. Some reporters seized the opportunity to write stories about Rosalynn Carter's total staff costs of $650,000 annually, with headlines such as "THE IMPERIAL FIRST LADY AND HER COSTLY COURT." A *Newsweek* cover story in November 1979 referred to Rosalynn as "The President's Partner," applauded her political sense as being greater than her husband's, and said "the real fear of Rosalynn's power may lie simply in the fact that she is an ambitious woman."

When Carter ran for reelection in 1980, Rosalynn Carter hit the campaign trial, leaving her husband in Washington to deal with the Iranian hostage crisis caused by militants who broke into the U.S. embassy in Tehran on November 4, 1979. Some fifty to sixty Americans were taken hostage in protest against Washington's decision to allow the deposed shah of Iran to receive medical treatment in the United States. The inability of the Carter administration to secure the release of the hostages (who remained in custody until Carter's term ended), coupled with an energy shortage that produced long lines for gasoline and the Soviet invasion of Afghanistan, sealed Carter's defeat by Ronald Reagan.

Rosalynn Carter did everything she could to keep this from happening. In the *Washington Post,* Sally Quinn described her as a "nurse" fighting valiantly against the odds to reach the public on behalf of her husband, "the patient." Comparing the first lady to a nurse "who has come to the waiting room to reassure the concerned relatives," Quinn wrote that "people seem to like her," but "they just don't know about her husband." When Carter lost the election, Rosalynn Carter said she was "bitter enough for both of us." She returned with her husband to Plains, where she spent the next three years writing her autobiography, which became a best seller. As first lady, she had made a commendable showing, with her approval rating of 59 percent in the fall of 1979 more than doubling her husband's—but not equal to the August 1976 approval rating of Betty Ford, at 71 percent. Rosalynn Carter was respected but perhaps a bit feared and not particularly beloved.

═══════════◇═══════════

SIX

FIRST LADIES AND IMAGE-MAKING: NANCY REAGAN AND BARBARA BUSH

The last decades of the twentieth century brought more emphasis on the packaging of presidents and their wives, as well as other family members, to make them acceptable to the country at large. The increased use of political consultants, "spin doctors," communication strategists, and public relations experts, combined with more competitive pressures in the news media, produced a climate geared to the favorable presentation of political figures to the public. What was said and how it came across in the media seemed more important than what was actually done, as sophisticated political communicators sought to make clients appear to their best advantage in the eyes of voters. With image blending into reality, the line between news and entertainment eroded further, creating a celebrity-driven culture in which the public avidly sought details on the personal lives of presidents and their spouses as a way of getting to know the "real persons." Journalists who once had reported on changes in political agendas now reported on changes in political images.

Concern with image-making reached new heights in

the administration of Republican Ronald Reagan, whose background as a Hollywood actor made him exceptionally attuned to politics that depended on effective communication. Reagan and his wife, Nancy, a former actress, understood the importance of personal appearances. As professional role-players, they knew how to present themselves to the public and how to play their parts to gain popularity with their audience. This was particularly true in the case of Nancy Reagan, who said she had no agenda other than to support her husband. The Reagans' successors, George and Barbara Bush, although they had a different style, built on the legacy created by a couple that turned a Hollywood romance into a successful political partnership that drew on media skills.

NANCY REAGAN

Americans both booed and applauded Nancy Reagan as first lady. Her standing bounced around in the polls, but one element dominated: she acted out a love story with Ronald Reagan and played a tremendously important role in the life of one of the pivotal political figures of the twentieth century. She got bad reviews at the start of his two terms as president and rave ones later, but she ended her tenure in the White House with continuing questions over her performance. Subsequently, her care for Ronald Reagan while he suffered from Alzheimer's disease and her dignity during his televised funeral in 2004 dimmed the criticism that once came her way. Still, Nancy Reagan's performance as first lady remains susceptible to varying interpretations.

In a memoir of his experiences with her, Michael K. Deaver, a public relations executive who served as assistant to the president and deputy chief of staff in the Reagan administration, "mused on the journey she . . . made—from a single mother's daughter to Hollywood, the White House and the unwinnable battle against Alzheimer's" and concluded that "Nancy's life has the arc of great drama.""Or maybe," he continued,"I should say 'lives' because there have always been two Nancy Reagans: the one the public thought it knew and the private one that was revealed to just a few of us." He expressed certainty that "Ronald Reagan would not have risen to such distinction without Nancy at his side."

Journalists covering the Reagans presented their personal drama in various ways—often cynically, sometimes affectionately, and even occasionally in terms of Nancy Reagan's possible impact on major public issues including nuclear arms reduction and the end of the Cold War. The facts were hard to ferret out in a political world that increasingly limited access to the president and the first lady and filtered information through public relations practitioners. Editorial writers criticized Nancy Reagan's ethics in accepting expensive clothing from designers, deplored her extravagant tastes, ridiculed her interest in White House china and decorating, and debated the sincerity of her "Just Say No" antidrug program, although many Americans applauded it. Highly placed members of Reagan's administration wrote tell-all memoirs that pictured the first lady as an unscrupulous power behind the throne who engineered the removal of presidential aides whom she disliked and insisted on consulting an astrologer before allowing the president's schedule to be set. Strains in the relationships between the Reagans and their children were aired in public. Yet journalists also wrote about her self-deprecating humor and liked her ability to make fun of herself. They publicized her numerous trips to drug treatment centers in her capacity as first lady and gave her credit for attempting to protect her husband's interests.

Reports on the intrigue within the Reagan White House raised questions over the lengths to which wives should go to protect their husbands from political fallout as well as over the propriety of the press intruding into the privacy of spousal advice. One prominent writer, Sally Quinn of the *Washington Post,* claimed that Nancy Reagan served to deflect criticism in the midst of political sparring by factions trying to influence the genial president. Quoting Nancy Reynolds, a confidant of the first lady, Quinn wrote: "She [Nancy Reagan] is very protective. If she has to be the hatchet man, the bad guy, she'll do it. Thank God for her, because he's Mr. Nice Guy."

This was one illustration of the way Nancy Reagan was presented in the media of the 1980s—as an example of women's presumed but unofficial power through marriage. With Americans divided over roles and expectations for women, the first lady remained a contested symbol of women's position in society. Not considered a feminist, Nancy Reagan did not support the equal rights amendment (ERA), which met defeat in 1982. Nevertheless, wedded to a conservative administration that opposed birth control and abortion, she became an ironic symbol of feminine power. According to Gil Troy, Nancy Reagan offered "America's middle-class women an energetic representative who understood that marital partnership did not mean total equality." In spite of attacks by radical feminists on the institution of marriage, many women still hoped to find happiness with their husbands and children, but this did not mean that American women saw themselves as passive victims.

Writing a feminist article in an academic journal in 1990, Catharine R. Stimpson, dean of the graduate school at Rutgers University, used Nancy Reagan to illustrate "a culture of resistance, which works through code . . . and through the indirection of irony and parody." She described an "'Unofficial White House Photograph,' which feminists like to send each other." She said it showed a smiling Nancy and Ronald Reagan standing in front of a window behind which "looms the Washington Monument, a pointed phallic column" that "looks foggy, misty." She continued, "Nancy's head (hatless) is placed on Ronnie's torso, clad in a business suit. Ronnie's head (hatless) is placed on Nancy's body, in beruffled blouse and skirt. Decapitation and transposition drain gender of its power." They also served as a graphic reminder that the power and mystique of one gender could be transferred to the other. Stimpson went on to note differences among women themselves: "For some, Nancy Reagan was a glamorous heroine; for others, an expensively clad creep." Either way, however, she conveyed symbolic importance.

This split in opinion regarding Nancy Reagan characterized much of her media coverage. She first became a target for criticism as the wife of the governor of California. Life in Sacramento, the state capital, had been uncomfortable for Nancy Reagan, a somewhat shy, slight, pretty woman who took little interest in politics or in socializing with ordinary citizens and demanded that her husband's staff make sure that he was not overworked. When Ronald Reagan won a surprisingly successful race for governor in 1966, she refused to live in the official residence, a rundown Victorian mansion deemed a firetrap in a downtown neighborhood, and insisted the family move to a well-off suburb. Some journalists called her "Queen Nancy," and political reporters commented sarcastically on her "gaze," the stare of rapt attention that she often fixed on her husband; while he was speaking, her face glowed. On the one hand, reporters characterized her as a throwback to pre–women's liberation days when she made statements such as, "I simply don't differ with Ronnie on anything." On the other hand, when they wrote about her demands on his staff members, some of whom called her "the Dragon Lady," she came across, to her displeasure, as Machiavellian.

Lou Cannon, a journalist and Reagan biographer, explained that "Nancy's interests were in fashion and money and the gossip of the wealthy, socialite circle she had left in Southern California. . . . She saw her role as protecting the privacy of 'Ronnie' and the life they enjoyed together. 'My life began when I got married,' she used to say." In keeping with Ronald Reagan's political conservatism, she projected herself and her husband as a couple upholding traditional moral values in opposition to the permissive social code of the 1960s. He called her "Mommy," and she called him "Ronnie." Not wanting to acknowledge that Reagan was divorced with two children by his first wife as well as two younger children by her, she told his campaign managers to ignore the older children and simply state, "He has two children."

With her love of style and elegance, Nancy Reagan received accolades from the society, if not the political, press.

Society pages showed the governor's wife shopping in expensive Beverly Hills stores, having lunch with Betsy Bloomingdale and other wives of millionaires, and attending social and cultural events around the state. Her social contacts kept her husband in touch with wealthy Republicans and may have helped him raise campaign funds. She also was pictured meeting with Vietnam veterans and advocating worthy projects, particularly the Foster Grandparents program that encouraged older Americans to develop contacts with handicapped children, but she was more identified with clothes than causes. While in California, she was named one of the best-dressed women in the United States.

A scathing profile titled "Pretty Nancy" in the *Saturday Evening Post* in 1968 set the tone for the initial coverage she received after Ronald Reagan defeated Jimmy Carter for the presidency in 1980. It also led to Nancy Reagan's permanent distrust of the media and her determination to maintain control of her press relations. After interviewing the governor's wife for a day in Sacramento, the author of the *Post* article, Joan Didion, pictured her as a phony individual with "the smile of a woman who seems to be playing out some middle-class American woman's daydream, circa 1948." Just prior to the inauguration, a profile by a reporter for the *Los Angeles Herald Examiner* was reprinted in the *Washington Post* and other newspapers, presenting Nancy Reagan as an imperious attention-seeker who had "been playing" Jackie Kennedy "forever."

"Of all the first ladies I've covered," Helen Thomas wrote in 1999, "this one [Nancy Reagan] got off to the worse start." Controversy immediately surrounded her desire to renovate the family quarters of the White House, which she found "dreary and uninviting." Commented Maureen Santini, who covered the Reagans, first for the Associated Press and then for the *New York Daily News,* "Stories before they got to the White House cast her in a controversial light; for example, there was one that she had asked the Carters to leave early (she denied it but who knows?)."

In an Associated Press story, Santini reported that members of the Reagan transition team "dropped broad hints that Nancy Reagan wants President and Mrs. Carter to vacate the White House before Inauguration Day so she can begin redecorating." The story included a denial from Nancy Reagan; however, it quoted Robin Orr, her press secretary, as saying the new first lady had suggested the Reagans themselves might break the tradition of staying in the White House until the inauguration of a new president "by moving to Blair House [a government residence for visiting dignitaries] a few weeks before the Reagan presidency ends." At the time, the Reagans were staying in Blair House, preparing to take a second tour of the White House living quarters with a Los Angeles decorator.

In her memoir, Mary Hoyt, Rosalynn Carter's press secretary, wrote that it was Orr, a California society reporter, who revealed "Mrs. Reagan can't understand why the Carters won't move out of the White House early so that her decorator can get started." Hoyt added that "in twenty-eight days she's [Orr is] gone." Her replacement was Sheila Patton (later Tate), a public relations expert.

The episode heightened the public perception of a clash between Nancy Reagan's lifestyle and Washington traditions. To the new first lady, it illustrated the kind of unfair press coverage to which she was subjected. In her autobiography, she wrote, "Somehow, a rumor got started—where do these stories come from?—that I wanted to renovate the White House *before* the inauguration, and that I had asked the Carters to move out early, so I could get started. I *never* asked the Carters to move out, and I wouldn't even think of it." She continued, "According to another report, I intended to knock down a wall in the Lincoln bedroom—the Lincoln bedroom! I would never dream of doing that, either."

Preinauguration stories by Santini and Thomas, based on a joint interview with the first lady–to–be, highlighted what appeared to be naïveté about and insensitivity to the issue of gun control, a particularly newsworthy topic at the time because of the recent shooting death of Beatle John Lennon. In her Associated Press dispatch, Santini wrote that Nancy Reagan had disclosed she kept a "tiny little gun" near her bed for protection in her California home and that her husband had taught her how to use it. She was afraid because he was frequently away, the story reported her saying, and she was left alone, but she had never used the gun and did not know what kind of a weapon it was. She joked she would not be likely to need it in the well-guarded White House. Thomas's story for United Press International reported the same information and ran under headlines such as "PISTOL-PACKIN' NANCY KEEPS A GUN IN HER BEDROLL" and "DON'T WORRY, NANCY: D.C. WILL BE DISARMING." Critics pointed out that gun control was not a trivial issue.

While plans went forward for the Reagan inauguration, the most expensive in history up to that time, magazines and newspapers provided details on Nancy Reagan's plans to restore splendor to the White House as well as to signal a changed atmosphere in Washington. The inauguration itself, said Haynes Johnson, a *Washington Post* journalist, was "an outpouring of wealth and privilege," highlighted by the fleet of corporate jets parked at National Airport as well as by streets crowded with limousines, "the preferred symbol of status."

Critics charged that the opulence of the inauguration at a time of economic hardship for many Americans represented, in Johnson's words, "a marriage of the New Right with the New Rich." They particularly disparaged "the lavish tone set by the First Lady–to–be, whose inaugural wardrobe was reported to have cost twenty-five thousand dollars (an amount that would purchase a year's supply of food stamps for fifty needy citizens) ... and whose new handbag alone cost more than sixteen hundred dollars." Unlike the Carter inauguration, which was billed as the "people's inaugural" and offered free events open to the general public, the Reagan inauguration required attendees to purchase costly tickets. Backers said it epitomized "class and dignity"—and free enterprise at its best.

As for Nancy Reagan herself, it appeared she looked to Jackie Kennedy as a role model. She employed Letitia Baldrige, Jackie Kennedy's social secretary, to help oversee the hiring of her staff. For the inaugural ball at the Smithsonian Museum of American History, the first lady wore a "flowing sheened white cape, with long white gloves, white jeweled shoes, and glistening one-shoulder beaded white gown," while, as Carl Anthony pointed out, on display nearby "was the white-caped, white-gloved, white-shoed and white-shoulderless-beaded bodiced ensemble of Jackie Kennedy."

Her first meeting with White House newswomen after

the "budget-busting inaugural," Thomas said, "did not get off to the most auspicious start. Much was made of her inaugural wardrobe—a red Adolfo dress, a black formal dress by Bill Blass and a white, beaded gown by James Galanos, all topped off by a full-length mink coat by Maximillan." One hundred journalists attended a press session on February 9, 1981, billed as an opportunity to learn about her plans to promote the Foster Grandparents program. The first lady said she was busy unpacking and left the group to watch a movie on the program for twenty minutes.

Nancy Reagan found media criticism hard to understand. "If the public really wants the first lady to look her best," she said in her autobiography, "why then was I attacked so strongly, and so often, for my wardrobe?" She speculated one reason might be "that some women aren't all that crazy about a woman who wears a size four, and who seems to have no trouble staying slim." She also seemed slow to realize that the orientation of many women reporters had changed from fashion to feminism during the twenty years between the Kennedy and Reagan administrations. As she explained in her autobiography, it was Katharine Graham who told her that younger women reporters "just couldn't identify with you." She said Graham commented, "You represented everything they were rebelling against."

In spite of having had her own acting career, Nancy Reagan appeared to personify the women whose lifestyles were based on the wealth and status of their husbands, not the personal achievements prized by feminists. Unlike Jackie Kennedy, she had not been born into an upscale world of privilege. In her early years, she had lived much lower on the social ladder.

Born in New York City to Kenneth Robbins, a car salesman, and Edith Luckett Robbins, an actress, she experienced a traumatic childhood. Although she gave her year of birth as 1923, her birth certificate and school records showed it was actually 1921. She was named Anna Frances, but her mother preferred to call her Nancy. In the wake of her parents' separation and divorce, she stayed for some five years in the modest home of her aunt and uncle in Bethesda, Maryland, while her mother pursued a stage career.

When her mother remarried in 1929, Nancy's fortunes improved. She was adopted by her stepfather, Loyal Davis, a Chicago neurosurgeon who sent her to the prestigious Girl's Latin School in Chicago and give her a debut. He also sent her to Smith College, where she majored in drama. Drawing on the contacts that her mother had with some of the most famous actors of the day, she went first to Broadway, where she dated Clark Gable, and then to Hollywood to seek work as an actress. She appeared in supporting roles in eleven films, but she maintained her real interest was in marriage. She met Ronald Reagan, a well-known B-grade actor who also was president of the Screen Actors Guild, in 1949, shortly after his divorce from Jane Wyman, whose acting career had eclipsed his own.

On March 4, 1952, Ronald Reagan and Nancy Davis were married, and on October 22, 1952, their daughter, Patricia Ann (called Patti), was born. The length of time between their marriage and the birth of their daughter gave rise to speculation that Nancy Davis had been pregnant before their marriage, a point made by some critics of the Reagans on grounds they were hypocrites when campaigning for a return to old-fashioned morality. Ronald Reagan never acknowledged this, although Nancy Reagan noted that her daughter had been born "a bit precipitously." Reagan himself was said to have told Patti when she asked about her birth, "If the studio hadn't made us change the wedding date, you wouldn't have been premature." Their son, Ronald, was born in 1958. Reagan also had two children with Wyman, a daughter, Maureen, and an adopted son, Michael.

All four children had difficulty growing up, suffering through varying degrees of estrangement from their parents, divorces, bouts with drugs, and years of misery. As Nancy Reagan said in her autobiography, the relationships with the children became a well-publicized issue during the Reagan presidency: "Our family and its problems were written about constantly. Ronnie had run for office on a platform of traditional family values, which both of us believe in and try to practice." Contending that the press was too critical in its portrayal of the situation, she said, "One of the disadvantages of living in the White House is that your family problems often end up on the front page."

In looking back on the growing-up years of the children, Nancy Reagan noted that her husband had been very involved in his work. As his acting career faded, he took a job as spokesman for General Electric, traveling around the country making speeches and meeting people on behalf of corporate America. He further developed his political ideas, called for cutbacks in government, and left the Democratic party, with which he long had been associated, to join the Republican party in 1962. Nancy Reagan was not politically inclined and disliked giving political speeches, but Loyal Davis was a strong conservative, and his views may have influenced his son-in-law. Proving that a background in acting was no bar to a political career, Reagan scored a surprising victory in his bid to become governor of California in 1966 and was reelected four years later.

Backed by antigovernment westerners, he attempted unsuccessfully to secure the Republican nomination for president in 1976 against Gerald Ford, but his strong showing in the primary campaign set him up to be the Republican candidate four years later. When he was elected president in 1980, Nancy Reagan realized that she had an opportunity to play a role far bigger than any she could have dreamed of getting in Hollywood. An actress friend told her, "You're the star of the whole world. The biggest star of all," and she replied, "Yes, I know, and it scares me." Perhaps the elegantly dressed first lady–to–be still harbored the insecurities of a little girl who had been separated from her mother.

As first lady, Nancy Reagan did not succeed in her initial efforts to emulate Jackie Kennedy. In Kennedy's day, Americans looked forward optimistically to putting a man on the moon and responded to calls that asked them to ponder "what you can do for your country." The handsome young Jack Kennedy and his wife intrigued news media—and a nation—eager to visit, via the relatively new magic of color television, a restored White House that served as a setting for the glamorous couple. Two decades later, Americans seemed more jaded. The Reagans presided over a different time.

As Carl Anthony pointed out, "Nancy Reagan suited her era. Glitzy glamour, conspicuous consumption, instant gratification, extravagant comfort—Nancy's image was all eighties." Her predilection for glamour and her quotable remarks were made to order for news columns and magazines, as well as for television and personal appearances. She created so much news that reporters found the East Wing of the White House, which housed the first lady's offices, a more desirable beat than previously. According to Anthony, "More stories appeared in print about Mrs. Reagan than even Mrs. Roosevelt." On television, she garnered more broadcast clips than Jackie Kennedy had.

Much of the attention during her first year was not welcome. Nancy Reagan said she was "called more names than I can remember." Among them were "Queen Nancy," "the Iron Butterfly," "the Belle of Rodeo Drive," "Fancy Nancy," and "the Cutout Doll." The news media attacked displays of style and elegance at a time when announcements of cuts in government social programs were making life more difficult for poor Americans.

To redecorate the White House, Nancy Reagan turned down the routine $50,000 appropriation from Congress given to each new president and sought some $800,000 from private donations. News stories pointed out that some contributions came from businesspeople who profited from Reagan's deregulation of oil and gas prices and used the donations for tax deductions, so that, in effect, the taxpayers were subsidizing the project. The press reacted with hostility, no longer enchanted by White House furnishings as in the days of Camelot.

The sharpest criticism came after a poorly timed announcement that $200,000 in donated funds had been spent for White House china, which was bordered in red, Nancy Reagan's favorite color. "The White House really badly, badly needs china," the first lady was quoted as saying, describing her fun in selecting a pattern with a border etched in gold. The announcement was made just as new standards for

school lunches were publicized, allowing catsup to be classified as a vegetable. A torrent of hostile publicity ensued, with
the Reagan administration accused of being more concerned
about china than children. A plaintive President Reagan
asked a reporter rhetorically, "Why wasn't the same thing said
about another first lady some years ago who set out to contribute to the beauty of the White House and there was
nothing but praise?"

More criticism resulted from the first lady's penchant
for wearing expensive outfits in a time of unemployment and
recession. Reporters wrote that she had accepted gowns on
loan from designers and did not return them, which appeared
to be a violation of federal law limiting gifts to public officials. In response, she donated a couple of gowns to fashion
museums but then returned to her previous habits. Dining in
expensive restaurants with old California friends also
brought her unfavorable notice.

The first lady remained an unpopular figure even after
Ronald Reagan was seriously wounded on March 30, 1981,
by a deranged John Hinckley, who shot the president outside
a Washington hotel. She was shown in numerous photographs arriving at the hospital where the president had undergone surgery, and she was pictured sympathetically in
news stories. But this coverage, depicting her as a worried
wife, did not change public attitudes toward her. Nor did her
image improve when she was seen attending the glittering
wedding of Prince Charles and Lady Diana while her husband stayed home.

Nancy Reagan certainly was not the first president's
wife to face criticism, but as she noted in her autobiography,
she "won the unpopularity contest hands down." By the time

1981 ended, she said, "I had a higher disapproval rating than any other first lady of modern times." Although it was easy to blame it all on journalists, she continued, she wished she "had tried harder to communicate to them who I really was."

Yet there was at least one subject that she definitely did not want to discuss in public—her reliance on an astrologer for the planning of public activities. The assassination attempt gave Nancy Reagan's long-standing concern about her husband's well-being renewed justification. After the shooting, the first lady began to check her husband's schedule with an astrologer, Joan Quigley, who made predictions as to "bad days" and "good days" for the president "to be around crowds." Deaver, who had more rapport with Nancy Reagan than other staff members did, had no problem with the use of the astrologer "if that's what she wanted to do." The news media did not learn of her reliance on the astrologer until near the end of Reagan's White House tenure, when it was revealed by Don Regan, the president's former chief of staff who had been fired from his position partly due to the first lady's insistence. The sensational news clouded the Reagans' departure from Washington.

By that time, however, Nancy Reagan had become a more popular figure. Afraid that she would be a political liability for the administration, Deaver and other advisers had launched what became known as "Project Nancy-Has-a-Heart." This undertaking consisted of efforts to prove that she was a warm, caring individual instead of a remote, snobbish clotheshorse.

The most obvious attempt was her performance, arranged by Sheila Tate through Helen Thomas, at what Kati Marton called "that sacred spring ritual of the Washington media and political establishment, the Gridiron dinner." A club of elite journalists, the Gridiron, holds a dinner annually to roast the president. When Nancy Reagan made fun of herself at the March 29, 1982, event by unexpectedly donning an odd collection of old clothes to impersonate a bag lady and singing "Second-Hand Rose," the capital's leading journalists suddenly loved her.

Thomas described the amusing scene in detail: "There she was, decked out in an aqua cotton shirt with red and yellow flowers, a navy polka-dot blouse and short-sleeved red sweater, white pantaloons decorated with blue butterflies, a big feathered hat, white feather boa, yellow rubber boots and big red earrings." Singing off-key, Nancy Reagan warbled lyrics written for her by Sheila Patton Tate and a White House speechwriter to the tune of "Second-Hand Rose":

> I'm wearing second-hand clothes
> Second-hand clothes
> They're quite the style
> In the spring fashion shows
> Even my new trench coat with fur collar
> Ronnie bought for 10 cents on the dollar
>
> Second-hand gowns
> And old hand-me-downs
> The china is the only thing that's new.
> Even though they tell me that I'm no longer queen
> Did Ronnie have to buy me that new sewing machine?
> Second-hand clothes, second-hand clothes
>
> I sure hope Ed Meese sews.

The crowd, including her husband, went wild, yelling for an encore, which she ended by smashing a "china" plate. The audience loved the act, although a few critics complained that it displayed callousness toward the poor. Nancy Reagan wrote in her autobiography, "This one song, together with my willingness to sing it, served as a signal to opinion-makers that maybe I wasn't the terrible humorless woman they thought I was—regal, distant, disdainful." Her image started to improve almost at once.

Even before the Gridiron performance, Nancy Reagan had shown that she could draw applause by making fun of herself. At a dinner in New York in October 1981, she called attention to a postcard picturing her as "Queen Nancy" wearing a crown and declared, "Now that's silly. I'd never wear a crown. It musses up your hair." The audience roared as she announced her new charity would be "The Nancy Reagan Home for Wayward China."

Washington, rather than New York, however, provided the setting for Nancy Reagan's transformation in the eyes of the media. Unlike the Carters, the Reagans quickly made contacts within the Washington power structure when they moved to the capital. They had no intention of spurning Washington society as their predecessors had done. The Reagans invited Katharine Graham to a reception as well as to one of their first official White House functions. The most powerful woman in media and the controlling force of *Newsweek* as well as the *Washington Post,* Graham, considered the honorary queen of capital society, "had the power to make or break almost anyone in Washington," according to one observer of the social scene.

Although the *Post,* with its liberal Democratic orientation, disagreed with the policies of the conservative Reagan administration, Graham hosted a dinner party for the first couple at her Georgetown home. She explained in her autobiography, "I consider it the role of the head of a newspaper to be bipartisan and to bring journalists together with people from government . . . it helps the publication by opening doors, and provides those who are covered in the news with the knowledge of whom they can suggest ideas to, complain to, or generally deal with." Before long, she and Nancy Reagan were close friends, often meeting for lunch and conferring by telephone.

While Graham took a hands-off approach to her news columns, her friendship with Nancy Reagan may have influenced the *Post* to be kinder to the Reagan White House than it might have been expected to be. Meg Greenfield, editorial page editor of the newspaper, who often attended lunches with the first lady at Graham's house, wrote that the "not for quotation" conversations that took place "confirmed disputes that the White House had officially denied and provided a lot of information about and insight into the ways of the people running the Reagan administration." Greenfield shared this "background corroboration" with the reporters who covered the Reagans, although frequently they "didn't need all that much help." Through these lunches, Greenfield said she came to appreciate Nancy Reagan's "indispensability to [her husband's] political career as a motivator, an activator, and an energizer without whose constant presence he would not have got where he was or been able to function once he got there."

Profiting from the journalistic willingness to view her in a better light, Nancy Reagan transformed her image from that of pampered queen obsessed with fashion and affectation to one of loyal wife and concerned mother. She continued her involvement with Foster Grandparents and published a ghost-written book, *To Love a Child,* praising the program. She also prevailed on her close friend Frank Sinatra to record a song to benefit it.

Her antidrug campaign, launched a month before the Gridiron dinner, was a far more ambitious activity. The campaign started with visits to drug treatment centers in Florida and Texas. An Associated Press story made it apparent that image-making lay at the heart of one such trip. The story began: "Nancy Reagan is venturing on a rare trip without her husband that will shift the spotlight from her free clothes and expensive china and focus it on her campaign against drug abuse." According to the story, all available press seats on the first lady's plane were filled because this was the first "substantive trip on which reporters were invited to accompany her." Previously, the article stated, the first lady had expressed concern about the drug problem but had limited her involvement to "giving a few speeches and visiting a few treatment centers."

That situation would soon change. Over the next few years, according to Deaver, Nancy Reagan "took her crusade to sixty-five cities in thirty-three states, to the pontiff's side in Rome, and to capitals the world over." Her travels drew a regular press following of some ten to twenty journalists and camera crews, augmented by scores of local media representatives at the stops she made. To combat drug abuse, she had, by the fall of 1985, appeared on twenty-three talk shows and cohosted a show for *Good Morning America* as well as a two-hour special for the Public Broadcasting Service. She also appeared briefly on the sitcom *Diff'rent Strokes*. Her campaign turned into the "Just Say No" movement after a child asked her, "What should I say if someone offers me drugs?" and she replied, "Just say NO! That's all you have to do." In 1985, she held an antidrug summit for seventeen first ladies from around the world. She also hosted a similar conference at the United Nations and was the first wife of the president of the United States to speak there. In 1986, her husband appeared with her on television to launch the National Crusade for a Drug-Free America.

After the Gridiron performance, journalists in the mainstream media changed their tune regarding Nancy Reagan. Major newspapers turned aside from personal attacks on the first lady that denigrated her appearance. One of the most cutting, which Tate said made the first lady cry, had been a column by Judy Bachrach in the *Washington Star* that referred to Nancy Reagan as having "a pair of piano legs." "The nature of that reporting was nasty," Tate said; "it came out of a decision by reporters to dislike her without knowing her."

The antidrug campaign provided an opportunity for reporters throughout the United States to meet the first lady in an activist role that was acceptable to editors. The touching stories of young drug addicts in treatment facilities brought tears to Nancy Reagan's eyes and moved onlookers who heard her tell the teenagers she loved them. At the end of one of her first visits in 1982, according to James Rosebush, her chief of staff, "we were all crying, even the Secret Service." He added, "It was hard to see how this type of raw feeling or caring could have been fabricated; and the writers and correspondents present began to see another side of this woman."

PLATE I. News photographers film Florence Harding and a delegation of women from the Philippines seeking better relations with the United States on the South Lawn of the White House in 1921.

PLATE 2. Eleanor Roosevelt meets with the female Washington press corps at one of her first White House press conferences for women reporters. The "press girls," as the reporters are called, stand around her or sit at her feet in the Monroe Room, March 13, 1933.

PLATE 3. Eleanor Roosevelt and four women reporters who were her close friends enjoy the countryside on a fact-finding trip to Puerto Rico in March 1934. *Left to right:* Emma Bugbee, *New York Herald Tribune;* Dorothy Ducas, International News Service; Eleanor Roosevelt; Ruby Black, United Press; and Bess Furman, Associated Press.

PLATE 4. Mamie Eisenhower cuts the cake given her by the Women's National Press Club in celebration of her sixty-third birthday at the Mayflower Hotel in Washington, D.C., in 1959.

PLATE 5. Jackie Kennedy entertains women reporters at a White House luncheon in April 1961.

PLATE 6. Lady Bird Johnson is interviewed at the White House by Barbara Walters for the *Today Show* on NBC on January 21, 1968.

PLATE 7. Betty Ford displays Christmas decorations to media representatives at the White House on December 10, 1974.

PLATE 8. Rosalyn Carter and her press secretary, Mary Finch Hoyt, meet on May 9, 1977, at the White House to plan for various media activities.

PLATE 9. Nancy Reagan speaks about drug abuse among youth to host Carol Randolph during a one-hour live broadcast July 23, 1984, of *Morning Break,* a program on WDVM-TV in Washington, D.C. Two former teenage drug users share the spotlight with her, while a hot-line service operates in the background.

PLATE 10. Barbara Bush records a selection in July 1991 for her children's program, *Mrs. Bush's Storytime*, which was broadcast over the ABC radio network.

PLATE 11. Hillary Rodham Clinton arrives at the National Press Club in Washington, D.C., accompanied by her aides to appear there in April 1996.

PLATE 12. Laura Bush delivers a luncheon address at the National Press Club on November 8, 2001, on patriotism and children in the wake of 9/11.

In his critique of the coverage of the Reagan administration, Mark Hertsgaard discussed an incident that reflected this change. When Nancy Reagan paid a visit to a New York drug rehabilitation center, he stated, a reporter for the *New York Times* "had the temerity to write a story lead noting the irony of Mrs. Reagan posing with impoverished junkies while wearing a designer dress worth thousands of dollars." A senior editor at the paper "stormed into the middle of the newsroom and, in front of numerous other reporters, loudly berated the reporter, warning that the reference to the dress was injurious both to the *Times* and to the reporter's career and ordering the lead changed immediately." Similarly, Lee Lescaze, transferred from the White House beat to the "Style" section of the *Washington Post,* remembered how "it suddenly became clear we were not to take swipes at Nancy Reagan." He said he was "never told specifically to do or not to do stories . . . but there was a kind of atmosphere of: enough is enough; she's not running the country."

Some critics argued that the first lady's antidrug campaign was hypocritical because her husband was cutting funds for drug prevention and education programs, but Nancy Reagan insisted the solution lay not in money but in private morality. Her advisers initially feared illegal drug use might not be a suitable project for a first lady because of political and budgetary implications, but Nancy Reagan carefully sidestepped these issues. Rosebush pointed out, "She never sought government money to fight drugs, attended only one meeting in the West Wing on drug policy, refused an invitation to testify before Congress, and insisted on keeping her efforts totally oriented toward the private sector." She saw her role, he said, as increasing "awareness, not spending."

According to Tate, today one of the top public relations practitioners in Washington, the antidrug effort was "a campaign that built credibility." The first year, she said, Nancy Reagan went "on the road and looked at facilities for treatment and prevention"; the second year, she "raised an enormous amount of money" for treatment facilities; and the third year, she "went on TV." The campaign moved forward in "concentric circles starting small and building and building so the first lady would be successfully identified with one issue." In Tate's view, "The public has come to expect public service from a first lady as a way of paying for her privileges."

The antidrug crusade, aimed particularly at children and teenagers, became the most successful project in history to be undertaken by a first lady. Nancy Reagan appeared on the cover of *Time* magazine and was complimented in an hour-long NBC special. With thousands of parents and children writing her about their own experiences with drugs, letters addressed to her at the White House increased from a 1982 total of 37,670 to a 1987 total of 85,930. The 1987 total was swelled by messages of support for Nancy Reagan herself, who underwent surgery for breast cancer that year. She chose to have a mastectomy rather than more limited surgery recommended by surgeons so that she could recuperate faster and continue in her role as first lady. Physicians argued in print over whether she had made the right choice, with one doctor quoted in the *New York Times* as saying that by not choosing a less traumatic option, she had set breast cancer treatment "back ten years." Nancy Reagan wrote she "resented" these statements and "wished that people would understand I was making this decision only for myself."

When Ronald Reagan started his second term in

1985, polls found that his wife was even more popular than he was. Respondents said they liked her because she supported the president and acted as a first lady should. To Rosebush, this response illustrated the underlying conservatism of Americans. "For a wife to support her husband with Nancy Reagan's fervency and attention is not an image popularized in society today," he said, so "there must be a value system that is much more traditional than what is portrayed by the media."

In addition to conducting her antidrug campaign, Nancy Reagan, occasionally on her own but usually with her husband, made more than a dozen diplomatic visits abroad, the most memorable of which included the summit meetings between Ronald Reagan and Soviet leader Mikhail Gorbachev. News accounts played up the friction between her and Gorbachev's wife, Raisa, a teacher who lectured her on communism. The press wrote about "style wars" between the two women, which Nancy Reagan characterized as "a little silly." Far more important was the first lady's effort to reduce Cold War tensions. "With the world so dangerous," she wrote in her autobiography, "I felt it was ridiculous for these two heavily armed superpowers to be sitting there and not talking to each other. I encouraged Ronnie to meet with Gorbachev as soon as possible." According to Helen Thomas, Nancy Reagan deserves "a special place in history for influencing her husband to take a softer line toward the Soviet Union."

To help carry out her duties, which included entertaining more foreign heads of state than any other first lady in history up to her time, she had a East Wing staff of about eighteen persons. In keeping with the Reagan administration's emphasis on reduced federal employment, she did not press for additional personnel. Staff turnover was high—perhaps because Nancy Reagan, in effect, acted as her own chief of staff, taking issues directly to Deaver until he left the White House in 1985. During her years as first lady, she went through three speechwriters, three social secretaries, three project directors, three press secretaries (not counting Robin Orr), and five chiefs of staff.

The drug campaign and other activities never overshadowed her zeal to protect her husband from both physical and political harm. As his second term unfolded, according to Helene Von Damm, an assistant to the president, Nancy Reagan's "influence grew even greater because there was an increasing vacuum of power at the White House." To attack those who she believed were not serving her husband well, Von Damm said, Nancy Reagan "learned to use all the weapons in her arsenal: social invitations, leaks to the press, and intramural scheming to work her will."

In particular, the first lady sought the ouster in 1987 of Don Regan, the White House chief of staff, whom she accused of trying to overschedule her husband following his colon cancer surgery in 1985 and prostate surgery two years later. She said he assumed too much authority and "saw himself as a kind of deputy president." She also blamed Regan for not heading off the Iran-contra scandal, which nearly brought down the Reagan presidency. The scandal involved selling arms to Iran with White House approval in exchange for the release of hostages and diverting proceeds to the contras, an anti-Communist military force in Nicaragua, in violation of U.S. law. The president contended the United States had not swapped arms for hostages but said that he had a faulty recollection of what had transpired.

Don Regan was forced to resign in early 1987, with newspaper coverage split in regard to Nancy Reagan's role in his departure. In a book giving his side of the debacle, Regan wrote that "Mrs. Reagan's concern for her husband's health was understandable ... but ... excessive, particularly since the President himself did not seem to think that there was any need for him to slow down to the point where he was lying dead in the water." He referred to Michael Deaver as a "manipulator" who "devised ways to communicate Mrs. Reagan's demands to the President by planting stories in the press that the President was bound to read."

Most shocking of all, he revealed the first lady's reliance on an astrologer to set the president's schedule, "the single most powerful tool in the White House, because it determines what the most powerful man in the world is going to do and where he is going to do it." Regan wrote, "By humoring Mrs. Reagan we gave her this tool—or, more accurately, gave it to an unknown woman in San Francisco who believed that the zodiac controls events and human behavior and that she could read the secrets of the future in the movement of the planets." This sensational disclosure, excerpted in a cover story in *Time* magazine, again made the first lady the center of controversy, toward the end of her White House stay. A Gallup Poll in 1987 reported that 62 percent of the people believed she had more influence on the president than any other first lady had had. In the firing of Don Regan, the American people supported her—two to one in a *Newsweek* poll.

In her memoir, *My Turn,* published a year after she left Washington, Nancy Reagan tried to downplay her interest in astrology, contending it had no influence on political or policy decisions. Still, she lost favor with the public. A 1989 poll gave Barbara Bush's approval rating at 58 percent, compared to Nancy Reagan's 19 percent. In recent years, public sympathy for her as she cared for her ill husband and then took part in his funeral in 2004 has restored her popularity.

Nancy Reagan's career as first lady resembled a ride on a roller coaster. In a speech to the American Newspaper Publishers Association in 1987, she defended her right to "look after your husband" and to speak up, if necessary, "to him or his staff." She concluded, "Once you're in the White House, don't think it's going to be a glamorous, fairy-tale life. It's very hard work with high highs and low lows." She spoke from bittersweet experience. The position of first lady, she said, is one "you can never get used to." Above all, she emphasized her role as her husband's intimate adviser and protector.

In *My Turn,* she wrote, "For eight years I was sleeping with the President, and if that doesn't give you special access, I don't know what does." In 1985, she had charmed Soviet ambassador Andrey Gromyko at a White House lunch, leading him to tell her, "Whisper the word peace to your husband every night." "I will," she shot back, "and I'll also whisper it in your ear ... peace." This incident illustrates the way Nancy Reagan turned her personal love story into a drama of White House power and intrigue that assured Ronald Reagan's legacy and may have affected the course of world affairs.

BARBARA BUSH

Barbara Bush, wife of one Republican president and mother of another, presented a far different image as first lady than Nancy Reagan did. A silver-haired, full-figured matriarch who scored high in public opinion polls, she came from a privileged background and was the descendant of another president, for her great-great-great uncle was President Franklin Pierce. As first lady, she drew favorable coverage that showed her surrounded by her grandchildren and patronizing good causes while acting as a supportive spouse, always loyal to her husband. Reporters aroused her ire, although she enjoyed good surface relationships with the press.

When George W. Bush, her oldest son, was inaugurated as president for a second term in 2005, his wife, Laura, revealed that whenever she and her mother-in-law had been together during the campaign, their favorite topic of conversation was the news media. She told the *New York Times*, "We loved to complain about various media." Asked if the complaints were about institutions or individuals, she answered, "All."

Although she did not elaborate on their objections, she said that Barbara Bush was a "terrific mother-in-law" but "more intimidating, maybe" than her father-in-law, the former president George H. W. Bush. Her remarks included oblique references to Barbara Bush being a more multifaceted person than her media image as the nation's grandmother suggested. Indicating that she was keenly interested in the way she and other members of the Bush family were portrayed, her comments hinted at the fact that Barbara Bush was a woman with a strong personality and a zest for politics—a woman absorbed by much more than domesticity.

Today, having been out of the White House for more than a decade, Barbara Bush continues to present an example of a first lady who, as Gil Troy put it, "took advantage of Americans' complicated attitudes toward women, power, aging, and beauty." She succeeded as first lady because she played herself, but she focused on only one dimension. The public saw a motherly but quick-witted figure, surprisingly blunt at times, who did not try to influence her husband's politics. Just before George H. W. Bush took office as president in 1989, when she was sixty-three years old, she said in a widely quoted interview that she might tell her husband she disagreed with him but never that she thought he had "messed up." She offered no specifics.

"We grew up in a world where you didn't talk about yourself all the time. I will confess, this whole fall I felt like I'd been on the couch," she continued, reflecting on numerous interviews held on the campaign trail. Apparently referring to the fact that those interviews had forced her to think back over her life, she said, "I still look in the mirror and see a young, sixteen-year-old whose tennis game could improve, but that isn't the way it is really."

The product of a patrician eastern upbringing in a society that expected men to make a financial mark in the world and women to stay home and bear children, Barbara Bush had been schooled to see a distinction between the public and the private. Perhaps she developed an antipathy toward the media because journalists tried to merge the two spheres. According to Kati Marton, Barbara Bush thought that "who she really was, or what her marriage was really like, was nobody's business but hers and her husband's."

As a realistic political wife, she knew she had to react to the pressure to present an acceptable public persona. And that she did, transforming what could have been handicaps—her weight, her wrinkles, and her age—into media assets. By displaying humor and what was her biggest weapon against criticism, her big and photogenic family, she endeared herself to a nation surfeited with Hollywood glitz during the Reagan years. As *Time* headlined a cover story on "the Silver Fox," the nickname given Barbara Bush by her children, "NOW FOR SOMETHING COMPLETELY DIFFERENT: A DOWN-TO-EARTH FIRST LADY."

In her preinauguration interview, Barbara Bush said, "My mail tells me a lot of fat, white-haired, wrinkled ladies are tickled pink." She added, "I think it makes them feel better about themselves. I mean, look at me—if I can be a success, so can they." Her comments, shortened for wire service dispatches, ran all over the country, promising that she would be a "role model for 'fat ladies.'" Her remarks took attention away from the cost of the inaugural ($25 million) and humanized the Bushes as ordinary Americans when, in fact, they were Yankee aristocrats who had become Texas millionaires.

Asked in the interview what she would do in the White House, she said it would be what she always had done—"I mean, truthfully, running the house, listening to my children's problems, passing them on to George, if they're important. I think we'll entertain an enormous amount there because George does that here [in the vice president's mansion]." What about accepting designer dresses like Nancy Reagan had done? She answered in the plural, meaning she and her husband, saying, "We've never done that," then adding she had accepted one dress once but "George paid taxes on it or whatever you do." She said she did not compare herself with Nancy Reagan because she would not come out well "on that scale."

On her own scale of backing her husband, however, she had done very well. Having become an accomplished public speaker after initial nervousness in facing an audience when her husband ran for office in Texas, she had mastered campaigning at the national level. Indeed, in two and a half months during the 1988 presidential campaign against Democrat Michael Dukakis, she had traveled 50,000 miles to 92 cities, granted 184 interviews, appeared at 77 campaign events, and been featured at 13 "press availabilities." When her husband decided to run for vice president in 1980, according to Myra Gutin, a scholar of first ladies, she "learned almost immediately that she would have to submerge her own opinions (pro–Equal Rights Amendment, and purportedly pro-choice) and ideas and support the Republican platform and Ronald Reagan." She willingly did so.

By staying out of the policy domain when her husband ran for president, she bolstered his image as a man who made his own decisions and countered the allegations of critics that he was a "wimp." Angered by the charge that her genial husband presented a "preppy" or "wimpy," rather than a macho, image, she insisted, "Nobody could be married to me and be a wimp." She had been a major factor in enabling him, as the candidate of traditional family values, to refute allegations that he had had a longtime affair with an aide, Jennifer Fitzgerald. By denying the issue, she was, as *Newsweek* correspondent Ann McDaniel put it, able "to control the story." She had become identified with public service, campaigning against illiteracy (seen as a worthy but totally noncontroversial cause), and writing a book, *C. Fred's Story,* under the name of her cocker spaniel to benefit her cause. Most of all, whether she had intended it or not, she had emerged as a public person in her own right after years of being in the background.

She also had learned to be extremely cautious in what she said to journalists. When Reagan and Bush had run for reelection in 1984 against Democrat Walter Mondale for president and Geraldine Ferraro for vice president, Bush had been "apprehensive to be the first man to run against the first woman." His anxiety seemed prophetic when two journalists with whom Barbara Bush had talked on a campaign plane reported a remark she made about his opponent. As Bush explained the incident, "Much to her dismay, Barbara became famous that campaign when in a moment of extreme frustration (the Mondale campaign kept referring to me as a rich elitist), she called Ferraro that 'four-million-dollar—' I can't say it but it rhymes with rich." He added, "She felt horrible and called Geraldine to apologize."

With her husband serving as vice president, Barbara Bush had been Nancy Reagan's understudy for eight years, but the star had given her few opportunities to perform. Making sure there was only one hostess of note in the Reagan administration—for example, in drawing up the guest list for a state dinner honoring Prince Charles and Princess Diana—Nancy Reagan violated rules of protocol and deliberately excluded Vice President and Mrs. Bush. According to Al Haig, Ronald Reagan's secretary of state, "Barbara was treated like dirt. And Barbara cried." Brought up to be socially correct, she managed to maintain the appearance of a cordial relationship with the Reagans in public and let Nancy Reagan stand in the national spotlight.

In her autobiography, Nancy Reagan placed her successor among those presidents' wives "who seemed not to care very much about fashion and appearance" but once in the White House "began to pay more attention to their hair and their clothing." In actuality, Barbara Bush had emerged as a person to be reckoned with on the capital scene before she had moved into the White House, exercising the wit and charm later used to good effect in the presidential campaign. The Bushes were not as involved in Georgetown society as the Reagans, but by the late 1980s, many influential Republicans had moved to Virginia, and Georgetown hostesses, with a few exceptions such as Katharine Graham, no longer had the influence they once enjoyed.

Two journalists reporting on the Washington power structure during the Reagan years ranked Barbara Bush slightly ahead of Nancy Reagan in social terms. Michael Kilian of the *Chicago Tribune* and Arnold Sawislak of United Press International contended, "That the gracious and totally unaffected Barbara Bush has little or no interest in where she might rank on someone's society list is just one reason why she belongs at the top . . . there's no one, including the first lady, who can't help but look up to Barbara Bush socially, no matter how unhappy it makes them." Describing her as an "attractive middle-aged matron," the reporters said that "she is wholly unlike most of the ladies in the Reagan crowd." Referring to her natural white hair, they said she did not need to "drape herself in $15,000 gowns or drag around

$1,600 handbags." Since she kept a low profile, the journal-
ists apparently did not know that she had begun to buy designer gowns as part of her transition to the national stage.

Although she covered up her feelings by making jokes,
Barbara Bush, like most women, was sensitive about her appearance. When her husband unsuccessfully vied with
Ronald Reagan for the Republican presidential nomination
in 1980, she was invited to a national press conference in
New York with other candidates' wives. She was dismayed
when she was told the women would be photographed but
not allowed to speak. In her autobiography, she wrote, "I had
the best candidate, but in a beauty contest or best-dressed
competition, I didn't have a chance."

About that time, she continued, "I had a very hurtful
conversation with a very loved sister-in-law" who told her
family members were wondering, "'What are we going to do
about Bar [her nickname]?' They discussed how to make me
look snappier—color my hair, change my style of dressing,
and, I suspect, get me to lose some weight." She said, "I know
it was meant to be helpful but I wept quietly alone until
George told me that I was absolutely crazy. . . . I certainly did
not expect all the personal criticism when he announced for
the presidency."

Particularly upsetting were jokes in the 1988 race that
she looked like George Bush's mother even though she was
one year younger than her husband. When *Saturday Night
Live,* a satirical television show, did a skit in which she was
introduced as Bush's mother, not his wife, she reportedly did
not appreciate the humor. Although she might employ sar-
casm herself, she found it hard to take from others. According to Sheila Tate, the press secretary for George H. W. Bush

when he was president-elect, "Barbara Bush has a self-deprecating personality." Tate explained, "She is a very funny person [who] uses humor to deal with issues that make her uncomfortable. She heads off people by making fun of herself. It hurt her when people said she looked like George Bush's mother."

In her autobiography, Barbara Bush said she was speechless when Jane Pauley on NBC's *Today* show referred to an apparent age gap between her and her husband. "We had a polite little interview until her last question," she recalled, "which went something like this: 'People say your husband is a man of the eighties and you are a woman of the forties. What do you say to that?'" Remembering that she felt slapped in the face, she said Pauley was "darn lucky I didn't burst into tears. . . . I finally answered, 'Oh, you mean people think I look forty? Neat! If you mean that I love my God, my country, and my husband, so be it. I am a woman of the forties.'"

The nature of the physical relationship between the Bushes emerged further as an issue in the 1988 campaign. After Michael Dukakis and his wife embraced in public, journalists reported on a lack of similar affectionate displays by the Bushes. In response, the Bushes made a point of smiling and touching each other. When Barbara Bush left the room during a CBS television interview, *Time* noted, her husband "pulled her back for a kiss." Although the magazine commented dryly that "romance is becoming the major non-issue of this campaign," voters apparently responded differently, as polls showed a so-called affection gap between the candidates narrowed in Bush's favor after he and his wife appeared to be more loving.

Regardless of the intent of Pauley's question, it was quite true that Barbara Bush's formative years had been in the 1940s. She was the daughter of Marvin Pierce, who rose to become president of McCalls publishing company, and Pauline Robinson Pierce, whose father was an Ohio Supreme Court justice. She grew up in affluent Rye, New York, a large-boned, athletic girl who lacked the beauty of her older sister and had a difficult relationship with her hard-to-please mother. Home for Christmas from Ashley Hall, an exclusive finishing school for young women in South Carolina, she met George Herbert Walker Bush, scion of an old New England family and a senior at Phillips Academy, at a country club dance in 1941. The young couple fell in love. They were married in 1945 after the nineteen-year-old bride had dropped out of Smith College and the twenty-year-old groom had returned from a World War II tour of duty in the Pacific as the youngest pilot in the U.S. naval air service. She joked years later that whenever she said "I married the first man I ever kissed," her children "just about throw up."

After World War II ended, George Bush, the son of Prescott Bush, who became a U.S. senator from Connecticut, enrolled at Yale University under the GI Bill of Rights. His wife worked in the Yale Coop (store) before their first son, George W., was born in 1946. After graduating with honors, Bush moved his family to the drab town of Odessa, Texas, where he set out to learn the oil business from the bottom up, since the Bush family expected its sons to make their own way in the world.

Subsequently, the Bushes had five more children, one of whom, a girl named Robin, died of leukemia at the age of three, leaving both parents grief-stricken. Barbara Bush nearly had a nervous breakdown, and her brown hair began to turn white. In subsequent years, she became virtually a single parent. Her husband traveled extensively to pursue business and political interests, benefiting from contacts with a network of family and friends. The family moved frequently, with Houston eventually becoming their permanent home and Kennebunkport, Maine, where the Bush family long had spent summers, a vacation residence. By the time the Bushes settled into the White House in 1989, they had lived in 28 different homes in 17 cities during their 44 years of marriage.

After making money in oil, George Bush sought public office, running unsuccessfully as a Republican for the U.S. Senate from Texas in 1964; two years later, he was elected to the House of Representatives, where he served two terms. After again losing a Senate race, Bush, a loyal party member, was appointed to a variety of posts: UN ambassador, Republican National Committee chairman, and U.S. envoy to China. In 1976, he went back to Washington as director of the Central Intelligence Agency (CIA).

With her children grown and with CIA security rules making it impossible for her to be involved in her husband's activities, Barbara Bush experienced a serious bout of depression. In her autobiography, she wrote, "I was very depressed, lonely, and unhappy." No one knew except her husband, who urged her to get professional help, but she refused. "Night after night George held me weeping in his arms while I tried to explain my feelings. I almost wonder why he didn't leave me." After about six months, she recovered, but she said the experience left her "more sympathetic of people with emotional problems."

By the time she became first lady, she had perfected her

semijoking style, saying simply, "What you see is what you get." What Americans saw, they liked: a no-nonsense wife and mother of five grown children who loved her dogs and eleven grandchildren, wore three strands of imitation pearls and size fourteen dresses, bought $29 shoes to wear with her inaugural gown, and was known for being feisty. She did not try to compete with her husband in running the country, saying, "I am not sure that the American public likes the spouse to be too front and center."

Only once did she differ from her husband on a policy issue, and then, in effect, she retracted her statement. Asked if she favored a ban on assault weapons following a school shooting, she replied, "Absolutely," but she said no more on the subject after her husband, who was against gun control, declared, "Absolutely not."

When Bush was inaugurated, she emphasized that she had different values than Nancy Reagan. "I want you all to take a look at me," Barbara Bush said, "please notice—hairdo, makeup, designer dress. Look at me good this week, because it's the only week." Her remark was both a put-down of her predecessor and a signal that the focus of the White House would not be elegance. It also obscured the fact that she herself actually had been wearing designer clothes and giving attention to her hairdo and makeup for years and would continue to do so.

Years earlier, she had been asked if she would like for George Bush to become president, and she had replied, "I'd like it because I'm going to be the first lady some time." She had kept her eye on that objective. Having attained it, she planned to add AIDS awareness to her causes because, she said, it "very definitely ties into literacy." She emphasized volunteerism and private partnerships, not public programs. She said, "I don't lobby George Bush and I don't lobby the federal government."

As first lady, Barbara Bush did what she said she would do, gaining extraordinary public approval ratings of more than 80 percent. Within a week of the inauguration, she visited a center serving the homeless in Washington, D.C. She made sandwiches and read to youngsters while journalists took notes and shot pictures. Subsequently, she initiated a visit to a home for babies with AIDS, hugging and kissing victims in widely distributed photographs to show that volunteer workers need have no fear of contracting the disease through personal contact.

Continuing with her campaign to promote reading, she set up the Barbara Bush Foundation for Family Literacy, a private grant-giving organization. With the proceeds going to the foundation, she published another book from the standpoint of a dog. *Millie's Book,* which topped the *New York Times* best-seller list, gave her new canine's view of White House life and raised $1 million for literacy efforts. In 1990, she launched a series of programs for children entitled *Mrs. Bush's Storytime* on ABC radio, also making available audiocassettes of the shows to aid the foundation.

Her East Wing staff, directed by Susan Porter Rose, sifted through hundreds of invitations to accept those most likely to enhance public backing for herself and her husband. Her press secretary, Anna Perez, the first African American to have an important East Wing role, set up luncheon meetings with reporters that led to generally good relationships between the first lady and the White House press corps. According to Maureen Santani, who covered her for the *New York Daily News,* "She could be barbed in her comments, even tart-tongued, and presidential aides confessed they tried to avoid getting on her wrong side." Yet, Santini said, "she often was refreshingly honest."

Accompanied by reporters, Barbara Bush became a frequent visitor to hospitals, schools, day care centers, libraries, and Head Start programs (federally funded preschool classes) across the nation. She maintained a busy schedule, delivering hundreds of formal and informal speeches even when being treated for Graves' disease, a thyroid ailment requiring radiation therapy and medication. Her visits and speeches did not generate exciting news, Santani said: "Her literacy campaign was a public service but also did not get a lot of publicity." Still, her efforts may have spurred her husband to support the National Literacy Act of 1991.

For the most part, Barbara Bush attracted little controversy as first lady. When she was invited to be the commencement speaker at Smith College and receive an honorary doctorate, however, 150 feminist students petitioned against her appearance. They contended she was not a good role model for them because she had done nothing in her own right except to marry a man who became president. The first lady managed skillfully to turn this public relations disaster into a success. Graciously agreeing with the students, she asked Raisa Gorbachev to join her on the platform so the audience could hear from both a university professor, Gorbachev, as well as a college dropout, herself. Her speech ended with a clever note of surprise as she remarked that "somewhere out in this audience may even be someone who will one day follow in my footsteps and preside over the White House as the President's spouse. I wish him well." With that line, she won over the press and most of the audience.

Although she acted the part of a homemaker, Barbara Bush was so occupied with public appearances that President Bush himself, a gregarious individual who liked to be surrounded by people, took responsibility for some of the White House entertaining. According to Barbara Matusow, a writer for the *Washingtonian* magazine, Barbara Bush delegated a great many details to her staff. Matusow said, "You picture her as a rather domestic woman when, in fact, she wasn't. It was George who sat there [and] wrote the guest list."

To the general public, Barbara Bush remained a symbol of the nation's homemakers. Her office received hundreds of requests for her recipes, but, as she confessed in her autobiography, many of the recipes that were sent out came from a White House volunteer. "There are cookbooks all over the country with 'Barbara Bush's favorite recipes' that I've never seen before," she said, adding "I just hope they're good."

When George Bush ran for reelection in 1992 following the Gulf War, polls showed that Americans liked his wife more than they liked him. In 1991 and 1992, she ranked number one in the Gallup Poll's list of "the most admired woman." She was a main speaker at the Republican National Convention that summer, presenting what was billed as a conversation on family values. Shortly thereafter, she campaigned on behalf of Republican members of Congress as well as for her husband.

In spite of her popularity, however, voters who were worried about the economy defeated George Bush in 1992. Both she and her husband were extremely disappointed that he lost. Barbara Bush blamed the defeat in part on the press, contending that most journalists wanted Bill Clinton to win because he was "one of them—baby boomers." She said, "The overall experience has left a bad taste in my month about the media." That taste apparently is shared by the entire Bush family.

If Barbara Bush left the White House without making an impact on the institution of the Office of the First Lady, she still had shown how an adroit performer could use the position to advantage. Pictures of her cuddling an AIDS baby may have made more of an impact on public attitudes toward the disease than any number of position papers. Nevertheless, her refusal to speak up on issues because she did not want to disagree with her husband left journalists in an ethical bind.

In her autobiography, Barbara Bush came out clearly for abortion rights. Should journalists have tried harder to make her position known while she was in the White House? And what of her persona as a kindly grandmother? Toward the end of the Bushes' White House tenure, a few journalists began to write about another side of her personality, with *Vanity Fair* referring to her as a calculating politician. Although this point might be debatable, it raises the question of whether journalists should be surprised to find that the wife of a political figure has ideas of her own regarding political strategies. Why would this be considered unbecoming? What right do journalists have to look long and hard for personal flaws in a president's wife when it is obvious that all human beings have their weaknesses? Are they trying to hold her to stereotypical standards as her husband's helpmate? If so, are they belittling her role as well as the role of all wives?

A related issue is the degree to which it is defensible to

attempt to penetrate the private relationship of a president and a spouse. How important is the role of a president's wife in a democratic government? Why should eyebrows go up if she serves as an adviser to her husband? Should her projects and good works, carried out in part with federal tax dollars, be accepted at face value without some tangible effort to measure the effectiveness of their impact? Is she in the White House only as window dressing for her husband? Should she not be expected to wield some kind of power, even though it may be derived from her position as a wife? If she does have a measure of power, should her relationship with her husband be privileged, in the way that a lawyer/client relationship is privileged? But since taxpayers fund her office, should not she be held accountable, at least to some degree, to the public for what she does? Perhaps there are no clear answers, but such questions seem of more importance than a first lady's dress size and the nature of her wardrobe.

If Americans want a president's wife to be a queen, then they naturally crave details of her looks and deportment. If they want an associate president or at least are willing to accept a first lady who wishes to be one, then they need to address the degree to which she can be an autonomous individual. This issue confronted the American public and the news media that strives to represent it in striking terms during the tenure of Barbara Bush's successor, Hillary Rodham Clinton.

SEVEN

HILLARY RODHAM CLINTON
AS MEDIA POLARIZER

Few individuals in U.S. history, let alone first ladies, have polarized the public as thoroughly as Hillary Rodham Clinton, the wife of President Bill Clinton. Making history by being elected to public office in her own right upon leaving the White House, she deftly deflected criticism of her style and past conduct, standing out as a role model for feminists as well as a target for those who accused her of overstepping her bounds as a wife. Campaigning while still in the White House, she won a U.S. Senate seat from the state of New York in 2000, reaffirming herself as a potent force in the Democratic party and a possible candidate for the presidency in 2008 or 2012.

Her tenure as first lady from 1993 to 2001 was notable in many ways, some emblematic of achievements for women, others fraught with embarrassment. She was the first president's wife to hold an advanced degree and to have been a practicing attorney before moving into the White House from Arkansas, where her husband had been governor. She was the first president's wife to set up an office alongside her husband's advisers in the West Wing of the White House as well as to have her own office for social affairs in the East Wing, the traditional domain of the first lady's staff. She was the first president's wife to chair an important task force— one entrusted with reforming the nation's fragmented health care system; although the effort failed, it identified her as a key policymaker. She was the first president's wife to insist on the appointment of several women to top administration posts, including Donna Shalala as secretary of health and human services. And she was the first president's wife to serve as a global advocate for women, delivering an acclaimed speech on human rights in 1995 at the United Nations Conference on Women in Beijing.

Other Rodham Clinton "firsts" smacked of scandal. She was the first president's wife forced to come to her husband's defense during impeachment proceedings against him, involving charges of lying about his sexual relations during Oval Office trysts with a government intern, Monica Lewinsky. She was the first president's wife to have a close legal associate and friend commit suicide as Vincent Foster did in 1993 while working as a White House deputy counsel, raising questions about what knowledge he might have had of the Clintons' personal and business affairs. Accusations that files were removed from his office fueled speculation, which proved unfounded, that he had been murdered.

She also was the first president's wife to be subpoenaed before a grand jury, being required to testify about her role in a complicated Arkansas land development transaction known as Whitewater. She was the first president's wife accused of making money unethically in cattle futures trading. She was criticized for allegedly having profited as a lawyer from her relationship to her husband when he was governor of Arkansas. She was called a liar in connection with missing billing records from the Rose Law Firm in Little Rock, where she had been a partner before her husband's election as president. She faced disapproval in connection with the firing of seven White House travel office employees, who supporters said were unjustly dismissed. When she and her husband moved out of the White House, they were accused of taking furniture that critics said had been given to the nation, not to the Clintons personally. In each of these instances, she denied any impropriety or wrongdoing.

In addition, she faced questions about her image, which critics claimed she altered repeatedly for political motives. Her hairstyles and clothing received extensive attention as evidence of her views on femininity. She discarded headbands after being ridiculed for wearing them during the 1992 campaign and experimented with different ways of wearing her hair during her White House years. With her wardrobe varying from business and professional attire to ladylike outfits and glamorous evening gowns, some speculated that she downplayed her feminism as elections approached. When she wore a teal blue pantsuit for a television interview with Barbara Walters, the host who introduced her asked if it was not odd for a first lady to wear pants. Reflecting on the incident, Neel Lattimore, one of her press secretaries, said, "Mrs. Clinton never wore the 'pants' in the family, but she did reinforce the fact there is no such thing as a 'traditional' first lady—every first lady creates her own traditions." In her case, the creation of tradition seemed equated with generating more controversy than any predecessor, with the possible exception of Eleanor Roosevelt.

On all sides, Hillary Rodham Clinton, as she announced her name would be in the White House, drew both
acclaim and condemnation. When he took office, President
Clinton made no secret of the fact that she was one of his
chief advisers and that he valued her contribution to his administration. In doing so, he gave public recognition to the
wielding of power by a wife, which led to arguments over the
appropriate dimensions of the first lady's role. Many first
ladies had exercised power, some more publicly than others,
but even in the cases of Roosevelt and Rosalynn Carter, two
of the most politically active first ladies, few doubted that the
final decisions rested with their husbands. Hillary Rodham
Clinton's influence, in contrast, appeared to approach that of
a copresident at the start of Bill Clinton's presidency.

By extension, the debate over her role turned into a
heated argument on the proper place of women in society as
a whole. In her memoir, *Living History,* Hillary Rodham
Clinton said, "We were living in an era in which some people still felt deep ambivalence about women in positions of
public leadership and power. In this era of changing gender
roles, I was America's Exhibit A."

The news media occupied a key position in the battle
between her supporters and her detractors, with both sides
vying for publicity to support their views. Commentators
were divided into two camps. Those for her praised her as an
inspiring professional woman; those against her, including
conservative talk show hosts such as Rush Limbaugh, labeled
her a "femi-Nazi" and intimated she was a lesbian. When her
husband appointed her to head the President's Health Care
Task Force five days after his inauguration, Betty Winfield, a
journalism historian, noted that skeptical columnists argued

"she risk[ed] being accused of using her marriage as a route to advancement (a variation of the old woman-sleeps-her-way-to-the-top story)." On one hand, reports surfaced of discord at the White House, with stories of the first lady engaging in shouting matches, hurling a lamp, and arguing with her husband. On the other hand, the first lady was given high marks as the concerned mother of a teenage daughter (who had been declared off-limits to the press) and the witty, fun-loving employer of a loyal personal staff of about twenty headed by Margaret Ann "Maggie" Williams. The first African American to hold such a position, Williams was named a special assistant to the president, elevating the Office of the First Lady in the White House bureaucracy and making her Rodham Clinton's emissary at high-level meetings.

As the years went by, with Bill Clinton winning a second term in 1996, supporters said his wife served as a whipping boy (or, in this case, girl) for conservative political opponents. It was these opponents who backed Kenneth Starr, the special prosecutor appointed over Rodham Clinton's objections, to investigate Whitewater and, subsequently, the Lewinsky affair. Detractors, by contrast, claimed the media were biased in the first lady's favor, a contention that she denied, insisting "the reality was that the loudest and most effective voices in the media were anything but liberal."

In the midst of this controversy, members of the White House press corps found themselves sidelined, illustrating a decline in their importance to the field of political communication. Instead of holding periodic press conferences and/or developing close relationships with the reporters at hand, Hillary Rodham Clinton choose to go directly to the public via television programs and to make use of a new White House Web site set up by the Clinton administration to publicize her activities. She gave some interviews, but these were carefully rationed. To the dismay of Washington reporters, her first major interview was with Marian Burros, a food writer, perhaps, in Betty Caroli's words, "to temper talk of too much clout in a first lady." Run on the front page of the *New York Times* on February 1, 1993, the article featured the first lady's ban on smoking in the White House, the decision to return broccoli to the White House menu (the vegetable had been banished by President Bush, who disliked it), and domestic themes related to entertaining.

According to Rodham Clinton, she had no idea that the story and the picture accompanying it, which showed her in a hostess role wearing an off-the-shoulder black dress, would lead to divisive arguments. While critics surmised "the story was contrived to 'soften' my image," she wrote, "ardent defenders" wondered "if I was really worrying about floral centerpieces and the color of table linens, how could I be substantive enough to head a major policy effort?" She concluded, "It was becoming clear to me that people who wanted me to fit into a certain box, traditionalist or feminist, would never be entirely satisfied with me as me—which is to say, with my many different, and sometimes paradoxical, roles."

Wary of the journalistic sound bite and efforts to simplify rather than to explain complexity, she kept herself apart from most reporters. Her experience under the glare of national publicity during the 1992 campaign had not been a happy one. In *Living History,* she referred to the 1992 election and noted the "tricky, delicate and important relationship" between political candidates and reporters, adding, "I didn't fully understand it."

In the White House, her staff feared that she would be made a scapegoat by the news media. According to Lattimore, "There was a tremendous trust issue between the first lady's staff and the White House press corp. We often said that if a snowstorm hit Washington and the power went out all over town that the press would find some way to blame Mrs. Clinton." Another factor, he said, was the staff's limited knowledge of how journalists operated: "I think as a staff we were terribly inexperienced and none of us really had long-standing relationships with the reporters that were covering Mrs. Clinton." He added, "Also, it is important to remember that reporters and media organizations were not sure how to cover the first lady."

Hillary Rodham Clinton did not fit into the existing patterns of first lady coverage, generally reserved for lifestyle and feature sections. As Lattimore said, "Here was a first lady [who] was photographed and appeared on the front page of the *New York Times* wearing a beautiful sexy gown, hosting the governors to dinner, and the next day she was wearing a pants suit and touring a hospital and talking to doctors about health care reform." Depending on the angle taken, journalists depicted her variously as a saint, a sinner, a career woman, a wife, a mother, a presidential adviser, a political strategist, a feminist, a ruthless power behind the throne, a high-powered lawyer, a global advocate for women and children, a public policy expert, a health care reformer, a hostess, a religious believer, and a sex symbol (after she was photographed in a seductive pose for *Vogue* magazine wearing a clinging, black Donna Karan dress). She refused to be typecast in any particular role. To a greater extent than even the pathbreaking Eleanor Roosevelt, Hillary Rodham Clinton presented a challenge to reporters attempting to offer an accurate picture of a nontraditional first lady.

Presidents' wives customarily had been portrayed as symbolizing the heart, not the head, of an administration and were not the subject of news articles on governmental policy. Rodham Clinton, however, displayed a perplexing mixture of intellect and emotions and defied placement in any single re-portorial category. Were her activities mainly political or so-cial or symbolic? Should the scandals that dogged her be written off as dubious political intrigue or treated as subjects for serious investigative reporting? Should the stories of her husband's infidelities affect her own coverage? What reporters should be assigned to her? Women of her own age group, some of whom acknowledged they identified with her as a role model? Veteran political reporters? Fashion and feature writers? Where should stories about her be placed in news-papers? In main news columns or in lifestyle sections? Her skittishness in dealing with the Washington press corps, which included her decision to hold health care task force delibera-tions in secret, did not help matters.

She held only one full-scale White House press confer-ence—on April 22, 1994, a day when journalists were expect-ing the imminent death of former president Richard Nixon. Since she wore a pink sweater set and a black skirt, which could be interpreted as an attempt to soften her image, she noted the event was called the "Pink Press Conference." At the time, both she and her husband were under attack. A month earlier, the story had broken about her commodity trading; she also was being criticized on ethical grounds in connection with Whitewater and the travel office firings. And President Clinton had just been accused of sexual harassment by Paula Jones. In the opinion of Ann Blackman, a *Time* correspondent, the first lady did not give a particularly convincing performance. She said, "Hillary does not want to be challenged. I'm not sure she's guilty of anything, but she acts as if she is." With the death of Nixon that night, her news conference got relatively little news play.

Although Rodham Clinton promised to be more open with the press, she did not attempt to court either White House reporters or the Washington elite. Helen Thomas, whose years as a United Press International correspondent made her the dean of the White House press corps, tried for nearly six years before she got an actual interview with the first lady. In her autobiography, Thomas wrote that Rodham Clinton "would talk to the media but her press lunch guests were mainly columnists from outside Washington." Thomas said she was told by an aide that the first lady "was afraid of what Washington reporters will ask."

According to another reporter, Barbara Matusow, Rodham Clinton was engaged behind the scenes in a lot of the activities traditionally carried out by first ladies, "but I think she didn't want to paint herself that way." She said the first lady "did cooperate with me on a piece for *Washingtonian* magazine [a local lifestyle publication] about her style of entertaining, and she posed in front of a doorway with tables set up for guests, looking very lovely." According to Matusow, "There was part of her that wanted to show that she was a regular woman and ... I actually think she did care about the color of the napkins but that wasn't the role she relished the best." Matusow said she "saw herself doing important policy work, which meant more to her."

In 1998, when the Helen Thomas interview finally took place, Rodham Clinton told the reporter she had learned that to cope with the pressure of White House life, "you have to fall back on the most basic values that you were raised with." In her case, they were values rooted in the Methodist Church and derived from her upbringing by mid-westerners who believed in hard work, education, and deter-mination to overcome obstacles. The brilliant daughter of a businessman and a homemaker, she grew up in Park Ridge, Illinois, a middle-class Chicago suburb.

After graduating from Wellesley College, where she was the first student selected to give a commencement speech, she entered Yale Law School. Concerned with legal issues af-fecting disadvantaged children, she interned with Marian Wright Edelman of the Children's Defense Fund and worked for her in Boston after graduating in 1973. In addi-tion, she was employed for several months as a staff attorney for the congressional committee considering impeachment proceedings against President Nixon in the wake of Water-gate. Theoretical work that she did on children's rights would be used against her in later years.

A chance encounter in the Yale Law Library with Bill Clinton, a classmate from Arkansas with political aspirations, resulted in a romance that took precedence over her career plans in the East. Against the advice of friends, she moved to Arkansas in 1974 to be with Clinton and taught at the Uni-versity of Arkansas Law School. The couple married in 1975, but she kept her maiden name and joined the prominent Rose Law Firm in Little Rock. Their only child, Chelsea, was born in 1980.

After Clinton won his first bid to be governor, the couple was shocked when he was defeated for a second term in 1980. When she learned that one of the reasons was perceived voter unhappiness with her bookish appearance and insistence on using her own name, Hillary Rodham quickly took his name and spruced up her wardrobe to present a more feminine image to the public. Bill Clinton went on to win five more elections, even though allegations of philandering were raised against him.

As Hillary Rodham Clinton advanced at the Rose firm, she became the family's chief breadwinner. Taking charge of the family finances, she made a profit of $100,000 from an initial investment of $1,000 in cattle futures trading, with the help of an experienced investor. The Clintons also joined two friends, James and Susan McDougal (who had connections with a failing concern, Madison Guaranty Savings and Loan), in the Whitewater Development Company, set up to invest in land for resale, although the proposed development was not a success. These financial activities led to investigations that plagued the Clintons on their road to the White House.

During her husband's tenure as governor, Hillary Rodham Clinton continued to be a practicing attorney of considerable stature, being named to the list of "100 Most Influential Lawyers in America." She also served on corporate boards, including that of Wal-Mart. At the same time, she was involved in Bill Clinton's gubernatorial campaigns and in policy matters at the state level. As governor, Clinton appointed her to chair a committee to reform public schools. Her efforts resulted in legislation to raise school standards.

When Bill Clinton decided to seek the Democratic presidential nomination in 1992, conservatives backing President George H. W. Bush, the Republican candidate for reelection, cited their commitment to traditional family values. They aimed their fire at both Clintons. They attacked Bill Clinton on grounds of having extramarital relations and his wife on grounds of holding liberal ideas related to her early legal interests. As news of Bill Clinton's alleged liaison with Gennifer Flowers, a nightclub singer, circulated, his wife saved his candidacy by stepping forward to show forgiveness and support.

She sat beside her husband on January 26, 1992, when he appeared for an interview on CBS's *Sixty Minutes,* in an effort to downplay the harmful effects of a story in the *Star,* a supermarket tabloid. The story alleged Bill Clinton, while governor, had carried on a twelve-year affair with Flowers. Although Clinton did not say whether he had committed adultery, he admitted having caused pain in his marriage. Hillary Clinton suddenly spoke up after the interviewer commented that the couple must have come to a marital "arrangement." She said heatedly, "I'm not sitting here— some little woman standing by my man like Tammy Wynette. I'm sitting here because I love him, and I honor what we've been through together. And, you know, if that's not enough for people, then heck, don't vote for him." Although she was forced to apologize to Wynette, a country-western singer, and her fans for what appeared to be a belittling reference to the singer's popular song "Stand by Your Man," Hillary Clinton's loyalty enabled Bill Clinton to stay in the race and win the nomination.

A few weeks later came a more infamous remark, one that was to haunt her for years and provoke hostility from wives who did not work outside the home, particularly after the comment was widely repeated on conservative radio talk shows. Denying a charge from a primary opponent of her husband that the Rose Law Firm had improperly benefited from her marriage to the governor, she told a reporter on March 16: "I suppose I could have stayed home and baked cookies and had teas, but what I decided to do was fulfill my profession, which I entered before my husband was in public life. And I've worked very, very hard to be as careful as possible, and that's all I can tell you." The first part of her statement—"I could have stayed home and baked cookies and had teas"—was immediately picked up by the news media.

She quickly tried to issue a clarification, stating, "The work that I have done as a professional, a public advocate, has been aimed . . . to assure that women can make the choices . . . whether it's full-time career, full-time motherhood or some combination." But CNN and other news organizations continued to reduce her remark to "I could have stayed home and baked cookies and had teas." In response, as the Democratic convention approached in July, she was said to "soften" her image. Emphasizing her domestic side, she participated in a good-natured cookie bakeoff contest sponsored by *Family Circle* magazine that pitted her chocolate chip cookie recipe against that of the first lady, Barbara Bush. In May, however, Barbara Bush's staff had demanded that she apologize (which she did) for alleging in a *Vanity Fair* interview that George Bush had a mistress, a story she contended the press was reluctant to probe.

During the election campaign, Republicans criticized positions Hillary Clinton had taken on family law issues before moving to Arkansas. Richard Bond, chair of the Republican National Committee, castigated reports on legal theory that she had written for the Carnegie Council on Children as radical cant that undermined the family unit. Pouncing on her abstract argument that children should have the same rights in court as their parents, he charged she was a "law-suit mongering feminist who likened marriage to slavery and encouraged children to sue their parents." Another critic was Richard Nixon, the disgraced former president, who declared in the pages of the *New York Times* that Bill Clinton was unlikely to be elected because his wife was too bright. Voters, he said, would not accept a man whose wife was "too strong and too intelligent." Opponents also looked askance at her work on the board of the nonprofit Legal Services Corporation, to which she had been appointed by President Jimmy Carter. The federally funded organization, set up to assist indigents, had provided legal aid for some controversial causes such as sex-change operations and Native American land claims in the state of Maine.

When Clinton was elected president in 1992, Hillary Rodham Clinton, like her husband, was still smarting from the effects of the bitter campaign, which had seen her denigrated in print as well as broadcast media. Conservative magazines caricatured her appearance viciously and attacked her with headlines such as "HILLARY FROM HELL." The *New York Times* commented that between January and September

1992, numerous articles in major publications made some comparison between her and Lady MacBeth.

Not comfortable with reporters, she tried to ignore the Washington press corps, even when she was in the midst of pushing her complicated health care reform proposal, which desperately needed public understanding and backing. She had little awareness of how journalists could be involved in efforts to build consensus, and she insisted on barring the public and press from task force meetings instead of seeking coverage that might have produced constructive feedback. Her preference for secrecy led to litigation that eventually reached a federal appeals court. The court held the first lady was, in effect, a government employee and consequently not bound to abide by laws forbidding advisory groups from meeting behind closed doors. The ruling was the first that established a legal basis for the position of the first lady.

Rodham Clinton's reticence to deal with Washington reporters frustrated Martha Sherrill, who was assigned to cover the first lady for the *Washington Post* in 1993. When Sherrill finally got an interview, she found her "warm and folksy but at the same time sort of preachy. . . . A mix of Bible and ancient wisdom. . . . She wasn't telling us who she was or what sort of first lady she wanted to be." Sherrill said reporters "ended up writing about her clothes and her hair, because that's all we had."

Later, Rodham Clinton saw that her aloofness had been a bad idea, telling Helen Thomas that if she had it to do over again, "I would try to learn more about what the press expected of me, because I really didn't understand that at all. . . . So my lack of experience in that area of public opinion and press coverage is something that I had to learn the hard way." But at the time, Thomas said, "she gave the impression that she neither needed nor cared for any kind of advice." Perhaps this was because she had been received so warmly on Capitol Hill as the first lady when she went there to testify on health care that she pressed forward blindly with an elaborate plan to give health coverage to all Americans.

Ultimately, she was outmaneuvered by the insurance interests that ran "Harry and Louise" commercials on television, effectively attacking her proposal by portraying average Americans fearing it might cause them to lose existing benefits. The reform effort died on Capitol Hill in 1994. As a result, Thomas said, the first lady was held responsible for votes by "angry white males" in the November 1994 election that "gave Republicans control of both houses of Congress for the first time in forty years."

She never held another policymaking post in her husband's administration, although she continued to be extremely active, speaking and writing on issues of particular concern to women and children in the United States and abroad and promoting breast cancer awareness. On September 5, 1995, she delivered a stirring address on human rights at the United Nations Conference on Women in Beijing, criticizing China and other countries for human rights violations regarding women. This was the first of many trips that established her as a global women's rights advocate. According to Lattimore, she visited more countries than any other first lady.

Maureen Santini, no longer covering the White House but observing the first lady from afar, saw Hillary Rodham Clinton's reluctance to meet the Washington press corps as reflecting indecision on how to present herself as the president's wife. Santini said, "Hillary Clinton tested a new model of first lady prematurely—before she'd had time to learn the ropes herself at the White House—and it didn't take." Santini continued, "After her first major defeat over health care reform, she retreated a bit and from then on obviously spent a lot of time and energy trying to be herself without incurring the wrath of the public." In Santini's view, "It may have annoyed her when her changing hair styles received attention but in a sense each new hairdo represented a new attempt to figure how to fit into the role and still be herself."

Rodham Clinton appeared uncomfortable with media attention that highlighted her personality or analyzed her attempts at defining herself, preferring, as she said in *Living History,* "to convey my thoughts and opinions directly to the public." Following in the footsteps of Eleanor Roosevelt, the first lady launched her own chatty syndicated newspaper column in the summer of 1995. Her weekly "Talking It Over" column, however, never hit a consistent tone or attained the popularity of her predecessor's "My Day" column. According to Mandy Grunwald, a close adviser, Rodham Clinton gave up on reporters because she "wanted them to focus on substance and they wrote only psychobabble pieces about her." Kati Marton attributed this to her misunderstanding of her times, not realizing that voters in the 1990s cared less about policy and projects than about character and personality.

Rodham Clinton's appearance in different types of attire, as well as different hairdos, led to continual coverage in terms of her image. Was she trying to appear less assertive, more appealing, more glamorous, and younger than before? What kind of statement was she trying to communicate? Lattimore said simply, "She changed her hair because she liked to." Her various outfits highlighted diverse aspects of the lives of today's women as wives, mothers, hostesses, and professional women, he noted: "The bottom line is that Mrs. Clinton was not very different than most working women [although] she was terribly aware of the image associated with being the first lady and when traveling overseas always dressed in a fashion that was respectful and stylish."

Unlike the presidential couples who preceded them, Hillary Rodham Clinton and Bill Clinton represented the baby boomers, members of the generation born after World War II. They modeled a new type of political marriage, with the wife being a well-educated professional and her spouse's equal, not his subordinate. Talk even emerged of a copresidency. Their model could have been expected to appeal to a nation of two-income families accustomed to both parents bringing home paychecks. By 1986, when the Clintons' daughter, Chelsea, started grade school, more than 50 percent of mothers with school-age children held a job. In the case of the Clintons, however, the model turned into a symbol of discordant gender relationships.

When Bill Clinton campaigned for president in 1992, he told his supporters, "Buy one, get one free!" Never before had a presidential candidate been so open about the advisory role that he expected his wife to play. Although there was some initial criticism on grounds of nepotism, much of the public responded positively to her appointment as head of the health care task force. Mainstream magazines loved her— she appeared in attractive photographs on the covers of *Time, Newsweek, U.S. News & World Report,* the *New York Times Magazine,* the *Los Angeles Times Magazine, People, Vogue,*

Mirabella, Parade, TV Guide, Redbook, Family Circle, and *Good Housekeeping,* with headlines such as "SAINT HILLARY" or "ASCENT OF A WOMAN." The press gave attention to a speech she made at the University of Texas, calling for a new "politics of meaning" with religious overtones. At the end of the first year of the Clinton administration, her poll standings ran well ahead of her husband's, with 62 percent approval for her performance as first lady compared to 48 percent approval of the job the president was doing. Conservative opponents, meanwhile, kept up a barrage of criticism.

Then the tide of mainstream support turned. Allegations of improprieties in the Whitewater affair resurfaced in news coverage after the suicide of Vince Foster, which set off rumors of foul play. In the spring of 1994, Michael Barone, of *U.S. News & World Report,* charged that journalists had tended to go easy on the first lady. He said many journalists were strong believers in feminism, did not want to attack a president's wife, and were not holding her "to the same standard as other people in public life." Health care reform flopped, and Democrats lost in the midterm elections.

In January 1995, a journalistic brouhaha developed when Rodham Clinton invited eleven women journalists, all of whom wrote gossip and advice columns along with traditional articles on first ladies' entertaining and fashions, to lunch at the White House. The *New York Times* carried a front-page story on the event on January 10. Headlined "HILLARY CLINTON SEEKING TO SOFTEN A HARSH IMAGE," the story by Marian Burros began: "Saying that she is eager to present herself in a more likable way, Hillary Rodham Clinton said today she had been 'naïve and dumb' about national politics and was to blame for the failure of the health care overhaul plan last year." The White House demanded an apology on grounds Burros had reported off-the-record remarks.

Burros claimed she had not violated any rules, but other reporters present agreed she had. Cindy Adams, a *New York Post* gossip columnist, said the story was particularly unfair because the previous week, Connie Chung, a CBS anchor, improperly had broadcast a comment by the mother of Newt Gingrich, the Republican Speaker of the House, that her son called the first lady a "bitch." Adams told the *Washington Post,* "Connie zapped her last week, and the *Times* is sandbagging her this week." The *Post*'s own story on the luncheon quoted the first lady as saying, "Sometimes I read stories or hear things about me and I go, 'Ugh! I wouldn't like her either.'"

Worse news coverage was to come. The surprising discovery at the White House of billing records from the Rose Law Firm conveyed an impression that Rodham Clinton might have been hiding them from the Whitewater grand jury, an allegation she denied. In addition, a memorandum turned up identifying her as responsible for the travel office firings. In January 1996, she was subpoenaed to appear before the grand jury in connection with the work she had done at the Rose firm for Madison Guaranty. William Safire, in his *New York Times* column, called her a "congenital liar." As conservative commentators, particularly on talk radio, tore further into her credibility, she sank lower in the polls. In June 1996, only 29 percent of the public surveyed in the joint CBS/*New York Times* poll expressed a favorable opinion, whereas 38 percent had an unfavorable impression.

At the same time, Bob Woodward, half of the famous

Woodward-Bernstein reporting team credited with exposing Watergate, revealed that the first lady, hurt by the health care fiasco and long interested in spiritual matters, had met in the White House with a New Age psychic philosopher, Jean Houston. According to Woodward, Houston led "reflective meditation" sessions in the spring of 1995, persuading the first lady to enact conversations with Eleanor Roosevelt and Mahatma Gandhi. Rodham Clinton denied that these sessions were séances, but they made the first lady an even more tempting target for media ridicule.

The White House said that Houston's primary role was to assist the first lady with her book *It Takes a Village and Other Lessons Children Teach Us,* which dealt with child rearing from a family and community viewpoint. In the book, she expressed her reservations about divorce. Published in 1996, the work became a best seller. It may have been a factor in causing her poll ratings to rebound as the 1996 presidential campaign intensified and after Bill Clinton was reelected.

Betty Winfield viewed coverage of Hillary Rodham Clinton as a "conflict story about the strange new species of political wife," which came at a time when the American press was "seeking an up-to-date coverage plan for this kind of postmodern woman." In Winfield's view, the press floundered about, and she said it set a "dangerous (and unfair) national cognitive connection between wrongdoing and the Clintons."

By the end of 1998, the year of the Lewinsky scandal, Hillary Rodham Clinton was popular again. Her ratings stood as high as they had been following the 1993 inauguration, with 67 percent of the public holding a favorable opinion of her. Ironically, Rodham Clinton's approval ratings went up in response to her conformity to a stereotypical feminine role. They reflected approval of her conduct as an aggrieved wife once again standing by her flawed husband. On January 21, 1998, the news broke that Special Prosecutor Starr was investigating her husband's sexual relationship with an intern, later identified as Monica Lewinsky, to determine whether the president had urged her to lie to cover up the affair. Rodham Clinton appeared on television expressing surprise and shock, but then she counterattacked by claiming the Clintons were victims of a "vast right-wing conspiracy" that included Starr, a "politically motivated" special counsel.

As Barbara Burrell, a public opinion researcher, noted, "Her image as the wronged wife staying in her marriage, however, was quite contrary to the image of the independent, professional achiever role she had adopted as first lady." She won sympathy by surmounting her personal pain and reaffirming values held by many traditionally minded Americans. Lattimore said, "People either thought she should have left the President or admired her for staying with the President. What few people understood was the role Mrs. Clinton's religious faith played in the healing process and how much she loved the President."

Interestingly, her poll ratings began to decline as soon as it became evident she would shatter precedent and seek political office in her own right. Eleven months before Bill Clinton's second term ended, Rodham Clinton announced that she would be a Democratic candidate for the U.S. Senate from New York. She said she would continue to serve as first lady too, and so she did, although she spent far more time raising money and campaigning in New York than in the

White House. Critics charged that her decision to run raised ethical concerns, saying it was hard to tell where the role of first lady, financed at taxpayer expense, ended and that of a candidate began. According to Dick Morris, a former White House adviser, Bill Clinton, in gratitude for her remaining with him, fixed his presidential power "on a solitary objective: electing Hillary."

As a candidate, Rodham Clinton was covered by a group of women reporters who found that she stuck to her campaign message without fail and was personally pleasant but still kept the journalists at arm's length. Beth J. Harpaz of the Associated Press attributed this situation to "her first lady trappings and her reserved personality." In the end, Rodham Clinton won a hotly fought contest in November 2000, and she has since announced that she intends to seek reelection in 2006. She is also thought to be considering a bid for the Democratic presidential nomination in 2008. Her successful pursuit of a Senate seat, particularly from a state where she had never lived until she decided to run for office, gives her a strong claim to being the most multifaceted and enigmatic first lady in U.S. history. To many in the media, she has been a flash point for national divisiveness.

The challenges that Hillary Rodham Clinton, a high-profile lawyer, faced in gaining public acceptance as first lady were greater than those confronting her more traditional predecessors. Even though she did not continue her legal career in the White House, her previous professional life opened the door for political attacks. When Kenneth Starr finally presented his report, the Clintons were exonerated in the Whitewater transaction. Impeachment charges were brought against President Clinton in connection with the

Lewinsky affair, but he was acquitted. If he returns to the White House as first gentleman, it will be interesting to see if he is given a policymaking post in the Hillary Rodham Clinton administration.

As first lady, Rodham Clinton was both idealized as a shining example of an independent woman and vilified as a power-mad consort, accused of overarching ambition that negated feminine nature. Historian Lewis Gould noted that she was a "first lady who took the institution to new levels of power and public controversy" as one of the "most loved and most hated presidential wives in American history." Winfield said one unexplored issue was whether "Americans— especially older male journalists—can accept a President's wife as an equal partner." Presumably, Rodham Clinton's election to the Senate proved that at least some Americans can, but the final answer to the question probably rests on whether she becomes a presidential candidate in her own right. If she is elected, the question then will be whether the country can accept a president's husband on the same terms.

EIGHT

LAURA BUSH AS EMBLEM OF NATIONAL CARING

If ever a first lady has personified the "heart" aspect of the American presidency, it is Laura Bush. With her serene demeanor and interest in children, she has epitomized the traditional family values lauded by her husband, President George W. Bush. His election in 2000, followed by reelection in 2004, restored the Republican party to the White House after his father, former president George H. W. Bush, was defeated in his campaign for a second term in 1992. With the two Bushes being the only father-son presidential team in history except for John and John Quincy Adams, the news media heralded a Bush dynasty comparable to those of the Roosevelt, Adams, and Kennedy families. Initially, the strong woman of the Bush dynasty seemed to be Barbara Bush, not Laura, a quiet former elementary school teacher and librarian.

On assuming the role of first lady, Laura Bush designated the noncontroversial areas of education and reading as her projects, in keeping with her husband's election promise to restore dignity to the White House after the Clinton scandals. Her role as a figure of strength and reassurance emerged only after the September 11, 2001, terrorist attacks on New York and Washington, affirming the vast potential importance of the first lady's position, particularly during perilous times. As the nation reeled from the destruction at the World Trade Center and Pentagon, Laura Bush—in person, print, and broadcast—stood out as the heart-warming counterpart to a militant George W. Bush in his role as commander in chief of the nation's armed forces.

Conveying a sense of both grieving and resilience, she "transformed her image," as *Us Weekly* put it, "from the behind-the-scenes presidential wife most comparable to Mamie Eisenhower to the nation's comforter-in-chief." She offered consolation via television, including an appearance on *The Oprah Winfrey Show*. She visited attack victims, attended memorial services, and was photographed steadily walking hand in hand with her husband, presenting a picture, according to the *Washington Post,* of "nurturing the nation." She was the "one member of the administration who offer[ed] quiet words of reassurance and empathy," the *Post* said, "while the President and his key aides use[d] the harsh rhetoric of war."

In short, she exhibited the dignified, womanly behavior associated with maternal caring and concern for human welfare. She struck a tone that resonated well in a stricken nation and proved her to be a major asset to her husband. Apparently motivated by no other goal than to reach out to others, she showed herself in command of her emotions and called on Americans to rally themselves.

In a speech to the National Press Club two months following the attack, she answered a question first asked by

Larry McQuillan of *USA TODAY* immediately after the horrific event: "What do you say to children?" "What I said then, and what I have said in nearly every interview since," the first lady stated, "is that we need to reassure our children that they are safe in their homes and schools. . . . We can turn off the television and spend time reading to our children. We can give them the gift of our time and attention."

She spoke movingly of her visits to classrooms, her church attendance with her husband at Camp David, and incidents of renewed patriotism and concern for others witnessed in her travels. She referred to God, country, and family, quoting from Psalm 27: "Your face, Lord, do I seek. I believe that I shall see the goodness of the Lord in the land of the living." That, she said, "[is] what has happened. We are seeing goodness throughout our land." A friend had reminded her, she noted, that "I had the great opportunity to reach a large audience and help them. . . . Helping others does make us feel good."

Her address to the National Press Club was her longest public speech up to that point. The third first lady to speak at a club luncheon, following Rosalynn Carter and Eleanor Roosevelt, she spoke for thirty minutes and took questions. She wowed a tough audience of Washington journalists and public relations professionals, impressed by her pose and humor. Asked whether she would write a book, Laura Bush responded that it would depend on "whether or not I can get that $8 million advance or whatever it is," a laughing reference to the amount given Hillary Rodham Clinton for *Living History,* her memoir. Someone else asked about her disagreements with her husband. A Democrat before her marriage, she had made a one-sentence statement on NBC's

Today show on inauguration eve saying she favored abortion rights, unlike her husband, although she agreed with him on the need to reduce abortions by "teaching abstinence." She finessed the subject at the press club by stating, "One thing about politics for sure is you nearly always have an opponent, so it doesn't have to be your spouse."

Her advice on comforting children had been given earlier on five television networks when she told anchors that parents ought to turn off their sets, eat meals with their children, and read them bedtime stories. The advice paralleled that offered in open letters to schoolchildren sent under her name to state school superintendents across the country, for distribution to children in middle and elementary schools. She told middle school children to talk about their emotions with parents, teachers, and counselors and younger children to express themselves by drawing pictures to share with "the adults in your life."

The success of the press club speech prompted Ellen Goodman, the Pulitzer Prize–winning feminist columnist, to suggest Laura Bush "take on some work more tangible than up-lifter in chief." She called on her to go "beyond her comforting and comfort zone" and pointed out that first ladies who "take on a powerful and public responsibility . . . go down in history as the great first ladies." There was reason to believe Laura Bush might be heading in that direction.

Less than two weeks after the press club speech, she became the first president's wife to give an entire Saturday presidential radio address; her predecessors Nancy Reagan, Hillary Rodham Clinton, and Barbara Bush had participated in the broadcasts but not as the sole speaker. Laura Bush delivered a solo address that newspapers said reflected both her elevated role in national affairs since September 11 and the Republican party's effort to court more women. She stressed that military action against al Qaeda terrorists, held responsible for the September 11 attacks, would benefit women and children.

In the speech, broadcast on November 17 from the Bush ranch in Crawford, Texas, the first lady applauded what she called "a worldwide effort to focus on the brutality against women and children by the al Qaeda terrorist network and the regime it supports in Afghanistan, the Taliban." The broadcast came six weeks after her husband authorized the bombing of Afghanistan to bring down the regime. It preceded a White House reception for a group of Afghan professional women who had fled repression under the Taliban.

Ann Gerhart, a *Washington Post* staff writer who covers Laura Bush and also has written her biography, described her moving beyond the "comforter-in-chief" role as she asked Americans to contribute to an Afghan children's school fund and traveled alone to Paris, Budapest, and Prague to broadcast the first Radio Free Europe address to Afghanistan. During her trip, she also spoke out against the recruitment of young people as suicide bombers in the Middle East but added diplomatically, "All of us in the world need to urge both of them—the Palestinians and the Israelis—to try to stop the violence and come to the table."

At the same time, according to Gerhart, the first lady "became more deft at avoiding what she did not want to say as a public figure, if it might conflict in even the smallest way with official United States positions." She was careful not to criticize the status of women in Saudi Arabia, a key U.S. ally.

She avoided saying whether she agreed or disagreed with the administration's refusal to release $34 million in contributions to the United Nations Population Fund, alleged to be allied with forced abortions in China.

Back in the United States, she returned to her signature issue of promoting education. On January 25, 2002, she became only the fourth first lady to testify before Congress, speaking to the Senate Education Committee on the need for early childhood education; her predecessor, Senator Hillary Rodham Clinton, was a rapt listener. Her testimony had been scheduled on the morning of September 11 but was postponed when the Secret Service rushed her away after receiving word of hijacked airplanes flying into the World Trade Center. The Democratic chairman of the Education Committee, Massachusetts senator Edward Kennedy, had spoken at an early childhood education summit hosted by the first lady at Georgetown University the previous summer. He endorsed her support of education reform legislation signed by President Bush earlier in the month, praising her "skillful advocacy."

In the wake of the attacks of September 11, Laura Bush had proven herself more than equal to a position she had not particularly wanted—that of first lady. Her picture on the cover sold Middle America magazines such as *People, Good Housekeeping, Reader's Digest,* and *Ladies' Home Journal;* her appearance with her husband on a Barbara Walters special featuring the White House Christmas decorations brought ABC's *20/20* program its highest rating for the month; and a USA TODAY/CNN poll at the end of 2001 gave her favorable ratings of 77 percent, about the same as her husband's.

Yet it seemed questionable that she would go down in

history as taking on the "powerful and public responsibility" that Goodman had advocated. On the eve of the invasion of Iraq in 2003, she told an interviewer, "I know my husband, and I have every confidence that he will do what's best for our country." She canceled a White House poetry event for fear some poets would use it to oppose President Bush's policies on the war in Iraq. When she appeared on the *Today* show in August 2004 to tone down the president's blunt remark that the war on terrorism could not be won, one columnist said while Barbara Bush occasionally "spoke her own mind, this Mrs. Bush speaks her husband's mind."

As George W. Bush put it, "I have the best wife for the line of work that I'm in. She doesn't try to steal the limelight." The story of the Bush marriage, as told in women's magazines, has an engaging plot: shy librarian meets wild young heir of a powerful political dynasty and settles him down so he can live up to expectations. Without his wife, it seemed unlikely that he ever would have become president.

Both Laura and George Bush grew up in Midland, Texas, a wealthy oil town, although they did not meet there until married friends introduced them at a backyard barbecue in August 1977. Within three months, they were married. Laura Bush, thirty-one and eager to have a family, left her job as a librarian at a predominantly Hispanic school in Austin. George Bush, also thirty-one, with a reputation for hard drinking and womanizing, hoped to follow his father in politics and knew he needed a wife. He was attracted to her looks, personality, and intelligence but said later the hardest decision he ever made was to get married. Presumably, that decision signaled the end of his riotous bachelor days.

Back-slapping George Bush said he found his wife

"one of the great listeners. And since I am one of the big talkers, it was a great fit." She never lost her self-possession. Barbara Bush recalled that her daughter-in-law, when asked what she did by George's aristocratic grandmother at the Bush family compound in Kennebunkport, Maine, replied, "I read, I smoke and I admire." A smoker since high school, she says she has given up the habit, but according to Gerhart, still has a cigarette "when she is among friendly troops." She is an avid reader, and one of her favorite novels is Dostoevsky's *The Brothers Karamazov,* a complicated psychological analysis of good versus evil.

As a teenager, George Bush moved with his family to Houston and attended a private New England prep school, Andover, before graduating from Yale University, where he distinguished himself in fraternity life if not scholarship. He received a master's degree in business administration from Harvard University in 1975. After Harvard, he returned to Midland to learn the oil business, like his father, from the ground up. Laura Bush, the introverted daughter of a builder and a homemaker who kept her husband's books, went to public school in Midland and to Southern Methodist University, where she obtained a degree in elementary education. She taught primary grades for two years before obtaining a master's degree in library science from the University of Texas in Austin in 1972. This makes her the second president's wife to have an advanced degree, following Hillary Rodham Clinton with her law degree.

As newlyweds, the Bushes honeymooned by campaigning together during George Bush's unsuccessful bid for Congress, when, his wife said, he broke the first promise he ever made to her—that she wouldn't have to give a campaign speech. Both of them were overjoyed at the birth of twin girls, Barbara and Jenna, in 1981 after an exceptionally difficult pregnancy. Gerhart said Laura Bush loved the girls so much that she was reluctant to set limits for them. After news media reported the twins were cited for underage drinking violations during their father's first term as president, the first lady spoke up with unusual passion on CNN. She accused the media of profit-driven exploitation of her children, saying the twins, both college students, should be "left totally alone."

When he was forty, George Bush gave up drinking, much to his wife's relief, but she denied the story that she told him it was "either me or Jack Daniel's." Her husband, who had joined her Methodist church in Midland, also became a "born-again Christian" and proclaimed his faith in language familiar to that of the religious Right, but he did not demand that she do the same. After selling his failing company for a huge profit, which critics alleged was due to his family connections, and working in his father's campaign for president in 1988, Bush headed a group that bought the Texas Rangers baseball team.

This move set him up to win the governorship of Texas, paving his way to the White House—and forcing Laura Bush to disclose a devastating teenage tragedy, which she previously had not mentioned openly. At seventeen, driving her parents' car, she had run a stop sign and hit another car, killing a high school student who had been her boyfriend. No charges were brought. She said in an interview with *Oprah* magazine, "It was a terrible thing to be responsible for an accident. . . . But at some point I had to accept that death is a part of life." She also had to accept the spotlight that went with politics, a friend told *Newsweek,* because "she loves her husband and this is what he does." As the governor's wife, she sponsored the successful Texas Book Festival, and as first lady, she has sponsored the National Book Festival in Washington.

In anticipation of the 2004 election, the Bushes gave an interview to the *Ladies' Home Journal,* foreshadowing campaign rhetoric to come. The president did most of the talking, saying that the United States was using its military might so "the guilty must fear, which makes it more likely that we'll win the war on terror and more likely the world will be peaceful." His wife spoke of the need for "saying we love you to the people we love and making time for family and for children."

During the campaign itself, USA TODAY reported Laura Bush was "considered such political gold that she's featured in most of President Bush's TV ads." Her favorable/unfavorable poll rating, according to the newspaper, stood at a glowing 74 percent versus 16 percent. By contrast, the rating of the outspoken Teresa Heinz Kerry, the wife of Bush's Democrat opponent, Senator John Kerry, was only lukewarm: 40 percent versus 34 percent, with a sizable segment undecided. The poll also showed that 53 percent of voters considered a spouse to be at least "somewhat" important in "considering which presidential candidate to vote for." In the close election, Laura Bush—conveying affection for her husband and, by extension, her fellow citizens with a set campaign speech sometimes repeated several times a day—may well have been the deciding factor.

As she began a second four-year term in the White House, Laura Bush, having discreetly slimmed down to a size six and patronizing fashionable designers, was not concerned she might be caricatured, in the words of the *New York Times,* "as too pretty, too perfect, too plastic to be true." She said, "I'm not trying to let people get to know me or whatever." Nevertheless, her depiction, like that of her White House predecessors, raises troubling questions about the coverage of both presidents' wives and American women more broadly as factors in political life. Lionized, trivialized, and occasionally demonized, first ladies can be used as a case study of societal attitudes toward women as reinforced by media bias.

---◇---

NINE

LOOKING AHEAD

Example (from the *New York Times,* February 7, 2005): A picture three and one-half columns wide of three individuals staring at the camera, appearing on page A16 of the national edition. The man in the middle has a medal around his neck and is standing close to the other man, who is dressed in a well-tailored suit and looks very distinguished. The woman is off to the side, wearing a stylish dress and a necklace of (probably real) pearls along with a lovely smile. The caption under the picture gives the names of the two men, President Bush and novelist Tom Wolfe. The woman's name is not mentioned.

The relatively large picture, nearly five inches in length and more than seven inches wide, appears inside a box to set it off from the rest of the page. The box also contains a sixteen-paragraph news feature on President Bush's reading preferences, set in two columns topped by a one-line italic headline, "*BUSH'S OFFICIAL READING LIST, AND A RACY OMIS-SION*"; that headline is placed under a "kicker—a short head-line leading into the main one that identifies the writer,

Elisabeth Bumiller, and the general subject, "WHITE HOUSE LETTER." Bush and Wolfe are quoted repeatedly in the sixteen paragraphs. The woman is not named at all, although in the eighth paragraph, there is a passing reference to "the first lady."

Example (from the *Washington Post*, February 9, 2005, A3): A news story, also in a box, on Laura Bush's visit to a "hardscrabble" elementary school in Baltimore to promote a community-based program aimed at helping deprived children, particularly boys, "avoid self-destructive choices." The story is accompanied by a fairly small picture (three inches long and four inches wide) of a beautifully dressed Laura Bush and a little African American boy. She is named; he is not. The ninth paragraph of the story reports that the effort is "nominally headed" by the first lady, whose name and title are given initially in the first paragraph. There is no explanation of who the actual head of the program is or what it means to be a "nominal" head.

Example (from MSNBC.com, February 3, 2005): Transcript of an interview by Brian Williams, anchor and managing editor of NBC's *Nightly News,* with Laura Bush. She is asked whether a new government program to curb gang violence originated with her or with her husband and whether she is "ready for the work this represents." She does not answer directly but says that she is "very interested in the work" and that "I hope I'm ready for it." Williams asks no follow-up question. He quickly moves on to talk about the "emotion" expressed in response to the president's state of the union speech and then asks if President Bush watches television news and if the couple "watch together at all in the evening."

These examples illustrate the way the news media, consciously or unconsciously, promote a stereotypical treatment of one of the most visible women in American life, the wife of the president of the United States. The first example shows how she is ignored, the second example shows how her activities are trivialized, and the third example shows how she is seen as important only as in relation to her husband. In actuality, her position, though ill defined, paradoxical, and confusing, has become increasingly important in the U.S. political system, particularly during campaigns. Yet the news media tend to ignore her except as a celebrity political wife whose status is derived totally from her husband and consequently not worth thoughtful coverage.

In the *New York Times* example, Laura Bush was not even given the dignity of being named as one of the three persons in the photograph used to illustrate her husband's interest in reading. Perhaps editors assumed it was not necessary to identify her because readers already know who she is and are aware that, as a former school librarian, she has urged more attention to books. If so, there would be little rationale for identifying George W. Bush either, since readers could be assumed to know who he is also. The caption said that President Bush was reading a new book, *I Am Charlotte Simmons,* by the novelist Tom Wolfe, pictured in the center.

Buried in the middle of the accompanying story was mention of the fact that Wolfe had been invited by "the first lady to the White House last year to speak at a salute" to three other writers. One might surmise Wolfe had received the medal he wore in the picture from her, but no information on it was given. Laura Bush's name was absent from the story, which focused on the president's liking for Wolfe's new work, set on a college campus and described as a "racy new beer-and-sex-soaked novel." The point of the story was that Wolfe's spicy novel did not appear on the official list of books, including the Bible, that President Bush says he reads.

There was no indication of whether Laura Bush liked the Wolfe book or not; apparently, the reporter had made no effort to find out. The story called attention to President Bush as the former president of a "jock fraternity at Yale" and identified him as the "father of two partying daughters, Jenna and Barbara." The fact that Laura Bush is their mother was omitted. The story said that President Bush reads before he goes to bed, but whether Laura Bush also does so was not noted. The reader was left with the impression that the *Times* considered her an unimportant figure, even though it has repeatedly been said that she reads extensively and has a far wider knowledge of literature than her husband.

While at least identifying Laura Bush, the *Washington Post* news story made it appear her efforts to help boys at risk were little more than window dressing for her husband's controversial faith-based initiative to shift social services from traditional agencies to community organizations allied with church groups. Under the headline "FIRST LADY FOCUSES ON KIDS AT RISK" is the subhead "COMMUNITY-BASED PROGRAMS TOUTED." The word *touted,* generally used in connection with racetrack information, conveys a pejorative connotation.

The story said Laura Bush visited the Baltimore school as part of a series of trips planned to call attention to effective community- and faith-based programs to keep boys out of gangs. She was quoted as praising the school for its use of a simple but effective technique to improve discipline—the

Good Behavior Game, which gives children daily rewards for attending to their tasks. Just how her visits would fit into President Bush's proposed $150 million program to combat conditions leading boys to join gangs or what this program would be was not specified. Neither was the leadership of the program, for which she was identified as the head in name only. Perhaps the actual head will be Jim Towey, director of the White House Office of Faith-Based and Community Initiatives, quoted twice in the article, but the reader would not know.

It appears that *Post* editors thought they were giving Laura Bush sufficient attention by running a story and picture on her visit because they considered it simply a public relations ploy for the administration. Maybe so, but this treatment means a lot of questions remain. True, the newspaper may run more stories on faith-based initiatives and community programs, but the *Post* prides itself on keeping a close watch on the federal government. Should it not make every effort to give readers as many facts on new programs as possible as soon as possible? In covering first ladies, unlike covering Congress, for instance, there seems to be a tendency to treat what they do superficially and then allege it should not be taken seriously because it is superficial.

In the case of the MSNBC interview, Brian Williams moved very quickly from the program to combat gangs to questions on how George and Laura Bush, particularly George, get their news. A viewer was left with the impression that Williams had little real interest in finding out whether Laura Bush herself was responsible for the administration's initiative to help boys avoid self-destructive actions. He made no attempt to find out why she was worried about her role in the initiative or what this role would be. He rapidly moved on to what he seemed to really care about—whether the president watched evening newscasts such as his own.

The three examples in themselves, of course, do not make a convincing case that the news media give short shrift to first ladies. Nevertheless, as the previous chapters show, there is abundant historical evidence that, unless they are being investigated as Hillary Rodham Clinton was, first ladies generally have been written off as inconsequential public figures. Consider Rosalynn Carter's complaint that the *Washington Post* was more interested in the White House policy on booze than her mental health commission. The president's wife obviously derives her importance from her husband's position, but she reinforces, reinterprets, strengthens, or weakens his position through her own performance.

First ladies may be seen as unimportant and incapable of personal autonomy, but such an interpretation involves a misreading of the contemporary political scene. Operating with the blinders of conventional practice, the news media have been slow to recognize their changing role. Sheilah Kast, a former ABC News White House correspondent, commented, "The press doesn't put much effort into covering people whose power derives from someone else, so stereotypes are often a convenient shorthand, and most of the press corps doesn't worry much if they're not accurate." Yet first ladies play a vital role in the intermixing of personal and political factors that marks the American presidency in a media age. Gil Troy contended "that the co-presidency of today, such as it is, focuses mostly on joint image-making, not power-sharing."

If the image of first ladies upholds outmoded ideas

about gender, then the news media have an obligation to look at their own part in shaping it. Images are totally dependent on media. Political figures use sophisticated advertising and public relations techniques, plus a plethora of high-paid advisers, to influence image creation, and the news media, in their rush to make deadlines and fill airtime, are too quick to accept at face value what is presented to them. They have the ability—indeed, the duty—to ask questions, to try to penetrate behind the scenes, and to keep watch on major institutions of political life. These include the institution of the first lady, which, perhaps surprisingly to some, now falls in that category in terms of its impact on voters as well as the amount of tax dollars spent to maintain it.

If the concept of the first lady is seen as an anachronism dating back to the days of George III, then it is time to launch a serious debate on whether the institution should be continued. The present mode of giving the institution and its occupant superficial pats on the head, look-how-the-nice-lady-stands-by-her-man coverage, not too far removed from that given White House pets, serves to confuse expectations concerning gender roles. The approach retards the progress of women in politics and limits the pool of possible presidential candidates to those who have suitable spouses.

Laura Bush, like other recent first ladies, has become a significant player in the national political game, which was transformed in the last decades of the twentieth century due to the emergence of television and the advent of state presidential primaries. In the 2004 presidential race, she contributed substantially to the victory of her husband, headlining events that raised $5.5 million for his campaign alone and about $10 million for the Republican party. From the days of

Lady Bird Johnson's whistle-stop tour of the South to the present, the ability of presidential contenders' spouses to campaign on their own has doubled the outreach of each candidate himself, allowing him to virtually be in two places at once. Women have voted in greater numbers than men in every presidential election since 1964, and they tend to make up a higher number of voters who are undecided until the last minute. The presence of Laura Bush, a popular figure who appeals particularly to traditional stay-at-home wives, may well have given George W. Bush his second four years.

As Robert Watson explained, "With a relatively weak political party structure and an emphasis on public opinion in governance, the President is forced to constantly campaign for public and political support for his programs and agenda." This phenomenon developed well before the end of the twentieth century, when a portion of the continuous campaigning was turned over to the first lady. At the same time, she was expected to carry out feminine functions as mistress of the White House. Being first lady is a taxing job, as Margaret Truman said, "undefined, frequently misunderstood, and subject to political attacks far nastier in some ways than those any President has ever faced."

Despite a first lady's contemporary political role, the news media covering her still seem mired in outworn ideas about women's status. These ideas go back to the concept of coverture in British common law, which meant that women were covered literally by their husband's status. Coverture's residue, according to three authorities on women in politics, is "a tradition that is still reluctant to view women as independent or separate from the men to whom they are related." In their book *Running as a Woman,* Linda Witt, Karen M.

Paget, and Glenna Matthews gave the background of Hillary Rodham Clinton's infamous "I could have stayed home and baked cookies" quote. They wrote that one of Bill Clinton's primary opponents, Jerry Brown, former governor of California, attacked her work at the Rose Law Firm as a conflict of interest while Clinton was governor of Arkansas. When Clinton pointed out that Pat Brown, himself a former governor of California and Jerry Brown's father, had not given up practicing law when his son was elected governor, Jerry Brown retorted, "Well, I don't control my father," implying that Clinton should not have "allowed" his wife to practice law.

The three authors noted the sexist perceptions of the significance of the first lady's role that were underscored by Clinton's phrase "You buy one, you get one free." The phrase, they said, resulted in "raising such fears of a too-powerful Jezebel meddling in the affairs of state that *Spy* magazine spoofed them with a cover picture of Hillary's face superimposed on the body of a leather-clad dominatrix." Suspicions of men with powerful wives feed into media stereotypes of "dragon ladies," which could be seen in the coverage of both Nancy Reagan and Hillary Rodham Clinton.

Such stereotypes disadvantage married women who are contemplating running for office as well as men with successful wives. They may impel some strong women to conceal their own interest in politics behind a nonthreatening persona, as Barbara Bush did in presenting herself as a grandmotherly figure. While no one favors reporters invading the bed chambers of presidents and their wives, there is good reason for journalists, as well as historians, to inquire into the issue of hidden power in presidential unions. Surely, it is not an invasion of privacy to try to determine the extent of a political partnership without casting aspersions on either party. Why should a husband or wife have to pretend that the "little woman" has little knowledge of political matters to avoid unflattering stereotypes?

According to Dick Morris, a longtime political consultant for the Clintons, Hillary Rodham Clinton hoped at the start of the 1992 campaign that the national press would be more receptive to her as an independent woman than the Arkansas press had been. He said she told him, "'I always thought that I had to watch myself in Arkansas because it was such a male-dominated culture and outspoken women were not accepted. I assumed it would be different on the national level. But really, it's just the same. Or worse.'" To Morris, "Hillary was serving as the classic lightning rod, drawing to herself the blows that might otherwise have landed on Bill." During Clinton's presidency, according to Morris, Hillary Rodham Clinton, after the failure of her health care task force, found an acceptable political role in foreign travel, "where she could be a spokesperson for women—and a symbol of their potential." He noted that during Clinton's second term, her foreign travel, paid for by the taxpayers, cost $12 million.

Witt, Paget, and Matthews attacked what they called "sexual apartheid that to this day colors political coverage of women." They charged that this apartheid has evolved little beyond the level shown at Eleanor Roosevelt's White House press conferences for women only. At those weekly gatherings, reporters for women's pages, barred from directly competing with men for front-page stories, focused on "the news-making first lady, her social life, her good deeds, as well as the threat that she might become too powerful." Even when stories on Eleanor Roosevelt made it out of the women's sections and onto the front pages, Witt, Paget, and Matthews continued, they tended to follow the "sob sister" style of women feature writers of the early twentieth century. The authors said this included "the attention to gesture, tone of voice, style of dress and manner that to this day often separates the coverage of men and women politicians."

Since the 1970s, women have made up an increasingly large proportion of the White House press corps. This development has not represented a revolution in the coverage of first ladies, mainly because the women, like their male colleagues, concentrate on coverage of the president. Unless a first lady draws attention in an unusual way—such as being accused of possible wrongdoing as Hillary Clinton was, stricken with a life-threatening illness as Betty Ford and Nancy Reagan were, or ridiculed for extravagant tastes as Reagan was—she gets relatively little media exposure in Washington. Her projects, interviews, and ceremonial appearances, carefully crafted by her staff, keep her in the public eye, but journalists do not make their careers by covering them.

"When I covered the White House I didn't want to be known as the 'woman's beat' first lady reporter, I wanted to be known as the White House reporter who covered the President," commented Jodi Enda, formerly a member of the Knight-Ridder Washington bureau. She said she stayed away from first lady stories until she had established herself at the White House. She would have liked to have accompanied Hillary Rodham Clinton on overseas trips, but her editors did not want to spend the money to send her, Enda continued, because they were "short-sighted in how many people would be interested in her [Hillary] separate from her husband."

Appearing on television, as they do with increasing frequency, first ladies tend to be treated like pop culture celebrities, judged on their appearance and asked as much or more about their husbands and families than about themselves. "It takes a lot of material to fill all these *People*-type magazines and shows like 'Entertainment Tonight,' and a glamorous or controversial first lady is fodder for them," writer Barbara Matusow noted. Yet when one potential first lady—Judith Dean, the wife of Howard Dean, a contender in the 2004 Democratic presidential primaries—declined to participate in media events, "look how shocked we were," Matusow said, adding that "she was so at variance with the usual picture of a candidate's wife." Citing her desire to continue her medical practice, Judith Dean did not join her husband in campaigning until pressed to do so by both his managers and the press just before he bowed out of the race. Her disinclination to take part highlighted the fact that the lack of a cooperative spouse can narrow the candidate pool.

Geneva Overholser, who holds the Hurley Chair in Public Affairs Reporting at the Washington Bureau of the Missouri School of Journalism, said coverage of first ladies is too narrow. She observed that reporters try to pigeonhole an individual woman as a traditionalist or an activist (meaning feminist), instead of presenting her as a real human being. "The tendency to make first ladies look like kooks is more applied to liberals than conservatives," she said. Overholser added: "Why do we have to go after them in such narrow ways? We still haven't figured out how comfortable we are with feminism."

Monitoring the coverage of the wives of the two presidential candidates in the 2004 election campaign, Sheila Gibbons, editor of *Media Report to Women,* found that "some reporting reduces these women to cookie-cutter stereotypes." She cited several examples. For instance, she remarked on "*Newsweek*'s May 3, 2004, cover that shouted 'Teresa: Is John Kerry's Heiress Wife a Loose Cannon—Or Crazy Like a Fox?'" and noted that "her passionate forthrightness seemed to concern reporter Melinda Henneberger, who wrote:'Does he [Kerry] worry that she communicates a perhaps too-European brand of confidence in herself as a "lot of woman"—at a time when he is being derided as "looking French"?'" Similarly, Gibbons pointed out that "CNN's Judy Woodruff reduced recent first ladies to labels ('controversial Hillarys,' 'glamorous Jackies,' and 'demure Lauras'). . . . Woodruff wrapped up the segment [of a broadcast] by commenting on the difference between Heinz Kerry's pumpkin spice cookie recipe ('different, an acquired taste') and Laura Bush's oatmeal chocolate chunk cookie recipe ('traditional') in a *Family Circle* readers' contest."Gibbons said she was surprised that Woodruff implied the cookies in the competition were "metaphors for the women themselves" and asked, "In the present strained geopolitical climate, isn't there much more to say about presidential partners? And at the beginning of the twenty-first century, what are *Family Circle*'s female editors doing orchestrating a bakeoff between candidates' wives, anyway?"

One answer was provided by Francine Prose, a novelist, in a *Washington Post* column on political wives. "As our culture grows more conservative, men (and many women, too) have less trouble admitting that actually they prefer our women compliant, supportive, free of troubling personality quirks like outspokenness or ambition." Surely, she continued, "this is what commentators mean when they say that the reserved Laura Bush is more of a campaign asset than the high-spirited, multilingual Teresa Heinz Kerry." If so, this situation shows a troubling news media bias against independent women, and it also reveals an obsession with personality that distracts the public from fundamental political decisions.

In Gibbons's eyes, "describing one woman by interpreting her in terms of her similarity or dissimilarity with the personality and views of another shortchanges them" both and "is journalistically lazy." Even worse, she said, "is media coverage that implies independence and critical thinking in first ladies are liabilities for their husbands and, by extension, the nation." The fact that some of this coverage is produced by women journalists themselves illustrates the influence of pat story lines on the shaping of news reports, with differences between women often being treated as variations of "cat fights" and outspoken women being depicted as "uppity."

Meanwhile, the workings of the Office of the First Lady receive little attention. The public is told that contemporary first ladies have offices in the East Wing of the White House, but there has been little additional explanation of what goes on there. In the case of Rodham Clinton, however, the press pointed out with some fanfare that an office for her had been set up in the West Wing, implying that she might be overstepping her appropriate role. Actually, according to *The White House* by Bradley H. Patterson Jr., which looked at support institutions of the presidency, Rodham Clinton had a "small but strategically located office space on the second floor of the West Wing, more spacious staff quarters in the Old Executive Office Building (which she often visited), and offices for the social secretary and her staff in the East Wing (their traditional location)."

Although Laura Bush has given up the West Wing space, her formal office structure follows the same organizational pattern used by Rodham Clinton and her predecessors. The Office of the First Lady today consists of about twenty-one persons, including a chief of staff (also a deputy assistant to the president), special assistants, press secretary, director of correspondence, director of projects, director of scheduling and advance, and one or more speechwriters (added during Rodham Clinton's tenure); in addition, the first lady's office oversees the White House social secretary (also a special assistant to the president) and social aides. The two presidential assistants have the right to attend White House staff meetings to coordinate East Wing and West Wing functions. The support staff is augmented by about ten interns and volunteers.

Although the White House itself does not issue an organizational chart, Patterson's research showed that the Office of the First Lady is one of the most important in the executive branch of government. On the chart he constructed, that office falls in third place, below the Office of the President and roughly equivalent to Office of the Vice President. Patterson referred to the first lady as "a senior counselor for the

President—perhaps his closest and most trusted. . . . The past four decades have shown that the president's spouse has the broadest turf of any White House counselor."

Patterson said it is difficult to tell from the White House budget exactly how much money is earmarked for the institution of the first lady, since there is not a separate budgetary line item for this purpose. Yet the taxpayers are funding a significant operation, one that bears journalistic attention. According to the U.S. Court of Appeals in 1993, the spouse of a president can be construed as a federal "officer or employee," even though the spouse is not an elected or appointed official.

Patterson described the institution of the first lady as "an evolving one" in terms of its role in the government. Can the same be said of the journalistic coverage of the president's spouse? Is it evolving too? Or is it still grappling with Victorian ideas that stressed three roles for upper-class ladies— women as wives and mothers, who presented living proof of the virility of their husbands; women as hostesses and home decorators, whose style and taste bore witness to their social status; and women as fashion icons, whose expensive wardrobes testified to their husbands' wealth and economic prowess? A fourth but less consuming idea called on women to personify the concept of noblesse oblige and take part in works of charity.

The first lady today gains favorable media attention by performing all four of these roles, unless she is accused of undue extravagance, as Nancy Reagan was, or of being indiscreet, as Betty Ford was when she commented frankly on the possibility of her daughter having an affair. If she appears to move into a policymaking position, her coverage becomes much more critical. As Betty Winfield said, "The media have always reinforced unwritten rules about female independence. . . . The first lady's position continues to reflect the anachronistic concept of an official consort to the President, a confining role."

Historian Lewis Gould of the University of Texas, who pioneered the scholarly study of first ladies, assessed attitudes toward first ladies as "a lagging indicator about where women are in the country." He said, "It's always seemed to me to be about half a generation behind what women in the workplace or in the cultural world or in the political world are doing." The term *first lady* itself conveys obvious sexist and elitist overtones, and the news media from the days of Martha Washington to Laura Bush have tended to reinforce stereotypical conduct along the lines of Victorian propriety.

According to Gil Troy, "We here in the twenty-first century are still stuck in the twentieth century in our conversation about first ladies. First ladies again and again [and] again run into the same set of expectations, the same demands they be traditional." Unfortunately, this conversation spills over to include women candidates. Writing in the *Boston Globe,* Wayne Woodlief argued that coverage of male candidates tends to be idea-based, whereas coverage of women tends to focus on personal stories.

Profiles of women candidates and personal details about them have more in common with coverage of first ladies than with news stories on positions taken by male candidates. When Elizabeth Dole unsuccessfully sought the Republican presidential nomination in 2000, reporters gave her primary opponents more coverage, while calling attention to her personal style and picturing her campaign negatively.

Commented Andrea Mitchell of NBC News, "I agree entirely that there were too many stories on her red suit and her matching red pumps and red handbag. But Dole also had problems within her own organization and reluctance to take on issues." If she failed to be outspoken, perhaps it was because she had been influenced by the campaign of 1996, when her husband, Senator Bob Dole, had run as the Republican candidate for president against President Bill Clinton and she, in effect, had campaigned for first lady. Perhaps neither the news media nor Elizabeth Dole herself took her presidential bid as seriously as they would have had she not previously been cast ac a first lady possibility.

Germaine Greer, a feminist author, has attacked the institution of the first lady, which she seeks to abolish, on grounds that it establishes a position of "decorative servitude," contrary to concepts of "both equality and democratic accountability." She said the president's wife, along with her children, perform the function of reassuring us "as to the head of state's active heterosexuality," which underlies recurring news stories in which first ladies announce bedroom arrangements in the White House. Greer also said, "The first lady must project a vivid image of the opulent American standard of living and encourage consumption by stimulating emulation of her style. Yet, even when their husbands had great private fortunes, Presidents' wives have been taken to task for spending too much." In her opinion, "No woman anywhere should be expected to relinquish her privacy and her own work, to diet and dress up and give interviews every day, simply because she has married a man who had a prospect of success in politics."

If this is true of a woman, it also will be true of a man

married to the nation's first female president, a figure bound to emerge later, if not sooner, according to polls and to experts. Senator Hillary Rodham Clinton is thought likely to make a presidential bid in 2008, giving a woman a chance at the nation's highest office in the first decade of this century. Her polling data show that she has a following, although not necessarily one strong enough for her election. A USA TODAY/CNN/Gallup Poll taken at the end of 2004 put her at the top of the list of the nation's most admired women, while President George W. Bush placed first among the most admired men. Closely behind Rodham Clinton came Oprah Winfrey, with Laura Bush ranking third on the women's most admired list.

If Rodham Clinton does not run, other women may be waiting in the wings, with or without spouses. Since 1980, political experts have referred to a gender gap in politics, meaning that women have been recognized as voting somewhat differently than men, although they by no means necessarily support women candidates. The nomination of Geraldine Ferraro for vice president on the unsuccessful Democratic ticket in 1984 was seen as a breakthrough for women, stemming from attention to the gender gap. Her ticket lost in a bitter campaign in which she was harassed with ethnic slurs and antiabortion epithets. Nevertheless, some political observers think a woman's most likely chance of becoming president is to be elected vice president and succeed to the presidency following the death of an incumbent.

In the 2004 elections, women won 14.8 percent of the seats in the U.S. Congress, eight governorships, more than 25 percent of statewide elective offices, and 22.5 percent of the seats in state legislatures. An increasing number of women are serving in the cabinet, including Condoleezza Rice as secretary of state. Yet women's progress in politics is slow, even though women constitute nearly 52 percent of the population. In 1992, dubbed the Year of the Woman, female representation in Congress nearly doubled. Since then, it virtually has hit a plateau, with the percentage of women holding congressional seats in 2005 only 1 percent greater than in 2004.

Nine out of ten Americans say they would be willing to vote for a qualified woman to be president. Still, perceptions of what constitutes qualified differ, and it is likely to be much harder for a woman to prove that she is qualified than for a man. In her essay in *Anticipating Madam President,* Karen O'Connor, a political scientist, wrote that "Gallup polls and others reveal that 42 percent of those queried think that a man would make a better President."

O'Connor saw this as a reflection of the news media's bias against women. She noted that a study showed the number of women on serious Sunday morning television talk programs dropped substantially (from 11 percent to 6.5 percent) following the September 11, 2001, tragedy, but that the news media responded poorly to the report. The *Washington Post* story began, "Most of the officials, lawmakers, experts, and pontificators who parade their opinions on Sunday morning television have something in common. They don't wear panty hose."

Even more striking than reluctance to accept women as leaders is the fact, according to USA TODAY, that voters "find it easier to picture a woman in the Oval Office than to envisage what her husband might do in the East Wing." Ob-

viously, a name change would be necessary. A male presidential spouse might be called simply that—a spouse—or he
could be given a title such as first gentleman or first man, although these may be incompatible with the sensibilities of
modern Americans. Presumably, the White House Office of
the First Lady could be renamed the Office of the Spouse,
and traditional responsibilities for entertaining could be
turned over to a paid staff, if a husband is disinclined to be
seen as a host.

The same would be true if a single individual of either
gender became president, although the public has shown a
strong preference for married heads of state. Only one unmarried president, James Buchanan, ever served a full term.
If there were no spouses, the functions now carried out by
first ladies could be entrusted to staff members, possibly assisted by presidential relatives, as happened in the nineteenth
century. Perhaps a woman president without a spouse might
be expected to handle many duties of the first lady as well as
those of the president, while a male president without a
spouse would rely more on staff support.

If spouses were left free to do whatever they cared to,
public opinion still would be likely to influence their
choices. Poll data show that an overwhelming majority of the
people approve of a spouse, male or female, serving as a
"trusted confidante." Employment is a stickier issue, but according to poll data, this is less so for men than for women,
with 64 percent saying it would be appropriate for a "first
man" to hold a paid job in the private sector versus 50 percent saying the same for a first lady.

It seems likely that a spouse's employment options
would be limited, however, because of potential conflicts of

interest. If a male spouse lived in the White House and did not work, he might be ridiculed as "riding on the woman's coat tails, so to speak," as one caller put it on a radio call-in show. To avoid difficulties of that type should Rodham Clinton be elected president, Bill Clinton, according to news reports, may be seeking a more permanent position with the United Nations (having served as a special UN envoy in the tsunami crisis). Perhaps voters would find this position acceptable for a spouse, although polls show that only 44 percent of Americans think it is appropriate for a male spouse to hold elective office and only 32 percent approve of a female spouse doing so. It seems likely that the most acceptable thing for a male spouse to do would be to stay out of the limelight, as was done by Denis Thatcher, the wealthy businessman who was the husband of former British prime minister Margaret Thatcher; his motto was "always present, never there."

Gender ideas change slowly, and the weight of American tradition lies on the side of a male president and a first lady. Biased coverage of women candidates certainly should be eliminated, but the news media also need to give immediate attention to the institution of the first lady. That institution is "always present," but it is "never there" in terms of being portrayed for what it is—an important part of the U.S. political system that bears witness to the ambiguities and inequalities of contemporary gender relationships.

NOTES

◈

CHAPTER ONE

1 *Fear and trembling:* Eleanor Roosevelt, *This I Remember* (New York: Harper, 1949), 102.

Newspaper girls: Ann Cottell Free, "Press Conferences," in Maurine H. Beasley, Holly Cowan Shulman, and Henry R. Beasley, eds., *The Encyclopedia of Eleanor Roosevelt* (Westport, Conn.: Greenwood Press, 2001), 413.

2 *By sign language:* Ishbel Ross, *Grace Coolidge and Her Era* (New York: Dodd, Mead, 1962), 108.

3 *Disguise as a Girl Scout:* Bess Furman, *Washington By-Line* (New York: Knopf, 1949), 58.

This untried field: Roosevelt, *This I Remember,* 103.

Him into trouble: Ibid.

4 *Organizational chart:* Bradley H. Patterson Jr., *The White House Staff: Inside the West Wing and Beyond* (Washington, D.C.: Brookings Institution Press, 2000), 44–45.

5 *Who loves life:* Richard Leiby, "Which Way to the Convent?" *Washington Post,* June 2, 2004, C3.

6 *Flexing their muscles:* Gil Troy, *Mr. & Mrs. President: From the Trumans to the Clintons,* 2nd ed. (Lawrence: University Press of Kansas, 2000), X.

Of newspaper staffs: Sheila Gibbons, "Media Report to Women Selected Statistics on Women and Media," *Media Report to Women* 27 (Winter 1999): 19.

7 *"Proper women's" place:* Linda Witt, Karen M. Paget, and Glenna Matthews, *Running as a Woman: Gender and Power in American Politics* (New York: Free Press, 1994), 182.

8   *Better than the men:* Roosevelt, *This I Remember,* 102.

9   *Of her influence:* Kati Marton, *Hidden Power* (New York: Pantheon, 2001), 5.

   A sexual relationship: Blanche Wiesen Cook, *Eleanor Roosevelt: 1884–1933,* vol. 1 (New York:Viking, 1992), 232.

   Noted in 1979: Interview with Mary Hornaday by Maurine Beasley, Red Bank, N.J., May 21, 1979, cited in Beasley, *Eleanor Roosevelt and the Media: A Public Quest for Self-Fulfillment* (Urbana: University of Illinois Press, 1987), 75.

10   *Stephen T. Early:* Maurine Beasley, ed., *The White House Press Conferences of Eleanor Roosevelt* (New York: Garland, 1983), 337.

   Off the record: Ishbel Ross, *Ladies of the Press* (New York: Harper, 1936), 319.

11   *Weekly, not daily, publications:* Betty H. Winfield, "Mrs. Roosevelt's Press Conference Association: The First Lady Shines a Light," *Journalism History* 8 (Summer 1981): 63.

   In 1940: William David Sloan, ed., *The Media in America,* 5th ed. (Northport, Ala.:Vision Press, 2002), 297.

   Readership demographics: Newspaper Association of America, *Facts about Newspapers, 2003* (Reston,Va.: Newspaper Association of America, 2003), 5.

12   *In the 1970s:* Maurine H. Beasley and Sheila J. Gibbons, *Taking Their Place:A Documentary History of Women and Journalism,* 2nd ed. (State College, Pa.: Strata, 2003), 147–48.

   For front-row seats: Free, "Press Conferences," in Beasley, Shulman, and Beasley, 413.

   Lead to temperance: Statement at Eleanor Roosevelt press conference, April 3, 1933, Bess Furman Papers, Box 76, Manuscript Division, Library of Congress, Washington, D.C. (hereafter referred to as BFP, MDLC).

13   *To write about:* Interview with Hope Ridings Miller by Maurine Beasley, Washington, D.C., May 3, 1979, cited in Beasley, *Eleanor Roosevelt and the Media,* 56.

   Gifts she had: Ibid., 86–87.

13 *And her children:* Betty Boyd Caroli, *First Ladies* (New York: Oxford, 1995), 120.

14 *Dinners and teas:* James MacGregor Burns and Susan Dunn, *The Three Roosevelts: Patrician Leaders Who Transformed America* (New York: Atlantic Monthly Press), 236.

Devious methods: Roosevelt, *This I Remember,* 102.

At the White House: Ibid. See also typescript of notes on Eleanor Roosevelt press conference, March 6, 1933, Box 76, BFP, MDLC.

Handled by him: Roosevelt, *This I Remember,* 102.

15 *To the unmarried:* See "Women's Forest Work Camps May Be Set Up," clipping, *New York Times,* May 24, 1933, Winifred Mallon Scrapbook, Box 154, BFP, MDLC.

Willing slaves: Dorothy Dunbar Bromley, "The Future of Eleanor Roosevelt," *Harper's Magazine* 180 (January 1940): 134.

16 *Filled columns:* Beasley, *Eleanor Roosevelt and the Media,* 53.

A President's wife: Reprinted in Furman, *Washington By-Line,* 194.

Of their history: Furman diary, entries for March 25, 1935, May 27, 1935, and February 10, 1936, Box 1, BFP, MDLC.

17 *Associated Press:* Furman diary, entry for November 16, 1935, Box 1, BFP, MDLC.

18 *With the first lady: Time,* February 19, 1934, 11.

On the defensive: Typed transcript of notes of Eleanor Roosevelt's press conference, January 5, 1942, Martha Strayer Papers, Box 2, University of Wyoming, Laramie.

19 *World War II:* Roosevelt, *This I Remember,* 261.

Meetings "precious": Minutes of meeting with Eleanor Roosevelt, December 7, 1942, Mrs. Roosevelt's Press Conference Association Papers, Franklin D. Roosevelt Library, Hyde Park, New York.

Quoted as saying: James T. Howard, "Males Squirm at First Lady's Parley," *PM,* September 27, 1943, 5, clipping, Ruby Black Papers, MDLC.

20   *Of the president:* Typed notes from Furman diary, March 15, 1933, Box 51, BFP, MDLC.

Of a rise: Typed notes from Furman diary, February 7, 1939, Box 78, BFP, MDLC.

With malice: Typed notes from Furman diary, May 4, 1939, Box 78, BFP, MDLC.

Circulation of 4,034,552: Beasley, *Eleanor Roosevelt and the Media,* 91.

21   *As president:* Ibid., 110.

Was taken: Interview with Anne W. Arnall by Maurine Beasley, Laurel, Md., April 27, 1984, cited in Beasley, *Eleanor Roosevelt and the Media,* 55.

22   *Eyes and ears:* Kathleen McLaughlin, "Mrs. Roosevelt Goes Her Way," *New York Times Magazine,* July 5, 1936, 7.

A lot: Frances Perkins, *The Roosevelt I Knew* (New York: Viking, 1946), 70.

With us: Hornaday interview, cited in Beasley, *Eleanor Roosevelt and the Media,* 97.

23   *Seldom betrayed:* Roosevelt, *This I Remember,* 103.

24   *For the president:* George Gallup, "Mrs. Roosevelt More Popular Than President, Survey Finds," *Washington Post,* January 5, 1939, section 3, 1.

25   *The newspaper women:* Roosevelt, *This I Remember,* 103.

CHAPTER TWO

27   *Hostess for the nation:* Edith P. Mayo, ed., *The Smithsonian Book of the First Ladies: Their Lives, Times and Issues* (New York: Holt, 1996), 11.

Virginia house-keeper: Edith P. Mayo and Denise D. Meringolo, *First Ladies: Political Role and Public Image* (Washington, D.C.: Smithsonian Institution, 1994), 13.

28   *Of the world:* Paul F. Boller Jr., *Presidential Wives* (New York: Oxford, 1988), 6.

To this day: Margaret Truman, *First Ladies: An Intimate Group Portrait of White House Wives* (New York: Fawcett Columbine, 1995), 21.

28 *Subsequent administrations:* Mayo and Meringolo, 12.
      Must not depart from: Quoted in Helen Bryan, *Martha Washington: First Lady of Liberty* (New York: John Wiley, 2002), 300.
29 *Prodigiously pleased:* Ibid.
      Respectful curtsy: Carl Sferrazza Anthony, *First Ladies: The Saga of the Presidents' Wives and Their Power, 1789–1961,* vol. 1 (New York: Morrow, 1990), 45.
      "Unaffected" personality: Truman, *First Ladies,* 20.
      Monarchy and aristocracy: Catherine Allgor, *Parlor Politics* (Charlottesville: University of Virginia Press, 2000), 20.
30 *Queen's Nightcap:* Anthony, *First Ladies,* 1:46.
      Coat-of-arms seal: Ibid., 48.
      If they could: Quoted in Phyllis Lee Levin, *Abigail Adams: A Biography* (New York: Thomas Dunne, 1987), 82.
      Heroes would fight: Ibid., 83.
31 *Power over Wives:* Ibid., 84.
      Years that followed: Mayo and Meringolo, 15.
      Her predecessor: Truman, *First Ladies,* 90.
32 *Toothless Adams:* Quoted in Boller, 19.
      Friendly newspapers: Levin, *Abigail Adams,* 339.
      Or malicious writings: Quoted in Sloan, 116.
      Was impossible: Ibid.
      Ridiculous pomp: Quoted in Truman, *First Ladies,* 92.
33 *Air her opinions:* Caroli, *First Ladies,* 32.
      Politically null: Allgor, 31.
      Baltimore newspaper: Anthony, *First Ladies,* 1:80.
34 *Mrs. Madison:* Quoted in ibid., 81.
      Her husband: David B. Mattern and Holly C. Shulman, eds., *The Selected Letters of Dolley Payne Madison* (Charlottesville: University of Virginia Press, 2003), 6.
      Mrs. Madison's crush or squeeze: Allgor, 75.
      Like a queen: Linda L. Gordon, *From Lady Washington to Mrs. Cleveland* (Freeport, N.Y.: Books for Libraries Press, 1972, reprint of 1888 ed.), 93.
35 *Project of a president's wife:* Anthony, *First Ladies,* 1:94.
      Grace a publication: Ibid., 83.

35 *For a half-century:* Quoted in Boller, 36.
   For the President's consort: Caroli, *First Ladies,* XX.
   Became popular: Betty Caroli, *America's First Ladies* (Pleas-
      antville, N.Y.: Reader's Digest Association, 1996), XI.

36 *Surrounding its development:* Robert P. Watson, *The Presidents'
      Wives: Reassessing the Office of First Lady* (Boulder, Colo.:
      Lynne Rienner, 2000), 7.
   Hid by dirty collars: Quoted in Boller, 51.
   Any body was there: Ibid., 58.

37 *Strongly assimilated:* Ibid., 55.
   Weekly Messenger: Anthony, *First Ladies,* 1:110.
   Submissiveness and domesticity: Barbara Welter, "The Cult of
      True Womanhood: 1820–1860," *American Quarterly* 18
      (Summer 1966): 151.

39 *As much as possible:* Quoted in Anthony, *First Ladies,* 1:122.
   And a Christian: Quoted in Boller, 80.
   Around tables: Anthony, *First Ladies,* 1:124.

40 *Resembling a crown:* Quoted in Bess Furman, *White House Pro-
      file* (Indianapolis, Ind.: Bobbs–Merrill, 1951), 129.
   Hail to the Chief: Caroli, *America's First Ladies,* 106.
   Reprinted in other papers: Anthony, *First Ladies,* 1:129.
   Woman of her age: Quoted in ibid.

41 *A spotless house:* Truman, *First Ladies,* 98.
   Salutary influence: Quoted in Boller, 90.
   A queen should be: Quoted in Caroli, *First Ladies,* 76.
   Unusual prominence: Ibid., 67.
   Even a "photograph": Anthony, *First Ladies,* 1:146.
   A large handkerchief: Ibid., 151.

42 *Among women:* Ibid., 152.
   Enemies apart: Watson, 63.

43 *First lady in the land:* Quoted in Mayo and Meringolo, 8.
   First lady: Ibid.
   Mrs. President: Carl Sandberg, *Mary Lincoln: Wife and Widow*
      (New York: Harcourt, Brace, 1932), 87.

43   *Republican Queen:* Quoted in Caroli, *First Ladies,* 71.

Throughout the land: Jennifer Fleischner, *Mrs. Lincoln and Mrs. Keckly* (New York: Broadway Books, 2003), 4.

Sympathetic figure: Kathleen Prindiville, *First Ladies* (New York: Macmillan, 1954), 148.

45   *Fair, fat and forty:* Emily Edson Briggs, *The Olivia Letters* (New York: Neale Publishing, 1906), 169.

Positive characteristics: Mary Clemmer Ames, *Life and Scenes in the National Capital* (Hartford, Conn.: Worthington, 1874), 253.

Deeply injured: John Y. Simon, ed., *The Personal Memoirs of Julia Dent Grant* (New York: Putnam, 1975), 186.

First lady of the land: Quoted in Emily Apt Geer, *First Lady: The Life of Lucy Webb Hayes* (Kent, Ohio: Kent State University Press, 1984), 138.

46   *Countless of our sex:* Quoted in ibid., 230.

And never will have: Quoted in Anthony, *First Ladies,* 1:237.

47   *American journalism contemptible:* Cited in Caroli, *First Ladies,* 290.

Fallen upon her: Gordon, 443.

48   *Buttons and souvenirs:* Mayo and Meringolo, 66.

Affectionate as mine: Quoted in William Seale, *The President's House: A History,* vol. 1 (Washington, D.C.: White House Historical Association, 1986), 570.

49   *In the United States:* Caroli, *First Ladies,* 321.

Docility over independence: Ibid., 111.

Doll-like appearance: Ibid.

50   *Aristocratic flavor:* Boller, 199.

Newspapers and magazines: Mayo and Meringolo, 67.

Late to begin now: Quoted in Sylvia Jukes Morris, *Edith Kermit Roosevelt: Portrait of a First Lady* (New York: Coward, McCann and Geoghegan, 1980), 477.

51   *The Presidential race:* George Griswold Hill, "The Wife of the New President," *Ladies' Home Journal,* March 1909, 6.

51   *Go away more cheerfully:* Quoted in Frances Wright Saunders, *First Lady between Two Worlds: Ellen Axson Wilson* (Chapel Hill: University of North Carolina Press, 1985), 276.

52   *President of the United States:* Quoted in Phyllis Lee Levin, *Edith and Woodrow* (New York: Scribner, 2001), 428.

    Matters to my husband: Edith Bolling Wilson, *My Memoir* (Indianapolis, Ind.: Bobbs-Merrill, 1938), 289.

    Consequential for all the world: Levin, *Edith and Woodrow,* 515.

    Real power: Lewis L. Gould, "Edith Bolling (Galt) Wilson," in Lewis Gould, ed., *American First Ladies, Their Lives and Their Legacy* (New York: Garland, 1996), 366.

53   *Do with it?:* Mary Randolph, *Presidents and First Ladies* (New York: Appleton-Century, 1936), 229.

    All girls together: Quoted in Beatrice Fairfax (Marie Manning), *Ladies Now and Then* (New York: Dutton, 1944), 204.

54   *"Chat" for attribution:* Carl S. Anthony, *Florence Harding* (New York: William Morrow, 1998), 324.

    "Revolted" one reporter: Ibid., 392.

    Carry it far: Ross, *Ladies of the Press,* 312.

55   *Dignity and warmth:* Ross, *Grace Coolidge and Her Era,* 85.

56   *Kept to herself:* Ibid., 94.

    President and his wife: Randolph, 17.

    To the Republican Party: Quoted in Anthony, *First Ladies,* 1:404.

    Or its interest: Caroli, *First Ladies,* 184.

57   *Consider her aloof:* Anne Beiser Allen, *An Independent Woman: The Life of Lou Henry Hoover* (Westport, Conn.: Greenwood Press, 2000), 121.

    Problem for the press: Ross, *Ladies of the Press,* 314.

58   *They were welcome:* Ibid., 315.

    Priority on accuracy: Debbie Mauldin Cottrell, "Lou Henry Hoover," in Gould, ed., *American First Ladies,* 415.

    On mutual trust: Ross, *Ladies of the Press,* 315.

59   *Legislation and appointments:* Caroli, *First Ladies,* 193.

    Living in Washington: Janet M. Martin, *The Presidency and Women: Promise, Performance and Illusion* (College Station: Texas A&M Press, 2003), 189.

59 *Let it use her:* Caroli, *First Ladies,* 322.

60 *Measure themselves against:* Sarah McClendon, with Jules Minton, *Mr. President, Mr. President: My Fifty Years of Covering the White House* (Santa Monica, Calif.: General Publishing, 1996), 19.

CHAPTER THREE

62 *Becoming First Lady:* Truman, *First Ladies,* 75.

Great White Jail: Ibid., 77.

White House occupants: Marton, 97.

Say to the public: Quoted in Marianne Means, *The Woman in the White House* (New York: Random House, 1963), 227.

Mother of his daughter: Quoted in Marton, 96.

Politics and substance: Troy, 24.

63 *Condemned criminals:* Edith Benham Helm, *The Captains and the Kings* (New York: Putnam, 1954), 257.

Comings and goings: Ibid., 285.

Council of Church Women: Quoted in Margaret Truman, *Bess W. Truman,* 276.

Made up her mind: Ibid.

Quarter of a century: Quoted in Maurine Beasley, "Bess (Elizabeth Virginia Wallace) Truman," in Gould, ed., *American First Ladies,* 460.

Prefer gray: Quoted in Boller, 328.

64 *Much as the president:* Truman, *Bess W. Truman,* 279.

Merits of the issue: Ibid., 278.

Condemn the DAR: Ibid., 279.

Last lady: Ibid.

Truman partnership: Ibid.

65 *Goldfish bowl business:* Quoted in Furman, *Washington By-Line,* 337.

Decision to make: McClendon, *Mr. President,* 267.

Idealized past: Troy, 43.

Husband in private: Means, 230.

Dignified and dutiful: Troy, 51.

66 *On the nerve centers:* Quoted in ibid., 51.

66 *Not enthusiastic:* Julie Nixon Eisenhower, *Special People* (New York: Simon and Schuster, 1977), 202.

A dipsomaniac: Quoted in "Mamie Eisenhower Dies in Sleep at 82 in Hospital in Washington," *New York Times,* November 2, 1979, B5.

No romance: Quoted in Susan Eisenhower, *Mrs. Ike* (New York: Farrar, Straus and Giroux, 1996), 324.

67 *50 electoral votes:* Quoted in Robert Wallace, "They Like Mamie, Too" *Life,* October 13, 1952, 149.

Up in pink: Means, 253.

Very unfeminine: Quoted in Anthony, *First Ladies,* 1:566.

68 *Asked a question:* Maurine Beasley and Paul Belgrade, "Media Coverage of a Silent Partner: Mamie Eisenhower as First Lady," *American Journalism* 3, no.1 (1986): 43.

By inexorable tea: Quoted in Caroli, *First Ladies,* 212.

From her husband: Interview with Mary Jane McCaffree Monroe by Maurine Beasley, Washington, D.C., November 19, 1983, cited in Beasley and Belgrade, 44.

Costume needs: Betty Beale, *Power at Play* (Washington, D.C.: Regnery Gateway, 1993), 49.

Lose the game: Quoted in Winzola McLendon and Scottie Smith, *Don't Quote Me: Washington Newswomen and the Power Society* (New York: Dutton, 1970), 68.

69 *Occupants of the White House:* Maxine Cheshire, with John Greenya, *Maxine Cheshire, Reporter* (Boston: Houghton Mifflin, 1978), 28.

Match her gowns: Ibid., 30.

Press neglect: Jack Anderson, with James Boyd, *Confessions of a Muckraker* (New York: Ballantine, 1980), 320.

Than their intelligence: Caroli, *First Ladies,* 215.

Best-dressed women: Karal Ann Marling, *As Seen on TV: Visual Culture of Everyday Life in the 1950s* (Cambridge, Mass.: Harvard University Press, 1994), 36.

First lady liked: Anthony, *First Ladies,* 1:583.

Offer a woman: Quoted in ibid., 565.

69 *Name is Ike:* Quoted in Boller, 344.
70 *Million Dollar Fudge:* Anthony, *First Ladies,* 1:564.
        First Lady: Ibid., 575.
        Please Vote: Quoted in Caroli, *First Ladies,* 218.
71 *Dry out:* Anthony, *First Ladies,* 1:585.
        Hated to leave: J. B. West and Mary Lynn Kotz, *Upstairs at the White House* (New York: Warner, 1974): 186.
        Smalltown dowdiness: Cheshire, 40.
        Noble deeds: Joyce Hoffmann, *Theodore H. White and Journalism as Illusion* (Columbia: University of Missouri Press, 1995), 178.
72 *Consolations of ritual:* "First Lady," *The New Yorker,* April 30, 1994, 4.
        Oversized T-shirts: Betty Boyd Caroli, "Jacqueline (Lee Bouvier) Kennedy (Onassis)," in Gould, ed., *American First Ladies,* 480.
        Vital to a campaign: Jacqueline (Mrs. John F.) Kennedy, "Campaign Wife," news release, Democratic National Committee, Washington, D.C., October 13, 1960.
73 *To be president?:* Quoted in Freda Kramer, *Jackie: A Truly Intimate Biography* (New York: Tempo Star, 1979), 68.
        Sable underwear: Quoted in C. David Heymann, *A Woman Named Jackie* (New York: Carol Communications, 1989), 223.
        Mrs. Nixon on clothes: Quoted in "That Fancy Fashion Fuss," *Life,* September 26, 1960, 18.
        Made in America: Quoted in Kitty Kelley, *Jackie Oh!* (Secaucus, N.J.: Lyle Stuart, 1978), 107.
        Same outfit twice: Ibid.
        $121,461.61: Heymann, *A Woman Named Jackie,* 363.
74 *Nurse for Caroline:* "Lovely Aspirants for Role of First Lady," *Life,* October 10, 1960, 156.
        More full-time: Mary Barelli Gallagher, *My Life with Jacqueline Kennedy,* edited by Frances Spatz Leighton (New York: David McKay, 1969), 50.

74   *Never have been so secure:* Letitia Baldrige, personal email to
         Maurine Beasley, November 3, 2004.
         Was ever printed: Marton, 120.

75   *Pretty drab:* Quoted in "Remembering Jackie, the Talk of the
         Town," *New Yorker,* May 30, 1994, 35.
         Became incensed: Heymann, *A Woman Named Jackie,* 330.

76   *"Complicated" to answer:* Caroli, *First Ladies,* 225.
         TV-oriented culture: Troy, 107.
         Jacqueline Kennedy to Paris: Quoted in "Ladies' Day at the
         Summit," *Newsweek,* June 12, 1961, 25.
         Jac-kie, Ni-na: Quoted in Letitia Baldrige, *A Lady First* (New
         York: Viking, 2001), 196.
         Superpower summit: Marton, 119.

77   *"Jack-ie, Jack-ie":* Quoted in Baldrige, *A Lady First,* 191.
         The summer: Ibid., 200.
         "LESS AGNELLI": Quoted in Heymann, *A Woman Named Jackie,*
         356.
         Asian splendor: Paul Grimes, "Mrs. Kennedy Gets a Festive
         Welcome on Arrival in India," *New York Times,* March 13,
         1962, A1.

78   *Virginia countryside:* "Benign Competition," *Time,* March 30,
         1962, 12.
         Queen Elizabeth II: "Mrs. Kennedy Guest of Queen at
         Lunch," *New York Times,* March 29, 1962, A1.
         On my own: Quoted in "Kennedy Greets Wife as Trip Ends,"
         New York Times, March 30, 1962, A4.
         Titular leaders: "The 'Image' Mrs. Kennedy Left in Asia," *U.S.
         News & World Report,* April 2, 1962, 15.
         Was "exorbitant": Quoted in ibid.

79   *Stay home?:* Quoted in Caroli, *First Ladies,* 326.
         Went after him: Quoted in Heymann, *A Woman Named Jackie,*
         273.

80   *Coverage of the family:* Baldrige email to Beasley.
         Merciless calculation: John H. Davis, *The Kennedys: Dynasty and
         Disaster 1848–1984* (New York: McGraw-Hill, 1985), 341.

80   *Her own:* "J," in "Life and Leisure," *Newsweek,* January 1, 1962, 32.

Ought to have been: Ibid.

Involved in those: Ibid.

More than fifty times: Troy, 120.

81   *Ill health:* Quoted in Baldrige, *First Lady's Lady,* 183.

Effort to explain: Marton, 123.

Like a saddle horse: Quoted in Peter Collier and David Horowitz, *The Kennedys: An American Drama* (New York: Summit, 1984), 281.

Politely, pleasantly, aloofly: Stephen Birmingham, *Jacqueline Bouvier Kennedy Onassis* (New York: Grosset and Dunlap, 1978), 111.

Who ever lived: Davis, 341.

82   *Space Agency:* Quoted in McLendon and Smith, 70.

Given the signal: Baldrige, *A Lady, First,* 168–69.

Maximum politeness: Quoted in Heymann, *A Woman Named Jackie,* 267.

Front-page news: Helen Thomas, *Dateline: White House* (New York: Macmillan, 1975), 11–12.

Twenty-four hours a day: Ibid., 12.

Thousand headlines: Ibid.

83   *Family used:* Helen Thomas, *Front Row at the White House* (New York: Scribner, 1999), 58.

Hot and cold: McLendon and Smith, 71.

What to do: Telephone interview with Winzola McLendon by Maurine Beasley, Washington, D.C., October 15, 2004.

Curtain closed: Thomas, *Dateline: White House,* 10–11.

As "harpies": Quoted in McLendon and Smith, 71–72.

Potted palms: Quoted in Heymann, *A Woman Named Jackie,* 275.

Her flesh: Ibid.

Near them: Quoted in ibid.

84   *Strange Spanish-looking women:* Quoted in Thomas, *Dateline: White House,* 7.

84 *Briefly arrested:* Heymann, *A Woman Named Jackie,* 272.
Of Arab descent: Ibid.
To attend: Thomas, *Dateline: White House,* 22.
White House: Thomas, *Front Row at the White House,* 58.
Through her own: Heymann, *A Woman Named Jackie,* 277.
Shot back: Ibid., 272.

85 *Stayed home:* Interview with Frances L. Lewine by Anne S. Kasper, Washington, D.C., November 18, 1991, Washington Press Club Foundation Oral History Project, Columbia University and other repositories, 44.
As it became: Ibid., 43.
Crucified her: Heymann, *A Woman Named Jackie,* 115.
At formal banquets: Quoted in ibid., 276.
In New York: Ibid.
First lady's representative: Carl Sferrazza Anthony, *First Ladies: The Saga of the President's Wives and their Power, 1961–1990,* vol. 2 (New York: William Morrow, 1991), 46.

86 *Dined alone:* Quoted in Beale, *Power at Play,* 71.
Parties in foreign lands: Quoted in "Caesar's Wife," *Newsweek,* October 28, 1962, 20.
A change of scene: Quoted in ibid.
Her reputation: Troy, 129.

CHAPTER FOUR

89 *As a species:* Meg Greenfield, *Washington* (New York: Public Affairs, 2001), 119.
And influence: Ibid.

90 *Come to this:* Lady Bird Johnson, *A White House Diary* (New York: Holt, Rinehart and Winston, 1970), 6.
An inevitable doom: Ibid., 9.
I never rehearsed: Ibid., 16.

91 *Felt that way:* Helen Thomas interview by Joe Frantz, Washington, D.C., April 19, 1977, Oral History Collection (hereafter referred to as OHC), Lyndon B. Johnson Library, Austin, Texas (hereafter referred to as LBJL), 6.

91 *Politically attuned:* Marjorie Hunter, "Public Servant without Pay: The First Lady," *New York Times Magazine,* December 15, 1963, 10.

The 1960 campaign: Ibid.

Cold-eyed: Nan Robertson, "Our New First Lady," *Saturday Evening Post,* February 8, 1964, 20.

92 *A pity:* Ibid.

Open heart: Ibid., 24.

At clotheshorsemanship: "The First Lady Bird," *Time,* August 28, 1964, 20.

Scorching envy: Ibid., 22.

For us: Quoted in ibid., 23.

93 *They were quiet:* Elizabeth Carpenter interview by Joe Frantz, Washington, D.C., December 3, 1968, OHC, LBJL, 13–14.

A woman was doing it: Ibid.

Values of beauty: Quoted in Lewis L. Gould, *Lady Bird Johnson and the Environment* (Lawrence: University Press of Kansas, 1988), 55.

94 *Involved in some way in the President's program:* Bess Abell interview by T. H. Baker, Washington, D.C., June 13, 1969, OHC, LBJL, 2.

Afraid of them: Johnson, 36.

95 *His purposes:* Liz Carpenter, *Ruffles and Flourishes* (Garden City, N.Y.: Doubleday, 1970), 57.

It's prissy: Quoted in Gould, *Lady Bird Johnson and the Environment,* 60.

Condensed it more: Elizabeth Carpenter interview by Joe B. Frantz, Washington, D.C., April 4, 1969, OHC, LBJL, 11.

"U.S. BEAUTY": Betty Beale, "A Plea for U.S. Beauty," *Washington Evening Star,* September 8, 1965, B1, and "First Lady Discusses Beauty," B5.

96 *Label beautification:* Gould, *Lady Bird Johnson and the Environment,* 61.

Beautification implied: Ibid.

Potomac River: Carpenter interview, April 4, 1969, 7.

97 *In the end:* Katharine Graham interview by Joe Frantz, Washington, D.C., March 13, 1969, OHC, LBJL, 31.

Got silly: Ibid., 32.

Would not have had: Ibid.

25,000 trees: Anthony, *First Ladies,* 2:130.

98 *Her adventures:* Thomas, *Dateline: White House,* 79.

Frontier mettle: Betty Beale, "Rain-Pelted News Reporters Challenge Snake River," *Washington Evening Star,* September 9, 1965, B2.

99 *Play on their stories:* Carpenter interview, May 15, 1969, 19.

Her activities: Katie Louchheim, *By the Political Sea* (Garden City, N.Y.: Doubleday, 1970), 220.

A tree somewhere: Ibid.

"FOR BEAUTIFICATION?": Isabelle Shelton, "Did the First Lady 'Lobby' for Beautification? *Washington Evening Star,* October 17, 1965, G2.

Describes her activities: Ibid.

100 *The words "Lady Bird":* Gould, *Lady Bird Johnson and the Environment,* 163.

Guarded: Ibid., 165.

More careful and less visible: Ibid.

Legislative aims: Quoted in Abigail McCarthy, *Private Faces: Public Places* (Garden City, N.Y.: Doubleday, 1972), 202.

Political wives: Ibid.

101 *Leave the floor:* "The First Lady Bird," 21.

Over splintered glass for Lyndon: Quoted in Troy, 134.

Was boorish: Thomas, *Dateline: White House,* 93.

Plant azaleas: Quoted in McLendon and Smith, 54.

Written for her: Quoted in ibid., 94.

We can better: Quoted in Anthony, *First Ladies,* 2:152.

102 *Vice president:* McCarthy, 259.

Into it: Katharine Graham, *Personal History* (New York: Vintage, 1989), 365.

Are today: Quoted in ibid.

Mr. President: Quoted in ibid.

Alleviated the tension: Ibid.

103 *Is undressing:* Ibid., 370.

His pajamas: Ibid.

Considered "style": Nancy Dickerson, *Among Those Present: A Reporter's View of Washington* (New York: Ballantine, 1976), 138.

104 *Accent was noticeable at all:* Graham interview, 34.

East Texas woods: Quoted in Gould, *Lady Bird Johnson and the Environment,* 9.

As a ladybird: Quoted in "The First Lady Bird," 21.

Happen to them: Robert A. Caro, *The Years of Lyndon Johnson: The Path to Power* (New York: Knopf, 1982), 297.

105 *We never will:* Quoted in Jan Jarboe Russell, *Lady Bird: A Biography of Mrs. Johnson* (New York: Scribner, 1999), 112.

She did: Caro, 304.

Setting the table and all: Quoted in ibid., 303.

106 *At $9 million:* Russell, 166.

Made a speech: Christine Sadler, "Our Very Busy First Lady," *McCall's,* March 1964, 81.

107 *Propositioned me once:* Dickerson, 159.

So did everybody else: Ibid., 158.

"The P.M.": Carpenter interview, April 4, 1969, 25.

This question: Ibid.

108 *Printed putdowns:* Beale, *Power at Play,* 98.

More liveliness: Ibid., 99.

Most Admired Women: Cited in Troy, 159.

Seething: Thomas, *Dateline: White House,* 100.

From the wedding: McLendon and Smith, 121.

109 *By and large:* Johnson, 756.

Confident and happy: Thomas, *Dateline: White House,* 91.

110 *Herself at all*: Quoted in Boller, 397.

Pat the robot: Quoted in ibid.

Peppy person: Quoted in Caroli, *First Ladies,* 250.

Her feelings completely: Thomas, *Dateline: White House,* 170.

111 *Defer to her:* Quoted in Anthony Summers, *The Arrogance of Power: The Secret World of Richard Nixon* (New York: Viking, 2000), 37.

111 *Embarrass him:* Quoted in Marton, 188.

112 *Some of those guys:* Quoted in Caroli, *First Ladies,* 250.

The end of it: Quoted in Summers, 37.

Good in anything: Ibid, 120.

To talk about it: Stephen E. Ambrose, *Nixon: Ruin and Recovery, 1973–1990* (New York: Simon and Schuster, 1991), 272.

113 *American political history:* Lester David, "Pat Nixon's Life Story: 'I Gave Up Everything I Ever Loved . . . ,'" *Good Housekeeping,* August 1978, 160.

Around or not: Thomas, *Dateline: White House,* 166.

114 *Had it easy:* Quoted in Caroli, *First Ladies,* 329.

Last four years: Quoted in Marton, 193.

Consideration: Quoted in David, 164.

115 *Ever loved:* Quoted in ibid., 158.

The little guys: Quoted in Caroli, *First Ladies,* 251.

Misplaced martyrdom: Ibid.

Right glove off: Julie Nixon Eisenhower, *Pat Nixon: The Untold Story* (New York: Simon and Schuster, 1986), 254.

116 *Her own right:* Ibid.

Home and abroad: Thomas, *Dateline: White House,* 165.

First lady in history: Eisenhower, *Pat Nixon: The Untold Story,* 254.

Trip of a first lady: Lewine interview, 45.

117 *As a prop:* Quoted in Troy, 196.

Dick has done: Quoted in ibid.

Music-filled home: Beale, *Power at Play,* 196–97.

Reporters over others: McLendon and Smith, 59.

118 *Husband and wife level:* Quoted in Troy, 187.

Work at night: Quoted in ibid., 181.

$150,000 a year: McLendon and Smith, 66.

Snow-job technique: Ibid., 65.

Environmentalism: Troy, 184.

Off the ground: Quoted in ibid.

119 *You can be proud of:* Quoted in ibid., 193.

Events and publicity: Ibid.

Never lied: Thomas, *Dateline: White House,* 162.

120 *In the press:* Quoted in Ambrose, 71.

 Substantive copy: Carl S. Anthony, "Patricia (Thelma Catherine Ryan) Nixon," in Gould, ed., *American First Ladies,* 532.

 One of them: Ibid.

 Anything else: Quoted in ibid.

 Top experience: Quoted in Beale, *Power at Play,* 199.

 Fault with him: Ibid., 200.

121 *NO "bad habits":* Thomas, *Dateline: White House,* 160.

 Have loved her: Quoted in Caroli, *First Ladies,* 248.

 Of her heart: Bonnie Angelo, "The Woman in the Cloth Coat," *Time,* July 5, 1993, 39.

 And the media: Ibid.

 I've covered: Thomas, *Front Row at the White House,* 258.

CHAPTER FIVE

124 *Presidents and presidential spouses:* Watson, 195.

 Fifth in another: Ibid.

 Presidential couples or partners: Ibid., 194.

 Holds government together: Quoted in Thomas, *Dateline: White House,* 259.

125 *My dear wife, Betty:* Quoted in Anthony, *First Ladies,* 2:220.

 A first lady: Ibid.

 Sat right down and cried: Betty Ford, with Chris Chase, *The Times of My Life* (New York: Ballantine, 1979), 163.

 Life as always: Quoted in Dickerson, 241.

 His favorite pot roast: Ibid.

 Terrifying: Ford, 167.

 Where it belonged: Ibid.

 Candor was established: Ibid.

126 *Blocking it out:* Ibid., 1.

 Since the Coolidges: Anthony, *First Ladies,* 2:227.

 Intimate lives: Thomas, *Dateline White House,* 273.

 Disgraceful and immoral: Ford, 173.

 Sleeping with his wife: Quoted in Sheila Rabb Weidenfeld, *First Lady's Lady* (New York: Putnam, 1979), 38.

 As often as possible: Ford, 183.

126 *Presidency imperial:* Marton, 200.

127 *On controversial subjects:* Thomas, *Dateline: White House,* 273.
Being a divorcee: Ibid.
With alcohol: Marton, 211.
Know what to do: Ibid., 212.

128 *Issue of abortion:* Ibid., 207.
Near zero: John Tebbel and Sarah Miles Watts, *The Press and the Presidency: From George Washington to Ronald Reagan* (New York: Oxford, 1985), 517.
The 1976 election: Ford, 197.

129 *By 300 to 400 percent:* Troy, 209.
Both breasts to cancer: John Pope, "Betty (Elizabeth Ann Bloomer) Ford," in Gould, ed., *American First Ladies,* 546.
As first lady: Ibid.
American Cancer Society: Ibid.
Contribution enough: Jane Roberts, "Forward Day by Day," *New York Times Magazine,* December 8, 1974, 36.

130 *Views of her husband:* Quoted in Anthony, *First Ladies,* 2:222.
The age of independence: Quoted in Weidenfeld, 146.
Much of the time: Boller, 421.

131 *Public officials:* Ibid., 422.
In the 1960s: Marton, 204.
Visible and active: Anthony, *First Ladies,* 2:224.
Perfectly mirrored it: Ibid.

132 *East Wing:* Karen M. Rohrer, "'If There Was Anything You Forgot to Ask. . . . ': The Papers of Betty Ford," in Nancy Kegan Smith and Mary C. Ryan, eds., *Modern First Ladies: Their Documentary Legacy* (Washington, D.C.: National Archives and Records Administration, 1989), 134.
Seem surly: Ford, 239–40.
I'm supposed to do: Quoted by Sheila Weidenfeld in interview by Maurine Beasley, Washington, D.C., September 20, 2004, 39.
Television is all about: Ibid.
Those [requested television] interviews: Ibid., 45.
Chat with it: Weidenfeld, 102.

133 *I pressed her to do the show:* Quoted in Lloyd Shearer, "Sheila Weidenfeld: The First Lady's Press Secretary," *Parade,* April 25, 1976, 4.

Your first cigarette: Ibid.

Having an affair: Quoted in Rohrer, 138.

Young to start affairs: Ibid.

Big girl: Ibid.

Blared the Los Angeles Times: Weidenfeld, 173.

134 *Parents' own:* Rohrer, 138.

Liability to Jerry: Ford, 225.

Twenty million: Rohrer, 140.

His wife's remarks: Quoted in Ford, 225.

An albatross: Dickerson, 271.

Speak her mind: Quoted in Marton, 210.

Share my views: Cited in Weidenfeld, 188.

To 23,232 against: Rohrer, 140.

135 *Asset to her husband:* Quoted in Caroli, *First Ladies,* 332.

Mrs. Ford's answer: "Mrs. Ford and the Affair of the Daughter," *Ladies' Home Journal,* November 1975, 118.

Moral sickness of Watergate: Quoted in ibid., 154.

Pillow talk: Quoted in Anthony, *First Ladies,* 1:232.

136 *Ribs at night:* Quoted in Troy, 223.

Own political stance: Anthony, *First Ladies,* 2:239.

Rock Washington: Ibid., 248.

Self-inflicted gunshot wound: Cheshire, 221.

I cried: Ford, 253.

137 *The* New York Daily News: Quoted in Troy, 227.

Use as centerpieces: Rohrer, 136.

Women of the Year: Troy, 227.

Million copies an issue: Ibid., 231.

"*BETTY IN THE WHITE HOUSE*": Ibid.

138 *Able to carry on:* Ford, 290–91.

140 *In the White House:* Boller, 443.

Wrong with that?: Quoted in ibid.

141 *Wouldn't go away:* Rosalynn Carter, *First Lady from Plains* (Boston: Houghton Mifflin, 1984), 174.

141 *A good one:* Ibid., 175.

Johnson and the environment: Quoted in Mary Finch Hoyt interview by Maurine Beasley, Washington, D.C., October 18, 2004, 2.

Most powerful: Quoted in Carter, 175.

Doing anything differently!: Quoted in ibid., 3.

142 *Really ever understood:* Beale, *Power at Play,* 243.

So raw: Hoyt interview, 5.

143 *Most of the meal:* Beale, *Power at Play,* 251.

Was shocked: Ibid.

Georgetown power elite: Quoted in C. David Heymann, *The Georgetown Ladies' Social Club* (New York: Atria, 2003), 266.

Great deal of resentment: Quoted in ibid.

Unofficial media adviser: Ibid.

Suffer us gladly: Thomas, *Front Row at the White House,* 82.

144 *Nice to them:* Ibid., 93.

Class in the White House: Ibid., 270.

Public relations advisors: McClendon, 276.

If she could speak: Ibid.

Very, very cautious: Ibid.

Of her predecessor: Kathy B. Smith, "(Eleanor) Rosalynn (Smith) Carter," in Gould, ed., *American First Ladies,* 566.

In my heart many times: Quoted in Troy, 236.

145 *Astonishingly political wife:* Ibid., 236–37.

Wouldn't tell you!: Quoted in Carter, 140.

Mind answering questions: Ibid.

No. 1 adviser: Quoted in Beale, *Power at Play,* 259.

Need your help: Quoted in ibid.

President needs your help: Quoted in ibid.

Attending Cabinet meetings: Carter, 175.

Something I wanted to do: Ibid.

146 *Sounding board for him:* Ibid., 164.

In each other's work: Ibid.

Other old timers: Caroli, *First Ladies,* 262.

147 *A Washington outsider:* Hoyt interview, 5.

148 *To the White House later:* Carter, 91.

148   *Carter from Plains, Georgia:* Ibid., 8.

149   *The White House doesn't:* Quoted in Abigail McCarthy, "The Family of the Man," *Washington Post,* Style section, March 3, 1980, B1.

Elect the family: Ibid.

On [Capitol] Hill: Quoted in Marton, 230.

Very male territory: Carter, 188.

Back to imperial times: Quoted in Smith, 574.

Policies to them: "Out on Her Own," *Newsweek,* June 13, 1977, 15.

150   *President of the United States:* Ibid.

For her actions: Caroli, *First Ladies,* 266–67.

Handle a Presidential errand: Quoted in Marton, 231.

Seen and heard: Ibid., 266.

Mental capabilities: Beale, *Power at Play,* 260.

No-nonsense woman: Ibid.

Radcliffe told Kati Marton: Marton, 228–29.

Her playful side: Ibid.

Apparently ended successfully: Quoted in Smith, 574.

151   *Almost to perfection:* Ibid.

More than almost anything: Quoted in Anthony, *First Ladies,* 2:297.

Able to go himself: Quoted in Caroli, *First Ladies,* 267.

152   *Good, substantive article:* Carter, 173.

Overtime to the staff: Ibid.

"Lemonade Lucy" Hayes: Anthony, *First Ladies,* 2:280.

Not a prude: Quoted in ibid.

Much to our chagrin: Carter, 173.

Obviously was: Ibid.

It didn't seem right: Ibid.

PBS's MacNeil/Lehrer Report: Smith, 576.

153   *Mental Health Systems Act:* Carter, 278.

To testify before Congress: Ibid.

Being paid at all: Mary Finch Hoyt, *East Wing: Politics, the Press and a First Lady,* 140 (book is available through the Internet at www.Xlibris.com).

153 *First lady's job:* Quoted in Anthony, *First Ladies,* 2:283.
154 *To supervise her offices:* Ibid.
"*HER COSTLY COURT*": Quoted in Troy, 266.
An ambitious woman: "The President's Partner," *Newsweek,* November 5, 1979, 36.
The patient: Sally Quinn, "Rosalynn's Journey," *Washington Post,* Style section, July 25, 1979, B1.
155 *Know about her husband:* Quoted in ibid.
Enough for both of us: Quoted in Carter, 342.
At 71 percent: Troy, 265.

CHAPTER SIX
159 *Arc of great drama:* Michael K. Deaver, *Nancy: A Portrait of My Years with Nancy Reagan* (New York: Morrow, 2004), 5.
Few of us: Ibid.
Nancy at his side: Ibid., 6.
160 *Mr. Nice Guy:* Quoted in Sally Quinn, "Scapegoats: The Essence of Washington Politics," *Washington Post,* Style section, January 25, 1981, G3.
Total equality: Troy, 306.
161 *Irony and parody:* Catharine R. Stimpson, "Nancy Reagan Wears a Hat: Feminism and Its Cultural Consensus," *Critical Inquiry* 14 (Winter 1988): 227.
Send each other: Ibid.
Looks foggy, misty: Ibid.
Gender of its power: Ibid.
Expensively clad creep: Ibid.
162 *Her face glowed:* Troy, 279.
Ronnie on anything: Quoted in ibid., 280.
Machiavellian: Ibid.
She used to say: Lou Cannon, *Reagan* (New York: Putnam, 1982), 141.
Has two children: Quoted in Troy, 279.
163 *Around the state:* James G. Benze Jr., "Nancy (Anne Frances Robbins Davis) Reagan," in Gould, ed., *American First Ladies,* 591.

163 *Best-dressed women:* Ibid.

Woman's daydream, circa 1948: Quoted in Marton, 254.

"Been playing" Jackie Kennedy "forever": Quoted in Anthony, *First Ladies,* 2:319.

Worse start: Thomas, *Front Row at the White House,* 272.

164 *Dreary and uninviting:* Nancy Reagan, with William Novak, *My Turn: The Memoirs of Nancy Reagan* (New York: Random House, 1989), 225.

But who knows?: Maureen Santini interview by Maurine Beasley, Washington, D.C., April 27, 2004, 1.

Can begin decorating: Maureen Santini, Associated Press dispatch, Washington, D.C.: December 12, 1980, Santini's personal files.

Before the Reagan presidency ends: Quoted in ibid.

Decorator can get started: Hoyt, *East Wing,* 204.

She's [Orr is] gone: Ibid., 205.

165 *Think of it:* Reagan, 225.

Dream of doing that: Ibid.

How to use it: Maureen Santini, Associated Press dispatch, Washington, D.C., December 11, 1980, Santini's personal files.

Weapon it was: Ibid.

"WILL BE DISARMING": Quoted in Kitty Kelley, *Nancy Reagan: The Unauthorized Biography* (New York: Pocket Star, 1991), 316.

166 *Symbol of status:* Haynes Johnson, *Sleepwalking through History: America in the Reagan Years* (New York: Anchor/Doubleday, 1992), 19.

With the New Rich: Ibid., 21.

Sixteen hundred dollars: Ibid.

Free enterprise at its best: Ibid., 23.

Ensemble of Jackie Kennedy: Anthony, *First Ladies,* 2:323.

167 *Most auspicious start:* Thomas, *Front Row at the White House,* 272.

Coat by Maximillan: Ibid.

For twenty minutes: Kelley, *Nancy Reagan,* 333.

167   *For my wardrobe?:* Reagan, 33.
          No trouble staying slim: Ibid., 41.
          Couldn't identify with you: Quoted in ibid., 34.
          Rebelling against: Ibid.
168   *Actually 1921:* Benze, 583.
169   *A bit precipitously:* Reagan, 103.
          Wouldn't have been premature: Quoted in Troy, 277.
          Years of misery: Ibid., 278.
          Try to practice: Reagan, 147.
          On the front page: Ibid., 148.
170   *It scares me:* Quoted in Boller, 449.
          Image was all eighties: Anthony, *First Ladies,* 2:360.
171   *Even Mrs. Roosevelt:* Ibid., 361.
          Jackie Kennedy had: Ibid.
          Than I can remember: Reagan, 37.
          The Cutout Doll: Ibid.
          Selecting a pattern with a border etched in gold: Maureen Santini,
             "First Lady Orders China," *Washington Post,* Style section,
             September 12, 1981, B1.
172   *Classified as a vegetable:* Caroli, *First Ladies,* 276.
          Nothing but praise?: Quoted in Marton, 262.
          Her previous habits: Benze, 596.
173   *Contest hands down:* Reagan, 39.
          First lady of modern times: Ibid.
          Who I really was: Ibid., 38.
          Around crowds: Quoted in Marton, 260.
          Wanted to do: Ibid.
          Project-Nancy-Has-a-Heart: Quoted in Boller, 459.
174   *The Gridiron dinner:* Marton, 263.
          Suddenly loved her: Ibid.
          Big red earrings: Thomas, *Front Row at the White House,* 274.
          Ed Meese sews: Reagan, 42.
175   *Regal, distant, disdainful:* Ibid., 43.
          Musses up your hair: Quoted in Boller, 460.
          Wayward China: Ibid.

175 *Official White House functions:* Heymann, *The Georgetown Ladies' Social Club,* 266.

Almost anyone in Washington: Ibid., 342.

176 *Generally deal with:* Graham, 610.

By telephone: Ibid., 266.

Reagan administration: Greenfield, 215.

All that much help: Ibid.

Function once he got there: Ibid., 216.

177 *Against drug abuse:* Maureen Santini, Associated Press dispatch, Washington, D.C., February 15, 1982, Santini's personal files.

Invited to accompany her: Ibid.

Few treatment centers: Ibid.

The world over: Deaver, 91.

Public Broadcasting Service: Benze, 597.

178 *You have to do:* Quoted in Boller, 461.

Crusade for a Drug-Free America: Ibid.

Piano legs: Quoted in Kelley, *Nancy Reagan,* 204.

Without knowing her: Telephone interview with Sheila Tate by Maurine Beasley, Washington, D.C., December 15, 2004, 3.

Even the Secret Service: James S. Rosebush, *First Lady: Public Wife* (Lanham, Md.: Madison, 1988), 44.

Another side of this woman: Ibid.

179 *Thousands of dollars:* Mark Hertsgaard, *On Bended Knee: The Press and the Reagan Presidency* (New York: Farrar, Straus and Giroux, 1988), 159.

Lead changed immediately: Ibid.

Swipes at Nancy: Quoted in ibid.

Running the country: Ibid.

Private morality: Boller, 461.

Private sector: Rosebush, 112.

Not spending: Ibid., 113.

180 *Campaign that built credibility:* Tate interview, 1.

Went on TV: Ibid

With one issue: Ibid.

180 *Paying for her privileges:* Ibid.

By a first lady: Troy, 291.

Total of 85,930: Carl Sferrazza Anthony, "She Saves Everything: The Papers of Nancy Reagan," in Smith and Ryan, eds., *Modern First Ladies,* 160.

Back ten years: Quoted in Reagan, 287.

Only for myself: Ibid.

181 *First lady should:* Benze, 597.

Portrayed by the media: 18.

A little silly: Quoted in Troy, 299.

As soon as possible: Reagan, 337.

The Soviet Union: Thomas, *Front Row at the White House,* 272.

182 *Five chiefs of staff:* Barbara Silberdick Feinberg, *America's First Ladies: Changing Expectations* (New York: Franklin Watts, 1998), 113.

Power at the White House: Helene Von Damm, *At Reagan's Side* (New York: Doubleday, 1989), 229.

Work her will: Ibid.

Deputy president: Reagan, 314.

183 *Dead in the water:* Donald T. Regan, *For the Record: From Wall Street to Washington* (San Diego, Calif.: Harcourt Brace Jovanovich, 1988), 72.

Bound to read: Ibid., 289.

Going to do it: Ibid., 74.

Movement of the planets: Ibid.

First lady had had: Boller, 464.

In a Newsweek *poll:* Anthony, *First Ladies,* 2:401.

184 *Nancy Reagan's 19 percent:* Sally Quinn, "Nancy Reagan Looks Back in Anger," *Washington Post Book World,* November 5, 1989, 1.

To him or his staff: Quoted in Boller, 465.

Low lows: Ibid.

Get used to: Quoted in Caroli, *First Ladies,* 279.

I don't know what does: Reagan, 60.

Husband every night: Quoted in Marton, 266.

184 *Your ear . . . peace:* Ibid.
185 *Various media:* Quoted in Todd S. Purdum, "A More Relaxed
        Laura Bush Shows Complexity under Calm," *New York
        Times,* January 20, 2005, A1.
        She answered, "All": Ibid.
        George H. W. Bush: Ibid.
186 *Power, aging, and beauty:* Troy, 343.
        Messed up: Donnie Radcliffe, "Barbara Bush, Being Herself,"
        Washington Post, Style section, January 15, 1989, F6.
        On the campaign trail: Ibid., F1.
        Way it is really: Quoted in ibid.
187 *And her husband's:* Marton, 275.
        DOWN-TO-EARTH FIRST LADY: Headline for Margaret Carlson,
        "The Silver Fox," *Time,* January 23, 1989, 22.
        Are tickled pink: Quoted in Radcliffe, F6.
        So can they: Ibid.
        "'Fat ladies'": Headline for United Press International dis-
        patch from Washington, D.C., *Columbia* (Mo.) *Missourian,*
        January 16, 1989, A2.
        Here [*in the vice president's mansion*]*:* Radcliffe, F6.
188 *Whatever you do:* Quoted in ibid.
        On that scale: Ibid.
        Press availabilities: Cited in Troy, 325.
        And Ronald Reagan: Myra Gutin, "Barbara (Pierce) Bush," in
        Gould, ed., *American First Ladies,* 616.
        Be a wimp: Anthony, *First Ladies,* 2:426.
189 *To control the story:* Quoted in Marton, 294.
        Against the first woman: George Bush, *All the Best: My Life in
        Letters and Other Writings* (New York: Scribner, 1999), 337.
        Rhymes with rich: Quoted in ibid., 340n.
        Geraldine to apologize: Ibid.
        Vice President and Mrs. Bush: Marton, 264.
190 *And Barbara cried:* Quoted in Peter Schweizer and Rochelle
        Schweizer, *The Bushes: Portrait of a Dynasty* (New York:
        Doubleday, 2004), 295.

190 *The national spotlight:* Gutin, 618.

Hair and their clothing: Reagan, 31.

They once enjoyed: Heymann, *The Georgetown Ladies' Social Club,* 291.

How unhappy it makes them: Michael Kilian and Arnold Sawislak, *Who Runs Washington* (New York: St. Martin's Press, 1982), 214.

The Reagan crowd: Ibid.

191 *Drag around $1,600 handbags:* Ibid.

Have a chance: Barbara Bush, *Barbara Bush: A Memoir* (New York: Scribner, 1994), 143.

Lose some weight: Ibid., 149.

Announced for the presidency: Ibid.

Appreciate the humor: Gutin, 616.

192 *Self-deprecating personality:* Tate interview, 5.

George Bush's mother: Ibid.

Say to that?: Quoted in Bush, 148.

Woman of the forties: Ibid.

For a kiss: Margaret Carlson, "The Candidates' Love Match," *Time,* September 26, 1988, 23.

193 *Naval air service:* Herbert Parmet, *George Bush: The Life of a Lone Star Yankee* (New York: Scribner, 1997), 47.

Just about throw up: Troy, 315.

194 *Depressed, lonely, and unhappy:* Bush, 135.

Leave me: Ibid.

Emotional problems: Ibid., 136.

195 *What you get:* Quoted in Thomas, *Front Row at the White House,* 279.

Too front and center: Bush, 214.

Absolutely not: Quoted in Marton, 300.

The only week: Quoted in ibid., 74–75.

Continue to do so: Ibid., 75.

First lady some time: Quoted in Parmet, 36.

Ties into literacy: Quoted in Radcliffe, F6.

196 *Lobby the federal government:* Ibid.

Personal contact: Anthony, *First Ladies,* 2:430.

196 *Herself and her husband:* Caroli, *First Ladies,* 285.
197 *On her wrong side:* Maureen Santini, email to Maurine Beasley, April 10, 2004.
    Refreshingly honest: Ibid.
    Radiation therapy and medication: Caroli, *First Ladies,* 284.
    A lot of publicity: Santini email.
    Who became president: Caroli, *First Ladies,* 286.
198 *I wish him well:* Text of speech by Barbara Bush, Wellesley College, Wellesley, Mass., June 1, 1990, in Bush, 540.
    Of the audience: Gutin, 622.
    The guest list: Barbara Matusow interview by Maurine Beasley, Bethesda, Md., March 2, 2004, 6.
    Hope they're good: Bush, 479.
    Most admired women: Caroli, *First Ladies,* 286.
199 *Baby boomers:* Bush, 498.
    About the media: Ibid., 499.
    Calculating politician: Troy, 341.

CHAPTER SEVEN

202 *In Beijing:* Marton, 334.
203 *Own traditions:* Neel Lattimore email interview by Maurine Beasley, January 25, 2005.
204 *America's Exhibit A:* Hillary Rodham Clinton, *Living History* (New York: Simon and Schuster, 2003), 141.
205 *Way-to-the-top story:* Betty Houchin Winfield, "'Madame President': Understanding a New Kind of First Lady," *Media Studies Journal* 8 (Spring 1994): 68.
    High-level meetings: Christopher Andersen, *American Evita: Hillary Clinton's Path to Power* (New York: Morrow, 2004), 118.
    Anything but liberal: Rodham Clinton, 291.
208 *Clout in a first lady:* Caroli, *First Ladies,* 303.
    Major policy effort?: Rodham Clinton, 140.
    Paradoxical roles: Ibid.
207 *Fully understand it:* Ibid., 105.
    Blame Mrs. Clinton: Lattimore email interview.

207 *Covering Mrs. Clinton:* Ibid.

Cover the first lady: Ibid.

Health care reform: Ibid.

208 *Pink Press Conference:* Rodham Clinton, 226.

209 *As if she is:* Quoted in Marton, 332.

Washington elite: Ibid.

Outside Washington: Thomas, *Front Row at the White House,* 286.

Will ask: Quoted in ibid.

Paint herself that way: Matusow interview, 3.

Very lovely: Ibid.

210 *Relished the best:* Ibid.

Meant more to her: Ibid.

Were raised with: Quoted in ibid., 287.

211 *Most Influential Lawyers:* Caroli, *First Ladies,* 296.

212 *Arrangement:* Rodham Clinton, 107.

Don't vote for him: Quoted in ibid.

213 *All I can tell you:* Quoted in ibid., 109.

Some combination: Quoted in Barbara Burrell, *Public Opinion, the First Ladyship, and Hillary Rodham Clinton,* rev. ed. (New York: Routledge, 2001), 31.

Had teas: Quoted in Rodham Clinton, 109.

Barbara Bush: Caroli, *First Ladies,* 302.

214 *Reluctant to probe:* Lewis L. Gould, "Hillary Rodham Clinton," in Gould, ed., *American First Ladies,* 640.

Sue their parents: Quoted in Burrell, 30.

Too intelligent: Ibid.

State of Maine: Caroli, *First Ladies,* 299.

HILLARY FROM HELL: Ibid., 301.

215 *Lady MacBeth:* Quoted in Burrell, 27.

She wanted to be: Quoted in Marton, 327.

All we had: Quoted in ibid., 326.

216 *Learn the hard way:* Quoted in Thomas, *Front Row at the White House,* 290.

Any kind of advice: Ibid.

216 *First time in forty years:* Ibid., 291.

Violations regarding women: Steven Mufson, "First Lady Critical of China, Others on Women's Rights," *Washington Post,* September 6, 1995, 1.

Any other first lady: Lattimore email interview.

217 *Didn't take:* Santini, email.

Wrath of the public: Ibid.

Still be herself: Ibid.

Directly to the public: Rodham Clinton, 291.

Psychobabble pieces about her: Quoted in Marton, 327.

Character and personality: Ibid., 328.

218 *Because she liked to:* Lattimore email interview.

Respectful and stylish: Ibid.

A job: Caroli, *First Ladies,* 290.

Get one free!: Troy, 356.

219 *ASCENT OF A WOMAN:* Howard Kurtz, "Hillary to the Pillory!" *Washington Post,* Style section, March 7, 1994, C1.

President was doing: Burrell, 45.

People in public life: Quoted in Kurtz, "Hillary to the Pillory," C3.

220 *Overhaul plan last year:* Quoted in Howard Kurtz, "Off the Record and in the Paper," *Washington Post,* Style section, January 11, 1995, C1 and C3.

A "bitch": Ibid., C3.

Sandbagging her this week: Ibid.

Like her either: Lois Romano, "First Lady, Eye to Eye with Herself," in "The Reliable Source," *Washington Post,* January 10, 1995, E3.

Congenital liar: Quoted in Burrell, 50.

Unfavorable impression: Ibid., 51.

221 *Eleanor Roosevelt and Mahatma Gandhi:* Evan Thomas, "Hillary's Other Side," *Newsweek,* July 1, 1996, 21.

Postmodern woman: Winfield, "Madame President," 59.

Wrongdoing and the Clintons: Ibid., 69.

Favorable opinion: Burrell, 51.

222 *"Politically motivated" special counsel:* David Maraniss, "First Lady's Energy, Determination Bind a Power Partnership," *Washington Post,* February 1, 1998, A1.

Adopted as first lady: Burrell, 51.

Loved the President: Lattimore email interview.

223 *Candidate began:* Roxanne Roberts, "The Double Life of Hillary Clinton," *Washington Post,* Style section, February 3, 2000, C9.

Electing Hillary: Dick Morris, with Eileen McGann, *Rewriting History* (New York: HarperCollins, 2004), 194.

Reserved personality: Beth J. Harpaz, *The Girls in the Van: Covering Hillary* (New York: St. Martin's Press, 2001), 267.

224 *Wives in American history:* Gould, ed., *American First Ladies,* 641

As an equal partner: Winfield, "Madame President," 68.

CHAPTER EIGHT

225 *Kennedy families:* Schweizer and Schweizer, 543–44.

226 *Comforter-in-chief:* Nina Burleigh, "Laura Bush," *Us Weekly,* October 15, 2001, 28.

Nurturing the nation: Ann Gerhart, "Laura Bush, Comforter in Chief," *Washington Post,* Style section, September 19, 2001, C4.

Rhetoric of war: Ibid.

227 *Say to children:* Quoted in text of Laura Bush speech to National Press Club, Washington, D.C., November 8, 2001, 2.

Time and attention: Ibid.

Land of the living: Quoted in ibid., 6.

Throughout our land: Ibid.

Feel good: Ibid.

Eleanor Roosevelt: Ann Gerhart, "Tending the Home Front," *Washington Post,* Style section, November 9, 2001, C1.

Her memoir: Ibid.

228 *Teaching abstinence:* Christopher Andersen, *George and Laura: Portrait of an American Marriage* (New York: Morrow, 2002), 239.

228 *Be your spouse:* Gerhart, "Tending the Home Front," C3.

Read them bedtime stories: Gerhart, "Laura Bush, Comforter in Chief."

Adults in your life: Ibid.

Up-lifter in chief: Ellen Goodman, "More than 'Comforter in Chief'?" *Washington Post,* November 11, 2001, B5.

Great first ladies: Ibid.

229 *Court more women:* Mike Allen, "Laura Bush Gives Radio Address," *Washington Post,* November 18, 2001, A14.

Afghanistan, the Taliban: Ibid.

Under the Taliban: Elisabeth Bumiller, "Women Trade Shadows for Washington's Limelight," *New York Times,* November 30, 2001, A19.

Address to Afghanistan: Ann Gerhart, *The Perfect Wife: The Life and Choices of Laura Bush* (New York: Simon and Schuster, 2004), 179.

Come to the table: Quoted in ibid., 180.

Official United States positions: Ibid.,182.

230 *Abortions in China:* Ibid., 183.

Skillful advocacy: Quoted in Ann Gerhart, "The First Lady's Second Reading," *Washington Post,* Style section, January 25, 2002, C7.

Same as her husband's: Ibid.

231 *Best for our country:* "Laura Bush: An Intimate Conversation," an interview with Ellen Levine, *Good Housekeeping,* February 2003, 97.

War in Iraq: Jim Brosseau, "George and Laura: How Faith Keeps Them Strong," *Women's Faith and Spirit* (Fall 2003): 31.

Her husband's mind: Alessandra Stanley, "The First Lady's Influence Is Starting to Reveal Itself," *New York Times,* September 1, 2004, P9.

Steal the limelight: Quoted in Marton, 351.

To get married: Ibid., 354.

232 *A great fit:* Quoted in ibid.

And I admire: Quoted in ibid.

232 *Friendly troops:* Gerhart, *The Perfect Wife,* 79.

233 *Give a campaign speech:* Tamara Lipper and Rebecca Sinderbrand, "The Reluctant Campaigner," *Newsweek,* September 6, 2004, 40.

Limits for them: Gerhart, *The Perfect Wife,* 71.

Left totally alone: "Mrs. Bush Criticizes Coverage of Daughter," *Washington Post,* Style section, July 31, 2001, C2.

Me or Jack Daniel's: Quoted in Gerhart, *The Perfect Wife,* 75.

Death is part of life: Ibid., 9.

234 *What he does:* Quoted in Lipper and Sinderbrand, 40.

World will be peaceful: George and Laura Bush interview by Peggy Noonan, "Be Proud of What We Stand For," *Ladies' Home Journal,* October 2003, 130.

Family and for children: Ibid., 134.

Bush's TV ads: Susan Page, *USA TODAY,* October 20, 2004, D1.

Versus 16 percent: Ibid., D2.

Segment undecided: Ibid.

Candidate to vote for: Ibid., D1.

235 *To be true:* Todd S. Purdum, "A More Relaxed Laura Bush Shows Complexity under Calm," *New York Times,* January 20, 2005, A1.

To know me or whatever: Ibid., A16.

CHAPTER NINE

237 *Tom Wolfe:* Caption, picture, *New York Times,* February 7, 2005, A16.

238 *WHITE HOUSE LETTER:* Partial headline, Elisabeth Bumiller, "Bush's Official Reading List, and a Racy Omission," *New York Times,* February 7, 2005, A16.

The first lady: Ibid.

Self-destructive choices: Michael A. Fletcher, "First Lady Focuses on Kids at Risk," *Washington Post,* February 9, 2005, A3.

Nominally headed: Ibid.

Ready for work: Brian Williams interview, "First Lady Looks Forward to New Role," February 3, 2005, MSNBC.com,

http://www.msnbc.msn.com/id/6909276, accessed on
February 25, 2005.

238 *Hope I'm ready:* Ibid.

Watch together at all in the evening: Ibid.

239 *To speak at a salute:* Bumiller, "Bush's Official Reading List,"
A16.

240 *Beer-and-sex-soaked novel:* Ibid.

Jenna and Barbara: Ibid.

COMMUNITY-BASED PROGRAMS TOUTED: Subhead, Fletcher,
"First Lady Focuses on Kids at Risk," A3.

242 *They're not accurate:* Sheilah Kast email message to Maurine
Beasley, February 12, 2005.

Not power-sharing: Troy, XIII.

243 *$10 million for Republican party:* "New Term Offers First Lady
Opportunities," Associated Press story posted on ABC
.com, January 16, 2005, http://abcnews.go.com/Politics
/Inauguration/wireStory, accessed on February 1, 2005.

244 *Two places at once:* Watson, 46.

Programs and agenda: Ibid.

President has ever faced: Truman, *First Ladies,* 5.

By their husband's status: Linda Witt, Karen M. Paget, and
Glenna Matthews, *Running as a Woman: Gender and Power in
American Politics* (New York: Free Press, 1994), 21.

To whom they are related: Ibid., 23.

245 *To practice law:* Ibid., 24.

Get one free: Quoted in ibid., 191.

Leather-clad dominatrix: Ibid.

246 *Arkansas press had been:* Morris, 87.

Or worse: Quoted in ibid.

Landed on Bill: Ibid., 89.

Symbol of their potential: Ibid., 131.

Cost $12 million: Ibid.

Colors political coverage of women: Witt, Paget, and Matthews,
190.

247 *Become too powerful:* Ibid., 191.

"Sob sister" style: Ibid.

247 *Men and women politicians:* Ibid.

Who covered the president: Jodi Enda interview by Maurine Beasley, June 21, 2004, Washington, D.C., 1.

248 *Separate from her husband:* Ibid.

Fodder for them: Matusow interview, 11.

Picture of a candidate's wife: Ibid., 12.

More applied to liberals than conservatives: Geneva Overholser interview by Maurine Beasley, December 3, 2004, Washington, D.C., 1.

249 *Comfortable we are with feminism:* Ibid., 3.

Cookie-cutter stereotypes: Sheila Gibbons, "Some Journalists Advancing Outdated Notions about the Role of First Ladies," *Media Report to Women* 32 (Summer 2004): 24.

Looking French: Quoted in ibid., 22–23.

Family Circle readers' contest: Ibid., 23.

Between candidates' wives: Ibid.

250 *Outspokenness or ambition:* Francine Prose, "What Do You Think She Was Thinking?" *Washington Post,* Outlook section, August 22, 2004, B4.

Teresa Heinz Kerry: Ibid.

Journalistically lazy: Gibbons, 23.

By extension, the nation: Ibid.

251 *Their traditional location:* Patterson, 293.

First lady's office: Ibid., 45.

Interns and volunteers: Telephone interview with Bradley Patterson by Maurine Beasley, February 14, 2005.

252 *White House counselor:* Patterson, 282.

Elected or appointed official: Ibid., 281–82.

253 *A confining role:* Betty H. Winfield, "The First Lady, Political Power, and the Media: Who Elected Her Anyway?" in Pippa Norris, ed., *Women, Media and Politics* (New York: Oxford University Press, 1997), 179.

Women are in the country: Quoted in Susan Page, "First Lady: Married to the Job," *USA TODAY,* October 20, 2005, 2D.

Half a generation behind: Ibid.

253 *Demands they be traditional:* Gil Troy comments, transcript, "The First Lady: Public Expectations, Private Lives," Part 1, Online NewsHour, PBS broadcast, October 25, 2004, 2, http://www.pbs.org/newshour/vote2004/first_ladies/, transcription accessed on October 27, 2004.

Focus on personal stories: Cited in Diane J. Heith, "The Lipstick Watch: Media Coverage, Gender, and Presidential Campaigns," in Robert P. Watson and Ann Gordon, eds., *Anticipating Madam President* (Boulder, Colo.: Lynne Rienner, 2003), 128–29.

254 *Take on issues:* Quoted in ibid., 129.

Democratic accountability: Germaine Greer, "Abolish Her: The Feminist Case against First Ladies," *New Republic,* June 26, 1995, 21.

Active heterosexuality: Ibid., 22.

Spending too much: Ibid., 23.

Success in politics: Ibid., 27.

255 *The most admired woman:* "George W. Bush Is Most Admired Man in 2004," Gallup Poll News Service, December 29, 2004, 2, http://www.gallup.com/poll/content/print.aspx?ci=14470, accessed on February 8, 2005.

Most admired list: Ibid.

The gender gap: Norris, ed., introduction to *Women, Media and Politics,* 4.

Antiabortion epithets: Max J. Skidmore, "Breaking the Final Glass Ceiling: When (Not If) a Woman Becomes President," in Watson and Gordon, 27.

256 *State legislatures:* "Women in Elective Office 2005," Fact Sheet, Center for American Women and Politics, Eagleton Institute of Politics, Rutgers University, New Jersey, 1.

Greater than in 2004: Ibid.

Qualified woman: S. Page.

A better president: Karen O'Connor, "Madam President: Sooner or Later?" in Watson and Gordon, eds., *Anticipating Madam President,* 211.

256 *Media responded poorly:* Ibid., 213.

Wear panty hose: Quoted in ibid., 214.

In the East Wing: S. Page.

257 *Trusted confidante:* Narrator, transcript, "The First Lady," part 3, 3, Online News/Hour, PBS broadcast, http://www.pbs .org/newshour/vote2004/first_ladies/, transcription accessed on October 27, 2004.

Job in the private sector: Ibid.

258 *Woman's coat tails:* Ibid., 2.

Elective office: See chart "First Lady vs. First Gentleman?" accompanying Page article.

Always present: Obituary, "Sir Denis Thatcher," BBC NEWS, June 26, 2003, http://newsvote.bbc.co.uk/mpapps /pagetools/print/news, accessed on February 14, 2005.

BIBLIOGRAPHY

BOOKS

Allen, Anne Beiser. *An Independent Woman: The Life of Lou Henry Hoover.* Westport, Conn.: Greenwood, 2000.

Allgor, Catherine. *Parlor Politics.* Charlottesville: University Press of Virginia, 2000.

Ambrose, Stephen E. *Nixon: Ruin and Recovery, 1973–1990.* New York: Simon and Schuster, 1991.

Ames, Mary Clemmer. *Ten Years in Washington: Life and Scenes in the National Capital.* Hartford, Conn.: Worthington, 1874.

Andersen, Christopher. *American Evita: Hillary Clinton's Path to Power.* New York: Morrow, 2004.

———. *George and Laura: Portrait of an American Marriage.* New York: Morrow, 2002.

Anderson, Jack, with James Boyd. *Confessions of a Muckraker.* New York: Ballantine, 1980.

Anthony, Carl Sferrazza. *First Ladies: The Saga of the President's Wives and Their Power, 1798–1990.* Vols. 1 and 2. New York: Morrow, 1990, 1991.

———. *Florence Harding.* New York: Morrow, 1998.

Baldrige, Letitia. *A Lady, First: My Life in the Kennedy White House and the American Embassies of Paris and Rome.* New York: Viking, 2001.

———. *Of Diamonds and Diplomats.* Boston: Houghton Mifflin, 1968.

Beale, Betty. *Power at Play: A Memoir of Parties, Politicians and the Presidents in My Bedroom.* Washington, D.C.: Regnery Gateway, 1993.

Beasley, Maurine. *Eleanor Roosevelt and the Media: A Public Quest for Self-Fulfillment.* Urbana: University of Illinois Press, 1987.

————, ed. *The White House Press Conferences of Eleanor Roosevelt.* New York: Garland, 1983.

Beasley, Maurine, and Sheila J. Gibbons. *Taking Their Place: A Documentary History of Women and Journalism.* 2nd ed. State College, Pa.: Strata Publishing, 2003.

Beasley, Maurine H., Holly C. Shulman, and Henry R. Beasley, eds. *The Eleanor Roosevelt Encyclopedia.* Westport, Conn.: Greenwood, 2001.

Birmingham, Stephen. *Jacqueline Bouvier Kennedy Onassis.* New York: Grosset and Dunlap, 1978.

Black, Allida M. *What I Hope to Leave Behind: The Essential Essays of Eleanor Roosevelt.* Brooklyn, N.Y.: Carlson, 1995.

Boller, Paul F., Jr. *Presidential Wives: An Anecdotal History.* New York: Oxford University Press, 1989.

Braden, Maria. *Women Politicians and the Media.* Lexington: University Press of Kentucky, 1996.

Briggs, Emily Edson. *The Olivia Letters.* New York: Neale Publishing, 1906.

Bryan, Helen. *Martha Washington: First Lady of Liberty.* New York: John Wiley, 2002.

Burns, James MacGregor, and Susan Dunn. *The Three Roosevelts: Patrician Leaders Who Transformed America.* New York: Atlantic Monthly Press, 2001.

Burrell, Barbara. *Public Opinion, the First Ladyship, and Hillary Rodham Clinton.* Rev. ed. New York: Routledge, 2001.

Burt, Elizabeth V. *Women's Press Organizations, 1881–1999.* Westport, Conn.: Greenwood, 2000.

Bush, Barbara. *Barbara Bush: A Memoir.* New York: Scribner, 1994.

Bush, George. *All the Best: My Life in Letters and Other Writings.* New York: Scribner, 1999.

Cannon, Lou. *Reagan.* New York: Putnam, 1982.

Caro, Robert A. *The Path to Power: The Years of Lyndon B. Johnson.* New York: Knopf, 1982.

Caroli, Betty Boyd. *America's First Ladies.* Pleasantville, N.Y.: Reader's Digest Association, 1996.

————. *First Ladies.* Expanded ed. New York: Oxford University Press, 1995.

————. *The Roosevelt Women.* New York: Basic Books, 1998.

Carpenter, Liz. *Ruffles and Flourishes.* Garden City, N.Y.: Doubleday, 1970.

Carter, Rosalynn. *First Lady from Plains.* Boston: Houghton Mifflin, 1984.

Cheshire, Maxine, with John Greenya. *Maxine Cheshire, Reporter.* Boston: Houghton Mifflin, 1978.

Collier, Peter, and David Horowitz. *The Kennedys: An American Drama.* New York: Summit, 1984.

Cook, Blanche Wiesen. *Eleanor Roosevelt: 1884–1938.* Vols. 1 and 2. New York: Viking, 1992, 1999.

Davis, John H. *The Kennedys: Dynasty and Disaster, 1848–1984.* New York: McGraw-Hill, 1985.

Deaver, Michael K. *Nancy: A Portrait of My Years with Nancy Reagan.* New York: Morrow, 2004.

Dickerson, Nancy. *Among Those Present: A Reporter's View of Twenty-five Years in Washington.* New York: Ballantine, 1976.

Eisenhower, Julie Nixon. *Pat Nixon: The Untold Story.* New York: Simon and Schuster, 1986.

————. *Special People.* New York: Ballantine Books, 1977.

Eisenhower, Susan. *Mrs. Ike.* New York: Farrar, Straus and Giroux, 1996.

Fairfax, Beatrice (Marie Manning). *Ladies Now and Then.* New York: Dutton, 1944.

Feinberg, Barbara Silberdick. *America's First Ladies: Changing Expectations.* New York: Franklin Watts, 1998.

Fleischner, Jennifer. *Mrs. Lincoln and Mrs. Keckly.* New York: Broadway Books, 2003.

Ford, Betty, with Chris Chase. *The Times of My Life.* New York: Ballantine, 1979.

————. *Betty: A Glad Awakening.* Garden City, N.Y.: Doubleday, 1987.

Furman, Bess. *Washington By-Line: The Personal History of a Newspaperwoman.* New York: Knopf, 1949.

————. *White House Profile*. Indianapolis, Ind.: Bobbs-Merrill, 1951.

Gallagher, Mary Barelli. *My Life with Jacqueline Kennedy,* edited by Frances Spatz Leighton. New York: David McKay, 1969.

Geer, Emily Apt. *First Lady:The Life of Lucy Webb Hayes.* Kent, Ohio: Kent State University Press/Hayes Presidential Center, 1984.

Gerhart, Ann. *The Perfect Wife: The Life and Choices of Laura Bush.* New York: Simon and Schuster, 2004.

Goodwin, Doris Kearns. *No Ordinary Time: Franklin and Eleanor Roosevelt—The Home Front in World War II.* New York: Simon and Schuster, 1994.

Gordon, Linda L. *From Lady Washington to Mrs. Cleveland.* Freeport, N.Y.: Books for Libraries Press, 1972, reprint of 1888 ed.

Gould, Lewis L., ed. *American First Ladies: Their Lives and Their Legacy.* New York: Garland, 1996.

————. *Lady Bird Johnson and the Environment.* Lawrence: University Press of Kansas, 1988.

————. *The Modern American Presidency.* Lawrence: University Press of Kansas, 2003.

Graham, Katharine. *Personal History.* New York: Vintage, 1998.

Greenfield, Meg. *Washington.* New York: Public Affairs, 2001.

Gutin, Myra G. *The President's Partner: The First Lady in the Twentieth Century.* Westport, Conn.: Greenwood, 1989.

Halberstam, David. *The Fifties.* New York: Fawcett Books, 1993.

Harpaz, Beth J. *The Girls in the Van: Covering Hillary.* New York: St. Martin's Press, 2001.

Helm, Edith Benham. *The Captains and the Kings.* New York: Putnam, 1954.

Hertsgaard, Mark. *On Bended Knee: The Press and the Reagan Presidency.* New York: Farrar, Straus Giroux, 1988.

Heymann, C. David. *The Georgetown Ladies' Social Club.* New York: Atria Books, 2003.

————. *A Woman Named Jackie.* New York: Lyle Stuart/Carol Communications, 1989.

Hoffmann, Joyce. *Theodore H. White and Journalism as an Illusion.* Columbia: University of Missouri Press, 1995.

Hoyt, Mary Finch. *East Wing: Politics, the Press, and a First Lady.* Available on the Internet at www.Xlibris.com.

Johnson, Claudia T. (Lady Bird). *A White House Diary.* New York: Holt, Rinehart and Winston, 1970.

Johnson, Haynes. *Sleepwalking through History: America in the Reagan Years.* New York: Anchor/Doubleday, 1992.

Kelley, Kitty. *The Family: The Real Story of the Bush Dynasty.* New York: Doubleday, 2004.

———. *Jackie Oh!* Secaucus, N.J.: Lyle Stuart, 1978.

———. *Nancy Reagan: The Unauthorized Biography.* New York: Pocket Star Books, 1992.

Kilian, Michael, and Arnold Sawislak. *Who Runs Washington?* New York: St. Martin's Press, 1982.

Klapthor, Margaret Brown. *The First Ladies.* Washington, D.C.: White House Historical Association, 1994.

Kramer, Freda. *Jackie: A Truly Intimate Biography.* New York: Tempo Star, 1979.

Lash, Joseph P. *Eleanor and Franklin: The Story of Their Relationship Based on Eleanor Roosevelt's Private Papers.* New York: Signet Book, 1973.

Lawn, Connie. *You Wake Me Each Morning.* San Jose, Calif.: Writers Club Press, 2000.

Levin, Phyllis Lee. *Abigail Adams: A Biography.* New York: St. Martin's Griffin, 1989.

———. *Edith and Woodrow.* New York: Scribner, 2001.

Louchheim, Katie. *By the Political Sea.* Garden City, N.Y.: Doubleday, 1970.

Marling, Karal Ann. *As Seen on TV: The Visual Culture of Everyday Life in the 1950s.* Cambridge, Mass.: Harvard University Press, 1994.

Martin, Janet M. *The Presidency and Women: Promise, Performance and Illusion.* College Station: Texas A&M Press, 2003.

Marton, Kati. *Hidden Power: Presidential Marriages That Shaped Our Recent History.* New York: Pantheon Books, 2001.

Mattern, David B., and Holly C. Shulman, eds. *The Selected Letters of Dolley Payne Madison.* Charlottesville: University of Virginia Press, 2003.

Mayo, Edith P., ed. *The Smithsonian Book of the First Ladies: Their Lives, Times and Issues.* New York: Holt, 1996.

Mayo, Edith P., and Denise D. Meringolo. *First Ladies: Political Role and Public Image.* Washington, D.C.: Smithsonian Institution, 1994.

McCarthy, Abigail. *Private Faces/Public Places.* Garden City, N.Y.: Doubleday, 1972.

McClendon, Sarah, with Jules Minton. *Mr. President, Mr. President! My Fifty Years of Covering the White House.* Los Angeles: General Publishing Group, 1996.

———. *My Eight Presidents.* N.p.: Wyden Books, 1976.

McLendon, Winzola, and Scottie Smith. *Don't Quote Me: Washington Newswomen and the Power Society.* New York: Dutton, 1970.

Means, Marianne. *The Woman in the White House: The Lives, Times and Influence of Twelve Notable First Ladies.* New York: Random House, 1963.

Morris, Dick, with Eileen McGann. *Rewriting History.* New York: HarperCollins, 2004.

Morris, Sylvia Jukes. *Edith Kermit Roosevelt: Portrait of a First Lady.* New York: Random House, 1980.

Neal, Steve. *The Eisenhowers.* Lawrence: University Press of Kansas, 1984.

Newspaper Association of America. *Facts about Newspapers.* Reston, Va.: Newspaper Association of America, 2003.

Norris, Pippa, ed. *Women, Media, and Politics.* New York: Oxford University Press, 1997.

Parmet, Herbert. *George Bush: The Life of a Lone Star Yankee.* New York: Scribner, 1997.

Patterson, Bradley H., Jr. *The White House Staff: Inside the West Wing and Beyond*. Washington, D.C.: Brookings Institution Press, 2000.

Perkins, Frances. *The Roosevelt I Knew*. New York: Viking, 1946.

Phillips, Kevin. *American Dynasty: Aristocracy, Fortune, and the Politics of Deceit*. New York: Viking, 2004.

Prindiville, Kathleen. *First Ladies*. New York: Macmillan, 1954.

Radcliffe, Donnie. *Hillary Rodham Clinton: A First Lady for Our Time*. New York: Warner Books, 1993.

Randolph, Mary. *Presidents and First Ladies*. New York: Appleton-Century, 1936.

Reagan, Nancy, with William Novak. *My Turn: The Memoirs of Nancy Reagan*. New York: Random House, 1989.

Regan, Donald T. *For the Record: From Wall Street to Washington*. San Diego, Calif.: Harcourt Brace Jovanovich, 1988.

Ritchie, Donald A. *Press Gallery: Congress and the Washington Correspondents*. Cambridge, Mass.: Harvard University Press, 1991.

Rodham Clinton, Hillary. *It Takes a Village, and Other Lessons Children Teach Us*. New York: Simon and Schuster, 1996.

———. *Living History*. New York: Simon and Schuster, 2003.

Roosevelt, [Anna] Eleanor. *The Autobiography of Eleanor Roosevelt*. New York: Harper, 1961.

———. *It's Up to the Women*. New York: Stokes, 1933.

———. *This I Remember*. New York: Harper, 1949.

———. *This Is My Story*. New York: Harper, 1937.

Rosebush, James S. *First Lady: Public Wife*. Lanham, Md.: Madison, 1988.

Ross, Ishbel. *Grace Coolidge and Her Era: The Story of a President's Wife*. New York: Dodd, Mead, 1962.

———. *Ladies of the Press*. New York: Harper, 1936.

Russell, Jan Jarboe. *Lady Bird: A Biography of Mrs. Johnson*. New York: Scribner, 1999.

Sandberg, Carl. *Mary Lincoln: Wife and Widow*. New York: Harcourt, Brace, 1932.

Saunders, Frances Wright. *First Lady between Two Worlds: Ellen Axson Wilson*. Chapel Hill: University of North Carolina Press, 1985.

Schweizer, Peter, and Rochelle Schweizer. *The Bushes: Portrait of a Dynasty*. New York: Doubleday, 2004.

Seale, William. *The President's House: A History*. Vols. 1 and 2. Washington, D.C.: White House Historical Association, 1986.

Simon, John Y., ed. *The Personal Memoirs of Julia Dent Grant*. New York: Putnam, 1975.

Sloan, William David, ed. *The Media in America*. 5th ed. Northport, Ala.: Vision Press, 2002.

Smith, Nancy Kegan, and Mary C. Ryan. *Modern First Ladies: Their Documentary Legacy*. Washington, D.C.: National Archives and Records Administration, 1989.

Summers, Anthony. *The Arrogance of Power: The Secret World of Richard Nixon*. New York: Viking, 2000.

Tebbel, John, and Sarah Miles Watts. *The Press and the Presidency*. New York: Oxford University Press, 1985.

Thomas, Helen. *Dateline: White House*. New York: Macmillan, 1975.

———. *Front Row at the White House*. New York: Scribner, 1999.

Troy, Gil. *Mr. and Mrs. President: From the Trumans to the Clintons*. 2nd ed. rev. Lawrence: University Press of Kansas, 2000.

Truman, Margaret. *Bess W. Truman*. New York: Macmillan, 1986.

———. *First Ladies: An Intimate Group Portrait of White House Wives*. New York: Fawcett Columbine, 1995.

Von Damm, Helen. *At Reagan's Side*. New York: Doubleday, 1989.

Watson, Robert P. *The Presidents' Wives: Reassessing the Office of First Lady*. Boulder, Colo.: Lynne Rienner, 2000.

———, ed. *American First Ladies*. Pasadena, Calif.: Salem, 2002.

Watson, Robert P., and Anthony T. Eksterowicz, eds. *The Presidential Companion: Readings on the First Ladies*. Columbia: University of South Carolina Press, 2003.

Watson, Robert P., and Ann Gordon, eds. *Anticipating Madam President*. Boulder, Colo.: Lynne Rienner, 2003.

Weidenfeld, Sheila Rabb. *First Lady's Lady: With the Fords at the White House*. New York: Putnam, 1979.

Wertheimer, Molly Meijer, ed. *Inventing a Voice: The Rhetoric of American First Ladies of the Twentieth Century.* Lanham, Md.: Rowman and Littlefield, 2004.

West, J. B., with Mary Lynn Kotz. *Upstairs at the White House: My Life with the First Ladies.* New York: Warner, 1974.

Wilson, Edith Bolling. *My Memoir.* Indianapolis, Ind.: Bobbs-Merrill, 1938.

Witt, Linda, Karen M. Paget, and Glenna Matthews. *Running as a Woman.* New York: Free Press, 1994.

SELECTED NEWSPAPER AND PERIODICAL ARTICLES AND BROADCASTS

Allen, Mike. "Laura Bush Gives Radio Address." *Washington Post,* November 18, 2001, A14.

Angelo, Bonnie. "The Woman in the Cloth Coat." *Time,* July 5, 1993, 39.

Anthony, Carl Sferrazza. "First Lady of Candor." *Washington Post,* Style section, April 8, 1993, D1 and D2.

Beale, Betty. "A Plea for U.S. Beauty." *Washington Evening Star,* September 8, 1965, B1 and B5.

———. "Rain-Pelted News Reporters Challenge Snake River." *Washington Evening Star,* September 9, 1965, B2.

Beasley, Maurine H., and Paul Belgrade. "Media Coverage of a Silent Partner: Mamie Eisenhower as First Lady." *American Journalism* 3, no. 1 (Winter 1986): 38–49.

Bromley, Dorothy Dunbar. "The Future of Eleanor Roosevelt." *Harper's Magazine* 180 (January 1940): 129–39.

Brosseau, Jim. "George and Laura: How Faith Keeps Them Strong." *Women's Faith and Spirit* [cover story] (Fall 2003): 28–31.

Bruck, Connie. "Hillary the Pol." *New Yorker,* May 30, 1994, 58–96.

Bumiller, Elisabeth. "White House Letter: Bush's Official Reading List, and a Racy Omission." *New York Times,* February 7, 2005, A16.

———. "Women Trade Shadows for Washington's Limelight." *New York Times,* November 30, 2001, A19.

Burleigh, Nina. "Laura Bush Comforter-in-Chief." *Us Weekly* [cover story], October 15, 2001, 27–32.

Carlson, Margaret. "At the Center of Power." *Time* [cover story], May 10, 1993, 28–37.

——. "The Silver Fox." *Time* [cover story], January 23, 1989, 22–26.

Chin, Paula. "The Silver Fox Speaks Her Mind." *People* [cover story], October 1, 1990, 82–88.

Cohen, Richard. "Rosalynn Carter's Role: Resolving the Mystery." *Washington Post,* Style section, July 31, 1979, C1 and 5.

David, Lester. "Pat Nixon's Life Story: 'I Gave Up Everything I Ever Loved.'" *Good Housekeeping,* August 1978, 113–15, 156–64.

"The First Lady: Public Expectations, Private Lives." Online News Hour transcript of PBS program produced by MacNeil/ Lehrer Productions. October 25, 2004. http://www.pbs .org/newshour/vote2004/first_ladies/transcript.

"The First Lady Bird." *Time* [cover story], August 28, 1964, 20–23.

"The First Lady Brings History and Beauty to the White House" [includes Hugh Sidey, "'Everything Must Have a Reason for Being There'"]. *Life* [cover story], September 1, 1961, 54–65.

Fletcher, Michael A. "First Lady Focuses on Kids at Risk." *Washington Post,* February 9, 2005, A3.

Gallup, George. "Mrs. Roosevelt More Popular Than President, Survey Finds." *Washington Post,* January 15, 1939, section 3, 1.

Gerhart, Ann. "The First Lady's Second Reading." *Washington Post,* Style section, January 25, 2002, C1 and C7.

——. "Laura Bush, Comforter in Chief." *Washington Post,* Style section, September 19, 2001, C1 and C4.

Gibbons, Sheila. "Some Journalists Advancing Outdated Notions about the Role of First Ladies." *Media Report to Women* 32 (Summer 2004): 22–24.

Goodman, Ellen. "More than 'Comforter in Chief'?" *Washington Post,* November 11, 2001, B7.

Greer, Germaine. "Abolish Her: The Feminist Case against First Ladies." *New Republic,* June 21, 1994, 21–27.

Grimes, Paul. "Mrs. Kennedy Gets a Festive Welcome on Arrival in India." *New York Times,* March 13, 1962, A1 and A3.

Hertz, Rosanna, and Susan M. Reverby. "Gentility, Gender and Political Protest: The Barbara Bush Controversy at Wellesley College." *Gender and Society* 9, no. 5 (October 1995): 594–611.

Howard, James T. "Males Squirm at First Lady's Parley." *PM,* September 28, 1943, 5.

Hunter, Marjorie. "Public Servant without Pay: The First Lady." *New York Times Magazine,* December 15, 1963, 10, 70–73.

"The 'Image' Mrs. Kennedy Left in Asia." *U.S. News & World Report,* April 2, 1962, 15.

"J" in "Life and Leisure." *Newsweek,* January 1, 1962, 31–35.

Kurtz, Howard. "Hillary to the Pillory!" *Washington Post,* March 7, 1994, C1 and C3.

———. "Off the Record and in the Paper?" *Washington Post,* January 11, 1995, C1 and C8.

"Ladies' Day at the Summit." *Newsweek,* June 12, 1961, 25.

Levine, Ellen. "Laura Bush: An Intimate Conversation, an Interview." *Good Housekeeping* [cover story], February 2003, 92–97, 190–91.

Lipper, Tamara, and Rebecca Sinderbrand. "The Reluctant Campaigner." *Newsweek,* September 6, 2004, 40.

"Lovely Aspirants for Role of First Lady." *Life,* October 10, 1960, 150–57.

MacPherson, Myra. "White House Confidential." *Washington Post,* Style section, December 14, 1978, C1 and C3.

"Mamie Eisenhower Dies in Sleep at 82 in Hospital in Washington." *New York Times,* November 2, 1979, B5.

Maraniss, David. "First Lady's Energy, Determination Bind a Power Partnership." *Washington Post,* February 1, 1998, A1 and A18.

McCarthy, Abigail. "The Family of the Man." *Washington Post,* Style section, March 3, 1980, B1 and B3.

McLaughlin, Kathleen. "Mrs. Roosevelt Goes Her Way." *New York Times Magazine,* July 5, 1936, 7, 15.

"Mrs. Ford and the Affair of the Daughter." *Ladies' Home Journal,* November 1975, 118, 154.

"Mrs. Kennedy Guest of Queen at Lunch." *New York Times,* March 29, 1962, A1 and A9.

Mufson, Steven. "First Lady Critical of China, Others on Women's Rights." *Washington Post,* September 6, 1995, A1 and A24.

Noonan, Peggy. "Be Proud of What We Stand For." *Ladies' Home Journal* [cover story], October 2003, 118–34.

"Out on Her Own." *Newsweek,* June 13, 1977, 15–18.

Page, Susan. "First Lady: Married to the Job." With graphs, charts, and sidebars. *USA TODAY,* October 20, 2004, D1, D2, and D7.

"The President's Partner." *Newsweek* [cover story], November 5, 1979, 36–47.

Prose, Francine. "What Do You Think She Was Thinking?" *Washington Post,* Outlook section, August 22, 2004, B1 and B4.

Purdum, Todd S. "A More Relaxed Laura Bush Shows Complexity under Calm." *New York Times,* January 20, 2005, A1 and A16.

Quinn, Sally. "Rosalynn's Journey." *Washington Post,* Style section, July 25, 1979, B1 and B2.

——. "Scapegoats: The Essence of Washington Politics." *Washington Post,* Style section, January 25, 1981, G1 and G3.

Radcliffe, Donnie. "Barbara Bush, Being Herself." *Washington Post,* Style section, January 15, 1989, F1 and F6.

Reed, Julia, and Annie Leibovitz. "The First Lady." *Vogue,* December 1993, 228–33.

Roberts, Roxanne. "The Double Life of Hillary Clinton." *Washington Post,* Style section, February 8, 2000, C1 and C9.

Robertson, Nan. "Our New First Lady." *Saturday Evening Post,* February 8, 1964, 20–24.

Sadler, Christine. "Our Very Busy First Lady." *McCall's,* 79–81, 187–88.

Santini, Maureen. Associated Press dispatch, Washington, D.C., December 11, 1980.

——. "First Lady Orders China." *Washington Post,* Style section, September 12, 1981, B1.

Shales, Tom. "The True Grit of Betty Ford." *Washington Post,* Style section, March 2, 1987, B1 and B2.

Shearer, Lloyd. "Sheila Weidenfeld: The First Lady's Press Secretary." *Parade,* April 25, 1976, 4–7.

Stanley, Alessandra. "The First Lady's Influence Is Starting to Reveal Itself." *New York Times,* September 1, 2004, P9.

Stimpson, Catharine R. "Nancy Reagan Wears a Hat: Feminism and Its Cultural Consensus." *Critical Inquiry* 14 (Winter 1988): 223–43.

"That Fancy Fashion Fuss." *Life* [cover story], September 26, 1960, 18–21.

Thomas, Evan. "Hillary's Other Side." *Newsweek,* July 1, 1996, 20–23.

Welter, Barbara. "The Cult of True Womanhood: 1820–1860." *American Quarterly* 18 (Summer 1966): 151–74.

William, Brian. "First Lady Looks Forward to New Role." Laura Bush interview, NBC Nightly News, February 3, 2005. Available at http://www.msnbc.msn.com.

Winfield, Betty H. "'Madame President': Understanding a New Kind of First Lady." *Media Studies Journal* 8 (Spring 1994): 59–71.

———. "Mrs. Roosevelt's Press Conference Association: The First Lady Shines a Light." *Journalism History* 8 (Summer 1981): 54–55, 63–67.

"The World of Nancy Reagan." *Newsweek,* December 21, 1981, 22–27.

DISSERTATIONS

Burns, Lisa M. "First Ladies as Political Women: Press Framing of Presidential Wives, 1900–2001." Ph.D. diss., University of Maryland, College Park, 2004.

ARCHIVAL MATERIALS

Bess Furman Papers, Manuscript Division, Library of Congress, Washington, D.C.

Carl Sferrazza Anthony Papers (Nancy Reagan), National First Ladies Library, Canton, Ohio.

Eleanor Roosevelt Papers, Franklin D. Roosevelt Library, Hyde Park, N.Y.

Francis L. Lewine. Oral History interviews by Anne S. Kasper. Washington, D.C. November 12, 1991, and November 18, 1991, and transcript of videotaped interview, April 20, 1993, for "Women in Journalism" project, Washington Press Club Foundation, in the Oral History Collection of Columbia University and other repositories.

Martha Strayer Papers, Archive of Contemporary History, University of Wyoming, Laramie.

Maureen Santini personal collection, Bethesda, Md.

Mrs. Roosevelt's Press Conference Association Papers, Franklin D. Roosevelt Library, Hyde Park, N.Y.

Oral History Collection, Lyndon Baines Johnson Library, Austin, Tex. Interviews with Bess Abell, June 13, 1969; Elizabeth Carpenter, December 3, 1968, April 4, 1969, and May 15, 1969; Katharine Graham, March 13, 1969; Helen Thomas, April 19, 1977.

Ruby Black Papers, Manuscript Division, Library of Congress, Washington, D.C.

Women's National Press Club/Washington Press Club Records, Cora Rigby Washington Journalism Archive, National Press Club, Washington, D.C.

PERSONAL INTERVIEWS BY AUTHOR

Baldrige, Letitia. Email and telephone interview. November 3, 2004.

Cimons, Marlene. Tape-recorded interview. College Park, Md. March 5, 2004.

Enda, Jodi. Personal interview. Washington, D.C. June 21, 2004.

Hoyt, Mary Finch. Personal interview. Washington, D.C. October 18, 2004.

Kast, Sheilah. Email comments. February 12, 2005.

Lattimore, Neel. Email interview. January 25, 2005.

Lawn, Connie. Personal interview. Bethesda, Md. January 3, 2004.

Matusow, Barbara. Taped interview. Bethesda, Md. March 2, 2004.

McLendon, Winzola. Telephone interview. October 25, 2004.

Overholser, Geneva. Personal interview. Washington, D.C. December 3, 2004.

Santini, Maureen. Personal interview. Washington, D.C. April 27, 2004.

Tate, Sheila. Telephone interview. December 15, 2004.

Thornton, Lee. Taped interview. College Park, Md. October 29, 2003.

Weidenfelt, Sheila. Taped interview. Washington, D.C. September 20, 2004.

INDEX

Maurine H. Beasley is a professor of journalism in the Philip Merrill College of Journalism at the University of Maryland, College Park. She is the author of *Eleanor Roosevelt and the Media: A Public Quest for Self-Fulfillment* and the coeditor of *Taking Their Place: A Documentary History of Women and Journalism* and *The Eleanor Roosevelt Encyclopedia.*

Caryl Rivers is a professor of journalism in the College of Communication at Boston University. A former White House correspondent, she is the author of *Slick Spins and Fractured Facts: How Cultural Myths Distort the News* and *Camelot,* a novel set in the Kennedy administration.